Texas
GoMath!

Volume 2

Houghton
Mifflin
Harcourt

Houghton
Mifflin
Harcourt

Texas
GoMath!

ISBN 978-0-544-08693-7

8 9 10   0868   22 21 20 19 18 17

4500648918   B C D E F G

Cover Image Credits: (astronaut) ©Cosmo Condina/Getty Images; (fox) ©Dean Flkar/Getty Images; (ranch) ©Stephen Saks/Lonely Planet Images/Getty Images; (starfish) ©Allyson Kitts/Shutterstock.

Dear Students and Families,

Welcome to **Texas Go Math!**, Grade 3! In this exciting mathematics program, there are hands-on activities to do and real-world problems to solve. Best of all, you will write your ideas and answers right in your book. In **Texas Go Math!**, writing and drawing on the pages helps you think deeply about what you are learning, and you will really understand math!

By the way, all of the pages in your **Texas Go Math!** book are made using recycled paper. We wanted you to know that you can Go Green with **Texas Go Math!**

Sincerely,

The Authors

Made in the United States
Printed on 100% recycled paper

Texas Go Math!

Authors

Juli K. Dixon, Ph.D.
Professor, Mathematics
    Education
University of Central Florida
Orlando, Florida

Matthew R. Larson, Ph.D.
K-12 Curriculum Specialist for
    Mathematics
Lincoln Public Schools
Lincoln, Nebraska

Edward B. Burger, Ph.D.
President
Southwestern University
Georgetown, Texas

Martha E. Sandoval-Martinez
Math Instructor
El Camino College
Torrance, California

Consultant

Valerie Johse
Math Consultant
Texas Council for Economic
    Education
Houston, Texas

Volume 1

Unit 1 • Number and Operations: Place Value, Fractions, Addition, and Subtraction

Look for these:

H.O.T. Problems
Higher Order Thinking
Multi-Step Problems

Module 1 Place Value

Homework and Practice

Homework and TEKS Practice in every lesson.

Module 2 Representing Fractions

GO DIGITAL Resources

DIGITAL RESOURCES
Go online for the Interactive Student Edition with Math on the Spot Videos. Use *i*Tools, the Multimedia *e*Glossary, and more.

Unit 2 • Number and Operations: Multiplication and Division

Module 6 Multiplication Concepts

TEKS

Module 7 Multiply with 2, 3, 4, 5, 6, and 10

TEKS

Module 8 Multiply with 7, 8, and 9

TEKS

Look for these:

Real World

H.O.T. Problems
Higher Order Thinking
Multi-Step Problems

GO DIGITAL Resources

DIGITAL RESOURCES
Go online for the Interactive Student Edition with Math on the Spot Videos. Use *i*Tools, the Multimedia *e*Glossary, and more.

Look for these:

Real World

H.O.T. Problems
Higher Order Thinking
Multi-Step Problems

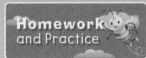

Homework and Practice

Homework and TEKS Practice in every lesson.

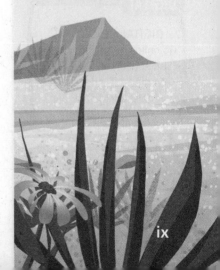

Volume 2

Unit 3 • Algebraic Reasoning

Module 14 Algebra

Volume 2

Unit 4 • Geometry and Measurement

Module 15 Two-Dimensional Figures and Three-Dimensional Solids

Look for these:

H.O.T. Problems
Higher Order Thinking
Multi-Step Problems

Homework and Practice

Homework and TEKS Practice in every lesson.

Volume 2

Unit 5 • Data Analysis

Module 19 — Graphs

Volume 2

Unit 6 • Personal Financial Literacy

Module 20 — Income and Spending

Algebraic Reasoning

Show What You Know

Check your understanding of important skills.

Name _____

▶ **Even and Odd Numbers** Draw counters to show the number. **Make pairs. Write *even* or *odd* for the number.**

1. 14   2. 17

_____   _____

▶ **Use a Multiplication Table** **Find the product.**

3. $4 \times 3 =$ _____   4. $7 \times 4 =$ _____   5. $5 \times 8 =$ _____

6. $3 \times 5 =$ _____   7. $9 \times 2 =$ _____   8. $10 \times 6 =$ _____

▶ **Relate Multiplication and Division**
Complete the equations.

9. $6 \times 5 =$ _____   10. $4 \times 9 =$ _____   11. $7 \times 2 =$ _____

$30 \div 6 =$ _____ $36 \div 4 =$ _____ $14 \div 7 =$ _____

12. $7 \times 6 =$ _____   13. $9 \times 3 =$ _____   14. $8 \times 6 =$ _____

$42 \div 7 =$ _____ $27 \div 9 =$ _____ $48 \div 8 =$ _____

GO DIGITAL Assessment Options:
Soar to Success Math

Vocabulary Builder

▶ **Visualize It**

Complete the flow map by using the words with a ✓.

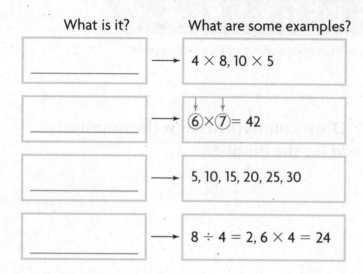

What is it?　　What are some examples?

$4 \times 8, 10 \times 5$

$\textcircled{6} \times \textcircled{7} = 42$

$5, 10, 15, 20, 25, 30$

$8 \div 4 = 2, 6 \times 4 = 24$

▶ **Understand Vocabulary**

Complete the sentences by using the review and preview words.

1. An _____ is a number sentence that uses the equal sign to show that two amounts are equal.

2. A _____ can be used to describe a pattern.

3. A _____ is the answer in a multiplication problem.

4. _____ are opposite operations, or operations that undo one another, such as multiplication and division.

5. An _____ is a part of a number sentence that has numbers and operations signs but does not have an equal sign.

Interactive Student Edition
Multimedia eGlossary

Name _____

Vocabulary

Multiplication and division are **inverse operations**.

You can use a related multiplication fact or a related division fact to help you divide.

Find 48 ÷ 8.

1. Use a related multiplication fact.

2. Use a related division fact.

3. Look at the two arrays. Use the Word Bank to label each part of the problem.

Word Bank

dividend

divisor

factor

product

quotient

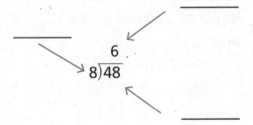   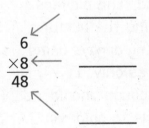

Writing How does knowing the product of 7 × 8 help you to find 56 ÷ 8? **Explain.**

Reading Look for this book in your library.
The Great Divide: A Mathematical Marathon,
by Dayle Ann Dodds and Tracy Mitchell

Block Out

Object of the Game Make arrays to cover more squares than the other player.

Materials

Number of Players 2

- 2 number cubes labeled 1–6
- 1-centimeter grid paper
- crayons

How to Play

1 Player 1 tosses the number cubes. One cube shows the number of rows. One cube shows the number of columns.

2 Player 1 shades an array on grid paper using the numbers tossed.

The array can be 3 rows of 5 or 5 rows of 3.

3 Player 2 repeats Steps 1–2 using a different color to shade the array tossed. The players take turns tossing the number cubes and shading arrays using uncolored squares only. If there are not enough uncolored rows and columns to color an array, that player's turn ends.

4 Play continues until each player has had 5 turns. The player with more squares shaded is the winner.

430

© Houghton Mifflin Harcourt Publishing Company

Name _____

Addition Strategies

TEKS **Algebraic Reasoning—3.5.A**
Also 3.4.A
MATHEMATICAL PROCESSES
3.1.A, 3.1.C, 3.1.E

? Essential Question

What strategies can you use to solve addition problems?

 Unlock the Problem

The table shows how many musicians are in each section of a symphony orchestra. How many musicians play either string or woodwind instruments?

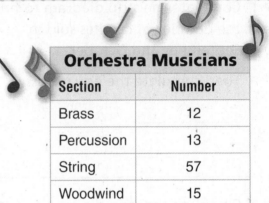

Orchestra Musicians	
Section	**Number**
Brass	12
Percussion	13
String	57
Woodwind	15

🔑 One Way Use the number line to find 57 + 15.

A Count on to the nearest ten. Then count by tens and ones.

Think: 3 + ▨ = 15

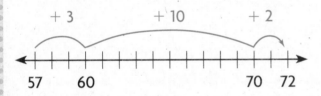

+ 3   + 10   + 2

57   60   70   72

B Count by tens. Then count by ones.

Think: 10 + 5 = 15

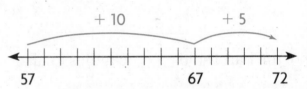

+ 10   + 5

57   67   72

Complete the equation.

57 + 15 = _____

So, _____ musicians play either string or woodwind instruments.

Remember

An equation is a number sentence that uses the equal sign to show that two amounts are equal.

Try This! Find 43 + 28. Draw jumps and label the number line to show your thinking. Then complete the equation.

So, 43 + 28 = _____.

🔑 Another Way Use strip diagrams to solve an addition problem.

During a fundraiser, the band sold 132 candles in September,
161 candles in October, and 125 candles in November. How many
candles did the band sell in all?

STEP 1 Complete the strip diagram to find
the number of candles sold in
September and October.

Then complete the equations.

$\underline{\hspace{1cm}} + \underline{\hspace{1cm}} = \blacksquare$

$\underline{\hspace{1cm}} = \blacksquare$

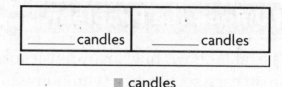

■ candles

STEP 2 Complete the strip diagram to find
the number of candles sold in all.

Then complete the equations.

$\underline{\hspace{1cm}} + \underline{\hspace{1cm}} = \blacktriangle$

$\underline{\hspace{1cm}} = \blacktriangle$

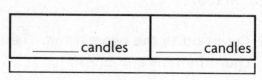

▲ candles

So, the band sold _____ candles in all.

Share and Show
MATH BOARD

✓ **1.** Count by tens and ones to find 63 + 27. Draw jumps
and label the number line to show your thinking.
Then complete the equation.

Think: Count by tens and ones from 63.

63

$63 + 27 = \underline{\hspace{1cm}}$

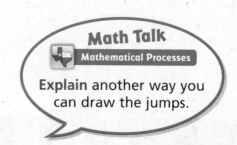

Math Talk
Mathematical Processes

Explain another way you
can draw the jumps.

Name _____

Complete the strip diagram to represent and solve. Then complete the equation for the strip diagram.

2. There are 512 students at Fairview Elementary. There are 454 students at Lincoln Elementary. How many students attend the two schools?

| _____ students | _____ students |

 students

_____ + _____ = ▇

_____ = ▇

Problem Solving Real World

Use the table for 3–6. You may use models, number lines, and equations to represent and solve.

3. **Apply** How many boys attended school on Thursday and Friday?

_____

4. **Analyze** How many girls attended school on Monday and Tuesday?

_____

5. **H.O.T.** **Multi-Step** How many students attended school on Tuesday and Wednesday? **Explain** how you found your answer.

Harrison School Attendance

Day	Boys	Girls
Monday	92	104
Tuesday	101	96
Wednesday	105	93
Thursday	99	102
Friday	97	103

_____

_____

6. **H.O.T.** **What's the Question** The answer is 201 students.

_____

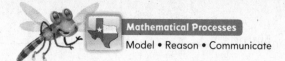
Daily Assessment Task

Fill in the bubble for the correct answer choice. You can use models, number lines, and equations to represent and solve.

7. **Use Tools** The Juice Hut sold 27 blueberry smoothies on Monday and 25 blueberry smoothies on Tuesday. How many blueberry smoothies were sold in all on Monday and Tuesday?

(A) 47

(C) 60

(B) 52

(D) 50

8. There are 198 adults and 124 children visiting a museum. What is the total number of people visiting the museum?

(A) 432

(C) 322

(B) 302

(D) 424

9. **Multi-Step** The table shows the number of books third and fourth graders collected for a book drive. In which week did the students collect the most books?

Number of Books Collected		
Week	Grade 3	Grade 4
1	24	31
2	38	21
3	29	27
4	32	26

(A) Week 4

(C) Week 3

(B) Week 2

(D) Week 1

 TEXAS Test Prep

10. On Monday, 46 boys and 38 girls bought lunch at school. How many students bought lunch?

(A) 74

(B) 76

(C) 84

(D) 73

434

Homework and Practice

Name _____

14.1 Addition Strategies

**Complete the strip diagram to represent and solve.
Then complete the equation for the strip diagram.**

1. The third grade class sells 127 tickets to the school play. The fourth grade sells 134 tickets. How many tickets do the two grades sell?

_____ tickets	_____ tickets

▨ tickets

_____ + _____ = ▨

_____ = ▨

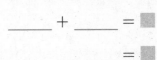 **Problem Solving**

Use the table for 2–5. You may use models, number lines, and equations to represent and solve.

Craft Fair Items		
Item	**Number Sold**	
	Saturday	**Sunday**
Picture frames	108	72
Flower baskets	95	113
Pencil holders	84	75
Candles	104	92

2. How many picture frames were sold at the Craft Fair?

_____

3. How many candles were sold at the Craft Fair?

_____

4. How many flower baskets and candles combined were sold on Sunday?

_____

5. If another 40 pencil holders were sold after the fair ended, how many pencil holders were sold in all?

_____

Fill in the bubble completely to show your answer. You may use models, number lines, and equations to represent and solve.

6. Beth reads 45 pages of a book in one week, and 66 pages the following week. How many pages does Beth read in all?

   Ⓐ 100

   Ⓑ 101

   Ⓒ 90

   Ⓓ 111

7. A museum has 165 oil paintings and 128 watercolor paintings. How many paintings does the museum have in all?

   Ⓐ 383

   Ⓑ 283

   Ⓒ 293

   Ⓓ 193

8. Pieto collects 89 bottles for recycling day. Ming collects 68 bottles. What is the total number of bottles that the children collect?

   Ⓐ 147

   Ⓑ 117

   Ⓒ 157

   Ⓓ 114

9. **Multi-Step** Mrs. Stein's classroom has 135 fiction books and 98 nonfiction books. Mr. Walter's classroom has 29 fewer books. How many books are in Mr. Walter's classroom?

   Ⓐ 194

   Ⓑ 204

   Ⓒ 233

   Ⓓ 262

10. **Multi-Step** The table shows the number of people that attended the School Fair. On which day did the most people attend the fair?

    Ⓐ Sunday

    Ⓑ Friday

    Ⓒ Saturday

    Ⓓ Thursday

Attendance at the School Fair		
Day	Adults	Children
Thursday	83	65
Friday	70	85
Saturday	79	75
Sunday	81	68

Name _____

TEKS Algebraic
Reasoning—3.5.A
Also 3.4.A
MATHEMATICAL PROCESSES
3.1.A, 3.1.C

14.2 Subtraction Strategies

? Essential Question

What strategies can you use to solve subtraction problems?

🔑 Unlock the Problem

A sunflower can grow to be very tall. Dylan is 39 inches tall. She watered a sunflower that grew to be 62 inches tall. How many inches shorter was Dylan than the sunflower?

🔓 One Way Use a number line to find 62−39.

Ⓐ Count up by tens and then ones.

Think: Start at 39. Count up to 62.

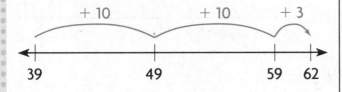

Add the lengths of the jumps to find the difference.

$10 + 10 + 3 =$ _____

Complete the equation. $62 - 39 =$ _____

So, Dylan was _____ inches shorter than the sunflower.

Ⓑ Take away tens and ones.

Think: Start at 62. Count back 39.

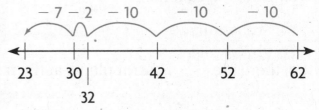

Take away lengths of jumps to end on the difference.

Try This! Find 74−38. Draw jumps and label the number line to show your thinking. Then complete the equation.

So, $74 - 38 =$ _____.

🔑 Another Way Use strip diagrams to solve a subtraction problem.

At Mr. Cruz's vegetable farm, there are 348 tomato plants.
There are 136 fewer pepper plants than tomato plants. There
are 92 fewer carrot plants than pepper plants. How many
carrot plants are at the farm?

STEP 1 Complete the strip diagram
to find the number of
pepper plants.

Complete the equations.

_____ − _____ = ■   _____ = ■

tomato | _____ plants |

pepper | _____ plants |

■ plants

STEP 2 Complete the strip diagram
to find the number of
carrot plants.

Complete the equations.

_____ − _____ = ▲   _____ = ▲

pepper | _____ plants |

carrot | _____ plants |

▲ plants

So, there are _____ carrot plants at the farm.

Share and Show

1. Yumi has 61 plant stickers. She has 24 fewer flower
stickers than plant stickers. How many stickers does
Yumi have in all? Use the number lines to represent and
solve. Then complete the equations.

61

$61 − 24 =$ _____

61

$61 +$ _____ $=$ _____

So, Yumi has _____ stickers in all.

438

Name _____

Complete the strip diagram to represent and solve.
Then complete the equation for the strip diagram.

2. On Monday, a large flower shop
sold 425 roses. The flower shop sold
123 fewer roses on Friday than on
Monday. How many roses did the
shop sell on Friday?

Monday | _____ roses

Friday | _____ roses

■ roses

_____ − _____ = ■

_____ = ■

Problem Solving

Use the table for 3–6. You may use models,
number lines, and equations to represent and
solve.

3. **Analyze** How many more people attended
the museum on Saturday than on Thursday?

_____

4. **Apply** How many fewer people attended the
museum on Monday than on Friday?

_____

| Nature Museum Attendance ||
Day	Number of People
Monday	306
Tuesday	415
Wednesday	345
Thursday	450
Friday	526
Saturday	585

5. **H.O.T.** **Multi-Step** How many
fewer people attended the museum
on Tuesday and Wednesday combined
than on Thursday and Friday combined?

_____

6. **H.O.T.** **Pose a Problem** Write a subtraction
word problem about the data in the table.
Then solve your problem.

_____

_____

Daily Assessment Task

Fill in the bubble for the correct answer choice. You can use models, number lines, and equations to represent and solve.

7. **Multi-Step** Jan and Dave are having a penny race. Dave will win the race if he finds at least 40 more pennies than Jan. Dave finds 213 pennies. Jan finds 172 pennies. Which is a true statement about Jan and Dave's penny race?

   (A) Jan wins because she finds 41 more pennies than Dave.

   (B) Jan wins because Dave finds 31 more pennies than she does.

   (C) Dave wins because he finds more pennies than Jan.

   (D) Dave wins because he finds 41 more pennies than Jan.

8. Kyle's basketball team scores 62 points. Kyle's team members score 51 of the points. Kyle scores the rest of the points. How many points does Kyle score?

   (A) 21   (B) 13   (C) 11   (D) 23

9. **Multi-Step** Suzi has 86 songs on her digital music player. Xavier has 112 songs on his digital music player. Then he deletes 18 songs. How many more songs does Xavier have now than Suzi?

   (A) 8   (B) 94   (C) 26   (D) 18

 TEXAS Test Prep

10. There were 87 sunflowers at the flower shop in the morning. There were 56 sunflowers left at the end of the day. How many sunflowers were sold?

    (A) 143   (C) 13

    (B) 31   (D) 41

14.2 Subtraction Strategies

**Complete the strip diagram to represent and solve.
Then complete the equation for the strip diagram.**

1. There were 285 visitors at the art show on Sunday. There were 173 visitors at the art show on Friday. How many more visitors were at the art show on Sunday than on Friday?

   Sunday | _____ visitors

   Friday | _____ visitors

   ▨ visitors

   _____ − _____ = ▨

   _____ = ▨

Problem Solving Real World

The table shows how many of each kind of fruit was sold at the Farmers' Market in one week. Use the table for 2–4. You may use models, number lines, and equations to represent and solve.

Farmers' Market	
Fruit	**Number Sold**
Peaches	218
Oranges	435
Grapefruit	347
Melons	212

2. How many more oranges than melons were sold?

   _____

3. How many fewer peaches than grapefruits and melons combined were sold at the market?

   _____

4. Write a subtraction word problem about the data in the table. Then solve your problem.

   _____

   _____

**Fill in the bubble completely to show your answer.
You may use models, number lines, and equations
to represent and solve.**

5. Jenna scores 87 points bowling. Karl
   scores 35 fewer points than Jenna.
   How many points does Karl score?

   (A) 122

   (B) 112

   (C) 52

   (D) 42

6. A toy store has 78 action figures. At
   the end of the day, 52 action figures
   are left. How many action figures
   were sold?

   (A) 130

   (B) 25

   (C) 26

   (D) 120

7. There are 278 people in a movie
   theater. Of those people, 145 are
   adults, and the rest are children.
   How many children are in the
   movie theater?

   (A) 133

   (B) 122

   (C) 100

   (D) 103

8. There are 295 people at a softball
   game. Of those people, 153 are
   adults, and the rest are children.
   How many children are at the
   softball game?

   (A) 300

   (B) 124

   (C) 142

   (D) 150

9. **Multi-Step** A market has 23 gift
   baskets of red apples and 35 gift
   baskets of green apples. If the
   market sells a total of 29 baskets,
   how many baskets are left?

   (A) 58

   (B) 39

   (C) 27

   (D) 29

10. **Multi-Step** There are 27 girls
    and 19 boys at the library. Fifteen
    students leave to go to class. How
    many students are still at the library?

    (A) 46

    (B) 61

    (C) 34

    (D) 31

14.3 Number Patterns

TEKS Number and Operations—3.5

MATHEMATICAL PROCESSES
3.1.E, 3.1.F, 3.1.G

? Essential Question

How can you use patterns to find rules and solve problems?

Unlock the Problem

A **pattern** is an ordered set of numbers or objects. The order helps you predict what will come next.

You can use the addition table to explore patterns.

+	0	1	2	3	4	5	6	7	8	9	10
0	0	1	2	3	4	5	6	7	8	9	10
1	1	2	3	4	5	6	7	8	9	10	11
2	2	3	4	5	6	7	8	9	10	11	12
3	3	4	5	6	7	8	9	10	11	12	13
4	4	5	6	7	8	9	10	11	12	13	14
5	5	6	7	8	9	10	11	12	13	14	15
6	6	7	8	9	10	11	12	13	14	15	16
7	7	8	9	10	11	12	13	14	15	16	17
8	8	9	10	11	12	13	14	15	16	17	18
9	9	10	11	12	13	14	15	16	17	18	19
10	10	11	12	13	14	15	16	17	18	19	20

Activity 1

Materials ■ orange and green crayons

- Look across each row and down each column. What pattern do you see?

_____

_____

- Shade the row and column orange for the addend 0. Compare the shaded squares to the yellow row and the blue column. What pattern do you see?

_____

What happens when you add 0 to a number?

_____

- Shade the row and column green for the addend 1. What pattern do you see?

_____

What happens when you add 1 to a number?

_____

_____

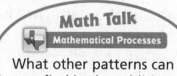

Math Talk
Mathematical Processes

What other patterns can you find in the addition table?

More Number Patterns

A **rule** can be used to describe a pattern.

🔑 **Look at this number pattern. Find a rule.**

Think: What do I do to 1 to get 4? What do I do to 4 to get 7?

1   4   7   10   13

_____   _____   _____   _____

What is a rule for this pattern? _____

- **Use the rule above to write the next three numbers.**

  1, 4, 7, 10, 13, _____ , _____ , _____

- **Use the rule above to find the missing number.**

  2, 5, _____ , 11, 14

🔑 Use the rule *Subtract 3* to create a pattern. Write the first five numbers in the pattern.

Think: What number should I start with? What numbers do I get when I subtract 3?

_____

Share and Show

Write a rule for the pattern. Then write the next two numbers.

✓ 1. 21, 26, 31, 36, _____ , _____   Rule: _____

Write a rule for the pattern. Then write the missing number.

2. 38, 35, _____ , 29, 26, 23, 20   Rule: _____

Use the rule to create a pattern. Write the first five numbers in the pattern.

✓ 3. **Rule:** Add 4.

_____

Name _____

Problem Solving 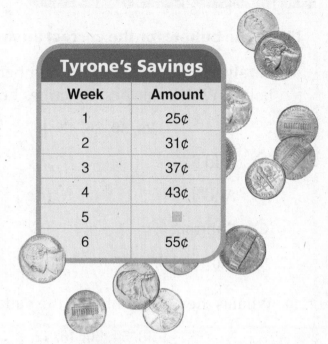 Real World

Use the table for 4–6.

4. How much money does Tyrone save each week after Week 1? _____

5. How much money has Tyrone saved by the end of Week 5? _____

6. **Write Math** ▶ Tyrone wants to buy a book that costs 75¢. If he continues his pattern of saving, will he have enough saved by Week 10? **Explain**.

_____

_____

_____

Tyrone's Savings	
Week	**Amount**
1	25¢
2	31¢
3	37¢
4	43¢
5	▪
6	55¢

7. **H.O.T.** **Use Math Language** Diego created the pattern below. Write a rule for the pattern. Then write the missing number.

42, 43, 45, 48, 52, _____

_____

_____

_____

8. **H.O.T.** **Multi-Step** Create your own pattern by starting with a 2-digit number. Write a rule for the pattern so that a 1-digit number is added to find the next number. Write the first five numbers in your pattern.

_____

_____

Daily Assessment Task

Fill in the bubble for the correct answer choice.

9. **Analyze** Shelly creates the number pattern shown below. Which rule best describes her pattern?

24, 30, 36, 42, 48, _____

Ⓐ Add 6.

Ⓑ Add 8.

Ⓒ Subtract 6.

Ⓓ Subtract 8.

10. What is the next number in the pattern shown below?

58, 54, 50, 46, 42, _____

Ⓐ 44   Ⓒ 38

Ⓑ 36   Ⓓ 41

11. **Multi-Step** Two patterns are shown below. Jerry wrote a third pattern. The first number of his pattern is the sum of the missing numbers below. What is the first number of the third pattern?

12, 17, _____, 27, 32

34, 30, 26, _____, 18

Ⓐ 5   Ⓒ 4

Ⓑ 22   Ⓓ 44

⭐ TEXAS Test Prep

12. Which rule best describes the pattern?

85, 80, 75, 70, 65, 60, 55, 50

Ⓐ Add 10.   Ⓒ Subtract 10.

Ⓑ Subtract 5.   Ⓓ Add 5.

Name _____

14.3 Number Patterns

Write the rule for the pattern. Then write the next two numbers.

1. 23, 26, 29, 32, _____ , _____   Rule: _____

2. 48, 44, 40, 36, _____ , _____   Rule: _____

Use the rule to create a pattern. Write the first five numbers in the pattern.

3. Subtract 5.

_____

_____

4. Add 6.

_____

_____

Problem Solving

Use the table for 5–7.

5. A craft club is making birdhouses to sell for charity. How many birdhouses do they make at the end of day 4?

_____

6. What is the rule for the pattern of making birdhouses?

_____

Birdhouses Made	
Day	Number
1	13
2	17
3	21
4	▪
5	29
6	33

7. The club wants to make a total of 45 birdhouses. If they continue the pattern of making birdhouses, on which day will they have 45 birdhouses?

_____

8. Nadia created the pattern below. Write a rule for the pattern. Then write the missing number.

10, 11, 9, 10, 8, 9, _____

_____

Lesson Check

TEXAS Test Prep

Fill in the bubble completely to show your answer.

9. Axle creates this number pattern. Which rule best describes his pattern?

   39, 34, 29, 24, 19, ____

   Ⓐ Subtract 4.
   Ⓑ Add 4.
   Ⓒ Subtract 5.
   Ⓓ Add 5.

10. Latisha creates this number pattern. Which rule best describes her pattern?

   5, 12, 19, 26, 33, ____

   Ⓐ Add 6.
   Ⓑ Add 7.
   Ⓒ Subtract 6.
   Ⓓ Subtract 7.

11. Darla writes the number pattern shown below. What is the next number?

   53, 50, 47, 44, 41, ____

   Ⓐ 42
   Ⓑ 40
   Ⓒ 39
   Ⓓ 38

12. Soo Jin writes the number pattern shown below. What is the next number?

   54, 60, 66, 72, 78, ____

   Ⓐ 85
   Ⓑ 80
   Ⓒ 79
   Ⓓ 84

13. **Multi-Step** Rodney writes this number pattern. Which of the patterns has the same number that comes next?

   13, 16, 19, 22, ____

   Ⓐ 5, 10, 15, 20, ____
   Ⓑ 16, 18, 20, 22, ____
   Ⓒ 6, 12, 18, 24, ____
   Ⓓ 12, 15, 18, 21, ____

14. **Multi-Step** The missing numbers in these two patterns add up to a secret number. What is the secret number?

   15, 21, ____ 33, 39
   19, ____ 27, 31, 35

   Ⓐ 27
   Ⓑ 23
   Ⓒ 40
   Ⓓ 50

Name _____

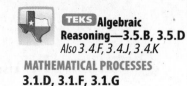
14.4 Relate Multiplication and Division

? Essential Question How can you use multiplication and division to solve problems?

🔑 Unlock the Problem

Pamela ordered a set of 6 books written by her favorite author. The set of books cost $48. Since she had already read them, Pamela sold 2 of the books to her friend Jody. If each book was the same price, how much did Jody pay?

- What operations will you use to solve the problem?

  _____

- Circle the numbers you need to use.

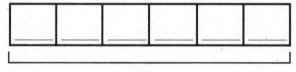

Example Use strip diagrams.

First, complete the strip diagram to show $48 divided into 6 equal groups.

$48

Complete the equation.

48 ÷ 6 = _____

So, each book cost $_____.

- What multiplication sentence can you write to solve the division problem?

  _____

Then, complete another strip diagram to show the cost of 2 books.

8	8

Complete the equation.

2 × 8 = _____

So, Jody paid $_____ for the 2 books.

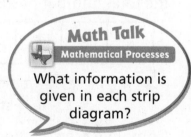

Math Talk
Mathematical Processes

What information is given in each strip diagram?

🔓 Example Use arrays.

Blair baked 4 batches of 9 cupcakes. He packed the cupcakes in 6 equal boxes. How many cupcakes did he put in each box?

Show an array with 9 counters in 4 equal rows by completing the drawing.

There are _____ counters.

Complete the equation. $4 \times 9 =$ _____

So, Blair baked _____ cupcakes.

Now, complete the array to show the number of cupcakes in each box.

There are _____ counters in each row.

Complete the equation. $36 \div 6 =$ _____

So, there are _____ cupcakes in each box.

Share and Show   MATH BOARD

The third grade students sat in 6 seats at 5 tables in the lunchroom. Show how the same number of students can sit in equal groups at 3 tables.

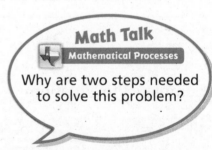

Math Talk
Mathematical Processes

Why are two steps needed to solve this problem?

✓ 1. Complete the strip diagram to show the total number of students.

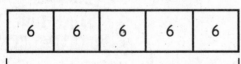

| 6 | 6 | 6 | 6 | 6 |

_____ students

Complete the equation.

$5 \times 6 =$ _____

So, there are _____ third grade students.

✓ 2. Complete the strip diagram to show the number of students at 3 tables.

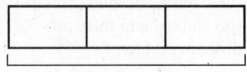

30 students

Complete the equation.

$30 \div 3 =$ _____

So, there are _____ students at each table.

Name _____

Use the table for 3–5. You may use arrays, strip diagrams, and equations to represent and solve.

Cochise County Fair	
Price of Admission	
Adults	$6
Students	$3
Children 5 and under free	

3. Mr. Patterson paid $24 for some students to get into the fair. How many students did Mr. Patterson pay for?

_____

4.  **H.O.T. Multi-Step** Garrett is 8 years old. He and his family are going to the county fair. What is the price of admission for Garrett, his 2 parents, and baby sister?

_____

5. **H.O.T. Multi-Step** Jose and Izzy are 8 years old. They go to the fair on a day when all rides are $2 and admission is $1 off. How much will they pay altogether to attend the fair and go on 5 rides each?

_____

6. There are 20 seats on the Wildcat ride. The number of seats in each car is the same. If there are 5 cars on the ride, how many seats are there in each car? Complete the strip diagram to show the problem. Then answer the question.

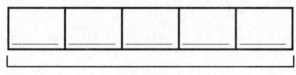

20 seats

_____

7. **Write Math** ▶ **Pose a Problem** How many days are there in 2 weeks? Write and solve a related word problem to represent the inverse operation.

_____

Daily Assessment Task

Fill in the bubble for the correct answer choice.
You may use arrays, strip diagrams, and equations
to represent and solve.

8. **Multi-Step** Paul is in charge of the egg toss at the World
Egg Day fair. There are 48 people participating in teams
of 8 people. Each team needs 1 egg. Paul is buying eggs
in cartons that each have 6 eggs. How many cartons does
Paul need?

Ⓐ 1   Ⓒ 8

Ⓑ 2   Ⓓ 6

9. **Apply** Kat is reading a book with 36 pages. She wants
to finish the book in 4 days. How many pages does she
need to read each day?

Ⓐ 8   Ⓒ 4

Ⓑ 6   Ⓓ 9

10. **Multi-Step** Roshan has 18 crackers. He shares the
crackers equally with his brother. Then Roshan eats
three crackers. How many crackers does Roshan
have left?

Ⓐ 21   Ⓒ 6

Ⓑ 15   Ⓓ 9

 TEXAS Test Prep

11. **Use Tools** There are 35 prizes in 5 equal rows.
How many prizes are in each row?

Ⓐ 9   Ⓒ 8

Ⓑ 7   Ⓓ 6

14.4 Relate Multiplication and Division

Complete the equations.

1.

2 rows of _____ = 14

$2 \times$ _____ $= 14$

$14 \div 2 =$ _____

2.

3 rows of _____ = 18

$3 \times$ _____ $= 18$

$18 \div 3 =$ _____

3. $6 \times$ _____ $= 24$ $24 \div 6 =$ _____

4. $8 \times$ _____ $= 56$ $56 \div$ _____ $= 8$

5. $8 \times$ _____ $= 64$ $64 \div 8 =$ _____

6. $5 \times$ _____ $= 45$ $45 \div 5 =$ _____

Problem Solving Real World

Use the table for 7–10. You may use arrays, strip diagrams, and equations to represent and solve.

7. Harry pays $16 for stuffed animals. How many stuffed animals does Harry buy?

Souvenir Shop	
Item	**Amount**
Stuffed animal	$4
Snow globe	$8
Calendar	$5

_____

8. Mrs. Kahn buys 3 snow globes for her children. How much money does Mrs. Kahn spend on the snow globes?

9. On Tuesdays, stuffed animals and calendars are each $1 off. How much will Marcus pay if he waits until Tuesday to buy 3 stuffed animals and 2 calendars?

_____

Fill in the bubble completely to show your answer. You may use arrays, strip diagrams, and equations to represent and solve.

10. Ned earns $15 delivering newspapers. He earns $5 each day. How many days does Ned deliver newspapers?

Ⓐ 20 days

Ⓑ 5 days

Ⓒ 3 days

Ⓓ 10 days

11. Janella buys some comic books. She spends $12. Each comic book costs $2. How many comic books does Janella buy?

Ⓐ 14

Ⓑ 10

Ⓒ 5

Ⓓ 6

12. There are 28 children going on a scavenger hunt. They need to make teams of 4. How many children are on each team for the scavenger hunt?

Ⓐ 7

Ⓑ 8

Ⓒ 6

Ⓓ 5

13. Mr. Brown wants to build a fence that measures 36 feet long. Each section of fencing is 6 feet long. How many sections of fence does Mr. Brown need?

Ⓐ 30

Ⓑ 42

Ⓒ 9

Ⓓ 6

14. Multi-Step A group of 30 people are going to the zoo. There are 4 cars. If each car seats 5 people, how many more cars will they need for the trip?

Ⓐ 10   Ⓒ 20

Ⓑ 2   Ⓓ 5

15. Multi-Step Paula has 21 shells she collected at the beach. She shares them equally with herself and 2 friends. Then she gives 3 shells to her mother. How many shells does Paula have left?

Ⓐ 7   Ⓒ 3

Ⓑ 4   Ⓓ 5

Multiplication Comparisons

TEKS Algebraic
Reasoning—3.5.C
MATHEMATICAL PROCESSES
3.1.D, 3.1.E, 3.1.F

 Essential Question

How can you model and describe multiplication comparisons?

You can use multiplication to compare amounts.

3 times as many as 5.   *5 times as many as 3.*

| 5 | 5 | 5 |

| 5 |

| 3 | 3 | 3 | 3 | 3 |

| 3 |

> An **expression** is part of a number sentence that has numbers and operation signs but does not have an equal sign.

$3 \times 5 \leftarrow$ multiplication expressions $\rightarrow 5 \times 3$

Unlock the Problem

Carly has 9 pennies. Jack has 4 times as much money as Carly. How can you use multiplication to show how much money Jack has compared to Carly?

🔑 **Draw a model and write an expression.**

Carly | _____ |

Jack | ____ | ____ | ____ | ____ |

Use the model to write an expression.

_____ × _____

Describe the expression as a comparison.

_____ times as much as _____

🔑 Example

Amelia made 8 cups of lemonade. Nathan made 4×8 cups of lemonade. They each wrote a comparison to describe the expression 4×8.

Amelia wrote: 4 times as much as 8   Nathan wrote: 4 more than 8

Who described the expression correctly? **Explain.**

_____

_____

1. There are 8 students in the art club. There are 3 times as many students in chorus. Draw a model and write a multiplication expression to represent the number of students in chorus compared to the art club.

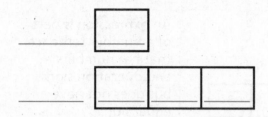

_____ × _____

Math Talk
Mathematical Processes

Explain how strip diagrams help you describe the multiplication.

Draw a model and write a multiplication expression to represent the comparison.

2. 6 times as many as 2

_____ _____ _____ _____ _____

_____

_____

3. 4 times as much as 5

_____ _____ _____ _____

_____

4. 3 times as much as 9

_____ _____ _____

_____

_____

5. 8 times as many as 6

_____ _____ _____ _____ _____ _____ _____ _____

_____

Describe the multiplication expression as a comparison.

6. 9 × 2

_____ times as many as _____

7. 8 × 4

_____ times as much as _____

8. 5 × 7

_____ times as much as _____

9. 6 × 9

_____ times as many as _____

Problem Solving · Real World

10. Use the picture at the right. John's big dog eats 10 times as much food as his cat eats. Write a multiplication expression to represent the amount of food that John's dog eats compared to his cat.

2 tazas

_____

11. **H.O.T.** **Pose a Problem** Write a problem about pet food that could be represented using the expression 4 × 3.

_____

_____

_____

12. **H.O.T.** **Multi-Step** Nando has 4 goldfish. Jill has 3 goldfish. Cooper has 2 times as many goldfish as Nando and Jill have combined. Write an expression that compares the number of goldfish that Cooper has with the number of goldfish that Nando and Jill have in all.

Write Math ▶ Show Your Work

_____

13. **H.O.T.** **Representations** How would the strip diagrams that represent *5 times as much as 11* look different from the strip diagrams that represent *50 times as much as 11*?

_____

_____

_____

_____

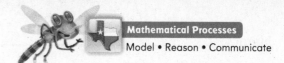
Daily Assessment Task

Fill in the bubble for the correct answer choice.

14. **Multi-Step** Karen has 2 blue hats, 3 green hats, and 1 red hat. Jonah has 3 times as many hats as Karen. Which expression represents the number of hats that Jonah has compared to Karen?

   Ⓐ 3×7 Ⓒ 6×3

   Ⓑ 3×6 Ⓓ $3 + 7$

15. Joseph's dog weighs 10 pounds. Shaunda's dog weighs 5 times as many pounds as Joseph's dog. Which expression represents the weight of Shaunda's dog compared to Joseph's dog?

   Ⓐ $5 + 10$ Ⓒ 10×5

   Ⓑ $10 \times 10 \times 10 \times 10$ Ⓓ 5×10

16. **Use Math Language** Juan has 21 pretzels. Eric's pretzels can be represented by 6×21. Which comparison statement best describes the expression?

   Ⓐ Eric has 6 more pretzels than Eric.

   Ⓑ Juan has 21 more pretzels than Eric

   Ⓒ Eric has 6 times as many pretzels as Juan.

   Ⓓ Juan has 6 fewer pretzels than Eric.

 TEXAS Test Prep

17. **Use Math Language** Which comparison describes the multiplication expression?

$$8 \times 4$$

   Ⓐ 8 more than 4   Ⓒ 4 less than 8

   Ⓑ 4 more than 8   Ⓓ 8 times as many as 4

14.5 Multiplication Comparisons

Draw a model and write a multiplication expression to represent the comparison.

1. 4 times as many as 7

___ ___ ___ ___

___

_____

2. 5 times as many as 3

___ ___ ___ ___ ___

_____

Describe the multiplication expression as a comparison.

3. 7×6

_____ times as many as _____

4. 3×8

_____ times as many as _____

5. 8×5

_____ times as many as _____

6. 9×2

_____ times as many as _____

Problem Solving *Real World*

Use information in the pictures for 7–9.

7. The toy store has 4 times as many whistles as yo-yos. Write a multiplication expression to represent the number of whistles compared to yo-yos.

_____

8. Write a comparison statement about the wind-up ducks that could be described using the expression 10×5.

_____

_____

9. The toy store has 8 times as many soccer balls as spinning tops. Write a multiplication expression to represent the number of soccer balls compared to spinning tops.

_____

_____

Fill in the bubble completely to show your answer.

10. Evelyn sells 5 boxes of greeting cards. Sam sells 3 times as many boxes as Evelyn. Which expression represents the number of boxes that Sam has compared to Evelyn?

Ⓐ $5 \times 5 \times 5$

Ⓑ $5 + 3$

Ⓒ $5 - 3$

Ⓓ 3×5

11. Kaitlin collects 6 bottle caps for a prize. Jin collects 4 times as many bottle caps as Kaitlin. Which expression represents the number of bottle caps that Jin collects compared to Kaitlin?

Ⓐ $6 + 4$

Ⓑ $6 \times 6 \times 6 \times 6$

Ⓒ 4×6

Ⓓ $4 \times 4 \times 4 \times 4 \times 4 \times 4$

12. Farrah has 18 crayons. John's crayons can be represented by 2×18. Which comparison statement describes the expression?

Ⓐ 18 more than 2

Ⓑ 2 times as many as 18

Ⓒ 2 more than 18

Ⓓ 2 fewer than 18

13. Justin writes the multiplication expression 3×9. Which comparison statement describes the expression that Justin wrote?

Ⓐ 3 more than 9

Ⓑ 9 more than 3

Ⓒ 3 times as many as 9

Ⓓ 3 fewer than 9

14. **Multi-Step** Bev has 5 books. She buys 3 more books. Dell has 3 times as many books as Bev. Which expression represents the number of books that Dell has compared to Bev?

Ⓐ 3×8 Ⓒ 5×8

Ⓑ 3×3 Ⓓ 3×5

15. **Multi-Step** Ryan has 5 crayons. He gets 4 more. Cindi has 6 times as many crayons as Ryan. Which expression represents the number of crayons that Cindi has compared to Ryan?

Ⓐ $9 + 6$ Ⓒ 4×6

Ⓑ 6×9 Ⓓ 6×5

Name _____

14.6 Real World Relationships

 TEKS Algebraic Reasoning—3.5.E
MATHEMATICAL PROCESSES
3.1.A, 3.1.E, 3.1.F

? Essential Question

What are some ways you can describe a pattern in a table?

🔑 Unlock the Problem Real World

The outdoor club is planning a camping trip. Each camper will need a flashlight. One flashlight uses 4 batteries. How many batteries are needed for 8 flashlights?

You can describe a pattern in a table.

Flashlights	1	2	3	4	5	6	7	8
Batteries	4	8	12	16	20	24	28	▨

Think: Count by 1s.

Think: Count by 4s.

🔒 One Way Describe a pattern across the rows.

STEP 1 Look for a pattern to complete the table. As you look across the rows, you can see that the number of batteries increases by 4 for each flashlight.

So, for every flashlight add _____ batteries.

_____

STEP 2 Use the pattern to find the number of batteries in 8 flashlights.

Add _____ to 28 batteries. $28 + 4 =$ _____

So, _____ batteries are needed for 8 flashlights.

> **! ERROR Alert**
>
> Check that your pattern will work for all the numbers in the table.

🔒 Another Way Describe a pattern in the columns.

STEP 1 Look for a pattern by comparing the columns in the table. You can multiply the number of flashlights by 4 to find the number of batteries that are needed.

_____

STEP 2 Use the pattern to find how many batteries are needed for 8 flashlights.

$8 \times 4 =$ _____

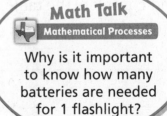

Math Talk
Mathematical Processes

Why is it important to know how many batteries are needed for 1 flashlight?

1. Describe a pattern for the table. Then write a sentence about the cost of 4 packs of batteries.

Packs of Batteries	1	2	3	4
Cost	$3	$6	$9	

_____

_____

Describe a pattern for the table. Then complete the table.

2.

Tents	Lanterns
5	10
6	12
7	14
8	16
9	
10	

_____

3.

Adults	Campers
1	6
2	12
3	18
4	
5	

_____

4.

Hours	1	2	3	4	5
Miles Hiked	2	4	6		

_____

5.

Cabins	3	4	5	6	7
Campers	27	36	45		

_____

6. Describe a pattern for the table at the right, and complete the table. Then complete each statement below.

Canoes	4	5	6	7	8
Campers	12	15	18		

_____

_____

_____ canoes have 12 campers.

_____ canoes have 21 campers.

5 canoes have _____ campers.

8 canoes have _____ campers.

Name _____

Problem Solving Real World

Use the pictograph for 7–9.

7. Jena bought 3 fishing poles. How much money did she spend?

_____

8. **Multi-Step** Noah bought 1 fishing pole, 2 corks, and 1 carton of worms. What was the total cost?

_____

9. **Write Math** ▶ Ryan bought 8 corks. **Explain** how you can use the Commutative Property to find the cost.

_____

_____

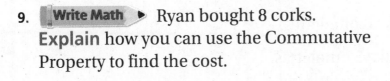

Cost of Fishing Supplies

Corks	🐟 🐟
Poles	🐟 🐟 🐟 🐟 🐟
Worms	🐟 🐟 🐟 🐟

Key: Each 🐟 = $2.

10. **H.O.T. Representations** Students made a craft project at camp. They used 2 small pine cone patterns and 1 large pine cone pattern. Complete the table to find how many patterns were used for the different numbers of projects.

Projects	1	2	3					
Small Pattern	2							
Large Pattern	1							

11. **H.O.T. Multi-Step** The cost to rent a raft is $7 per person. A raft can hold up to 6 people. There is a $3 launch fee per raft. What is the total cost for a group of 6? **Explain**.

_____

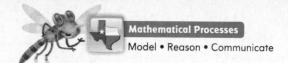

Daily Assessment Task

Fill in the bubble for the correct answer choice.

12. Greg has orchids growing in his garden. Each orchid has 6 blooms. Which of the following describes a pattern in the table?

Orchids	1	2	3	4	5
Blooms	6	12	18	24	30

Ⓐ Add 5.　　　　Ⓒ Multiply by 2.

Ⓑ Multiply by 5.　Ⓓ Add 6.

13. A chef uses eggs to make omelettes as shown in the table at the right. Which statement below is true?

Omelettes	1	2	3	4	5
Eggs	3	6	9	12	15

Ⓐ The chef uses 2 eggs to make 6 omelettes.

Ⓑ The chef uses 12 eggs to make 3 omelettes.

Ⓒ The chef uses 9 eggs to make 3 omelettes.

Ⓓ The chef uses 4 eggs to make 12 omelettes.

14. **Multi-Step** A group of students and adults are going on a field trip in vans. In each van, there will be 8 students and 2 adults. How many people will be in 4 vans?

Ⓐ 40　　　　Ⓒ 14

Ⓑ 10　　　　Ⓓ 32

 TEXAS Test Prep

15. Which of the following describes a pattern in the table?

Lifeguards	1	2	3	4	5
Swimmers	10	20	30	40	50

Ⓐ Add 9.　　　　Ⓒ Subtract 9.

Ⓑ Multiply by 2.　Ⓓ Multiply by 10.

Homework and Practice

Name _____

14.6 Real World Relationships

Describe a pattern for the table. Then complete the table.

1.

Wagons	2	3	4	5	6
Wheels	8	12	16		

_____

2.

Cars	3	4	5	6	7
Riders	15	20	25		

_____

3.

Tricycles	4	5	6	7	8
Wheels	12	15	18		

_____

4.

Van	5	6	7	8	9
Riders	30	36	42		

_____

Problem Solving Real World

Use the pictograph for 5–7.

5. How many students chose vanilla as their favorite flavor?

Favorite Flavors	
Flavor	**Students**
Vanilla	☺ ☺ ☺ ☺ ☺ ☺
Chocolate	☺ ☺ ☺ ☺
Strawberry	☺ ☺ ☺
Key: Each ☺ = 5 students	

_____

6. Two more students voted for strawberry. Now how many students chose strawberry as their favorite flavor?

7. How many more students need to vote for chocolate to tie for votes with vanilla?

_____

Fill in the bubble completely to show your answer.

8. Meg puts 5 tails on 1 kite. How many tails does she need for 5 kites?

Kites	1	2	3	4	5
Tails	5	10	15		

(A) 16

(B) 20

(C) 30

(D) 25

9. Shanaz puts 3 dimes in her bank each day. How many dimes will she have on day 4?

Day	1	2	3	4	5
Dimes	3	6	9		

(A) 15

(B) 12

(C) 9

(D) 7

10. Which describes a pattern in the table?

Vans	1	2	3	4	5
Riders	6	12	18	24	30

(A) Subtract 6.

(B) Multiply by 5.

(C) Add 6.

(D) Multiply by 2.

11. Which describes a pattern in the table?

Vases	1	2	3	4	5
Flowers	4	8	12	16	20

(A) Add 5.

(B) Add 4.

(C) Multiply by 6.

(D) Multiply by 5.

12. **Multi-Step** Isaac uses 4 red beads and 3 blue beads to make a belt. How many beads will Isaac use to make 4 belts?

(A) 48

(B) 12

(C) 28

(D) 16

13. **Multi-Step** Corey uses 5 yellow tiles and 4 green tiles to make a design. How many tiles will he need to repeat the design 5 times?

(A) 45

(B) 9

(C) 25

(D) 20

Find Unknown Numbers

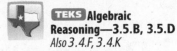
TEKS Algebraic
Reasoning—3.5.B, 3.5.D
Also 3.4.F, 3.4.K
MATHEMATICAL PROCESSES
3.1.E, 3.1.G

 Essential Question

How can you use an array or a multiplication table to find an unknown factor or product?

🔑 Unlock the Problem

Tanisha plans to invite 24 people to a picnic. The invitations come in packs of 8. How many packs of invitations does Tanisha need to buy?

An equation is a number sentence that uses the equal sign to show that two amounts are equal.

A symbol or letter can stand for an unknown factor. You can write the equation, $n \times 8 = 24$, to find how many packs of invitations Tanisha needs. Find the number, n, that makes the equation true.

- How many people is Tanisha inviting? _____
- How many invitations are in 1 pack? _____

🔓 One Way Use an array.

- Show an array with 24 tiles with 8 tiles in each row by completing the drawing.

Math Talk
Mathematical Processes

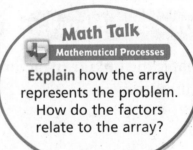

Explain how the array represents the problem. How do the factors relate to the array?

$$n \quad \times \quad 8 \quad = \quad 24$$
$$\uparrow \qquad\quad \uparrow \qquad\quad \uparrow$$

factor   factor   product
number of   number in   total
rows   each row   number

- Count how many rows of 8 tiles there are. **Think:** What number times 8 equals 24?

There are _____ rows of 8 tiles. The unknown factor is _____. $n =$ _____

      _____ $\times 8 = 24$ Check.

      _____ $= 24$ ✓ The equation is true.

So, Tanisha needs _____ packs of invitations.

🔑 Another Way Use a multiplication table.

$$24 \div 8 = \blacksquare$$

Think: $\blacksquare \times 8 = 24$

Find the factor, 8, in the top row.

Look down to find the product, 24.

Look left across the row from 24.

The unknown factor is _____.

$$\blacksquare = \underline{\hspace{1cm}}$$

$$\underline{\hspace{1cm}} \times 8 = 24 \quad \text{Check.}$$

$$\underline{\hspace{1cm}} = 24 \checkmark \text{ The equation is true.}$$

×	0	1	2	3	4	5	6	7	8	9	10
0	0	0	0	0	0	0	0	0	0	0	0
1	0	1	2	3	4	5	6	7	8	9	10
2	0	2	4	6	8	10	12	14	16	18	20
3	0	3	6	9	12	15	18	21	24	27	30
4	0	4	8	12	16	20	24	28	32	36	40
5	0	5	10	15	20	25	30	35	40	45	50
6	0	6	12	18	24	30	36	42	48	54	60
7	0	7	14	21	28	35	42	49	56	63	70
8	0	8	16	24	32	40	48	56	64	72	80
9	0	9	18	27	36	45	54	63	72	81	90
10	0	10	20	30	40	50	60	70	80	90	100

Share and Show 🖊 MATH BOARD

1. What is the unknown factor shown by this array?

$$35 \div \blacksquare = 5$$

$$\blacksquare = \underline{\hspace{1cm}}$$

Find the unknown number.

2. $d \times 3 = 27$

$d = \underline{\hspace{1cm}}$

3. $30 \div \triangle = 6$

$\triangle = \underline{\hspace{1cm}}$

✅ 4. $c = 4 \times 5$

$c = \underline{\hspace{1cm}}$

✅ 5. $\blacksquare \times 2 = 14$

$\blacksquare = \underline{\hspace{1cm}}$

6. $36 \div 9 = b$

$b = \underline{\hspace{1cm}}$

7. $8 \times e = 64$

$e = \underline{\hspace{1cm}}$

8. $7 \times \star = 42$

$\star = \underline{\hspace{1cm}}$

9. $8 \times 9 = z$

$z = \underline{\hspace{1cm}}$

10. $\blacksquare \div 6 = 3$

$\blacksquare = \underline{\hspace{1cm}}$

11. $36 = p \times 6$

$p = \underline{\hspace{1cm}}$

12. $9 \times 7 = m$

$m = \underline{\hspace{1cm}}$

13. $40 \div \triangle = 4$

$\triangle = \underline{\hspace{1cm}}$

Name _____

Problem Solving

H.O.T. **Algebra** Find the unknown number.

14. $3 \times 6 = k \times 9$

    $k =$ _____

15. $4 \times y = 2 \times 6$

    $y =$ _____

16. $30 \div g = 36 - 26$

    $g =$ _____

17. $2 \times 4 = \blacksquare \div 3$

    $\blacksquare =$ _____

18. $9 \times d = 70 + 2$

    $d =$ _____

19. $8 \times h = 60 - 4$

    $h =$ _____

Problem Solving **Real World**

Use the table for 20–23.

20. Tanisha needs 40 cups for the picnic. How many packs of cups should she buy?

    _____

21. **H.O.T.** **Write Math** ▶ **What if** Tanisha needs 40 bowls for the picnic? **Explain** how to write an equation with a letter for an unknown factor to find the number of packs she should buy. Then find the unknown factor.

    _____

    _____

    _____

22. **Multi-Step** Ms. Hill buys 3 tablecloths and 2 packs of napkins. How much money does she spend?

    _____

23. **H.O.T.** **What if** Randy needs an equal number of bowls and cups for his picnic? How many packs of each will he need to buy?

    _____

Picnic Supplies		
Item	Number in 1 Pack	Cost
Bowls	6	$10
Cups	8	$3
Tablecloth	1	$2
Napkins	36	$2
Forks	50	$3

Write Math ▶ Show Your Work

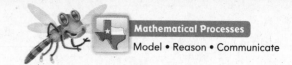

Daily Assessment Task

Fill in the bubble for the correct answer choice.
You can use arrays or equations to represent and solve.

24. What is the unknown product?

$$a = 5 \times 9$$

Ⓐ 30   Ⓒ 14

Ⓑ 45   Ⓓ 40

25. **Representations** The first row of an array is shown below. If the entire array has 40 tiles, how many rows are in the array?

Ⓐ 35   Ⓒ 5

Ⓑ 8   Ⓓ 12

26. **Multi-Step** Lenny and Kristen each made a batch of 24 brownies. Lenny cut his brownies into 3 equal rows. Kristen cut her brownies into 4 equal rows. How many more brownies are in each of Lenny's rows than are in Kristen's rows?

Ⓐ 6   Ⓒ 1

Ⓑ 2   Ⓓ 8

 TEXAS Test Prep

27. What is the unknown factor?

$$m \times 6 = 48$$

Ⓐ 8   Ⓒ 7

Ⓑ 6   Ⓓ 5

470

Name _____

14.7 Find Unknown Numbers

Find the unknown number.

1. $b \times 4 = 32$

   $b =$ _____

2. $m \div 3 = 7$

   $m =$ _____

3. $\blacksquare \times 7 = 49$

   $\blacksquare =$ _____

4. $20 \div 5 = y \times 2$

   $y =$ _____

5. $h \times 6 = 9 \times 4$

   $h =$ _____

6. $8 \times \blacksquare = 40 + 8$

   $\blacksquare =$ _____

Problem Solving

Use the table for 7–10.

7. Miss LaBlanc needs 32 markers for her art class. How many packs should she buy?

   _____

Stationery Store Supplies	
Item	Number in 1 Pack
Notepads	5
Sticky notes	4
Markers	8
Envelopes	30

8. Brian spent $18 on sticky notes and envelopes. Each pack of sticky notes costs $3. A pack of envelopes costs $6. If he buys an equal number of packs of each, how many packs of each did Brian buy?

   _____

9. Joshua needs an equal number of notepads and sticky notes. How many packs of each item does Joshua need to buy?

   _____

   _____

10. Mr. Garcia needs 28 notepads for his class. **Explain** how to write an equation with a letter for the unknown factor to find how many packs he should buy. Then find the unknown factor.

    _____

    _____

Fill in the bubble completely to show your answer.

11. Fiona does 30 sit-ups in sets of 5 sit-ups each. How many sets of sit-ups does Fiona do?

   (A) 35

   (B) 5

   (C) 25

   (D) 6

12. Kalon does 48 jumping jacks in sets of 6 jumping jacks each. How many sets of jumping jacks does Kalon do?

   (A) 6

   (B) 8

   (C) 46

   (D) 40

13. Rich draws this first row of an array. If the entire array has 36 circles, how many rows are there in the array?

   (A) 36

   (B) 45

   (C) 4

   (D) 6

14. Mrs. Spencer arranges one row of 7 chairs in her classroom. If she arranges 28 chairs in equal rows, how many rows of chairs are there?

   (A) 4

   (B) 7

   (C) 35

   (D) 28

15. **Multi-Step** Coz and Amelia each make a tile design with 36 tiles. Coz puts his in rows of 4. Amelia puts hers in rows of 6. How many more tiles are in each of Coz's rows than Amelia's?

   (A) 6

   (B) 9

   (C) 3

   (D) 2

16. **Multi-Step** Denny buys 3 boxes of cereal for $4 each and 5 boxes of oatmeal for $3 each. How much money does Denny spend in all?

   (A) $15

   (B) $7

   (C) $27

   (D) $8

Name _____

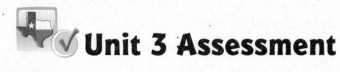

✓ Unit 3 Assessment

Vocabulary

Choose the best term from the box to complete the sentence.

Vocabulary
expression
pattern
rule

1. An _____ is a part of a number sentence that has numbers and operation signs but does not have an equal sign. (p. 455)

2. A _____ is an ordered set of numbers or objects in which the order helps you predict what comes next. (p. 443)

Concepts and Skills

Write a rule for the pattern. Then write the missing number. ⬇ TEKS 3.5

3. 50, 45, 40, 35, 30, _____   Rule: _____

4. 32, 35, 38, _____, 44, 47, _____   Rule: _____

Find the unknown number. ⬇ TEKS 3.5.B, 3.5.D

5. $m \times 5 = 30$

   $m =$ _____

6. $48 \div \blacksquare = 6$

   $\blacksquare =$ _____

7. $20 = 2 \times n$

   $n =$ _____

8. $p \div 8 = 4$

   $p =$ _____

9. $7 = 63 \div y$

   $y =$ _____

10. $1 \times 10 = \star$

    $\star =$ _____

Describe a pattern for the table. Then complete the table. ⬇ TEKS 3.5.E

11.

Weeks	1	2	3	4	5
Days	7	14	21		

12.

Tickets	2	3	4	5	6
Cost	$8	$12	$16		

_____

_____

Fill in the bubble for the correct answer choice.

13. Sally has 4 comic books. Renaldo has 6 comic books. Jay has 2 times as many comic books as Sally and Renaldo combined. Which expression represents the number of comic books Jay has compared to Sally and Renaldo combined? TEKS 3.5.C

    (A) $4 + 6$

    (B) 2×6

    (C) 2×10

    (D) $2 \div 10$

14. The camping club rents 4 rafts. How many people can 4 rafts hold? TEKS 3.5.E

Rafts	1	2	3	4
People	8	16	24	

    (A) 20

    (B) 30

    (C) 40

    (D) 32

15. There are 24 students in Mr. Smith's class and 30 students in Mr. Becker's class. The students sit in chairs in the gymnasium in rows with 6 chairs in each row. How many rows of chairs are there in all? TEKS 3.5.B, 3.5.D

    (A) 54

    (B) 4

    (C) 9

    (D) 5

16. Use the array. Which number makes the equation true?
    TEKS 3.5.B, 3.5.D

    $24 \div 4 =$ _____

    (A) 6   (C) 20

    (B) 8   (D) 12

Fill in the bubble for the correct answer choice.

Use the table for 17–20. You may use models, number lines, and equations to represent and solve.

17. Susie's Sweater Shop sells sweaters online. The table shows the number of sweaters sold in three months. How many more sweaters were sold in January than in March? ↴ TEKS 3.5.A

Susie's Sweater Shop	
Month	Numbers of Sweaters Sold
January	402
February	298
March	171

Ⓐ 231

Ⓑ 371

Ⓒ 331

Ⓓ 573

18. How many sweaters were sold in January and February? ↴ TEKS 3.5.A

Ⓐ 600

Ⓑ 700

Ⓒ 800

Ⓓ 690

19. How many more sweaters were sold in February and March than in January? ↴ TEKS 3.5.A

Ⓐ 66

Ⓑ 167

Ⓒ 67

Ⓓ 871

20. Susie sold only 28 sweaters in June, 19 sweaters in July, and 11 sweaters in August. How many sweaters did she sell in June, July, and August? ↴ TEKS 3.5.A

Ⓐ 57

Ⓒ 48

Ⓑ 56

Ⓓ 58

Fill in the bubble for the correct answer choice.
You can use models or equations to solve.

 **TEXAS Test Prep**

21. Brooklyn has 10 dolphin stickers. Jorge's stickers can be represented by 3×10. Which comparison statement describes the expression? ↓ TEKS 3.5.C

Ⓐ Brooklyn has 10 more stickers than Jorge.

Ⓑ Jorge has 3 times as many stickers as Brooklyn.

Ⓒ Brooklyn has 3 more stickers than Jorge.

Ⓓ Jorge has 3 fewer stickers than Brooklyn.

22. Which of the following multiplication equations can be used to find $42 \div 7$? ↓ TEKS 3.5.B

Ⓐ $6 \times 6 = 36$ Ⓒ $8 \times 6 = 48$

Ⓑ $5 \times 8 = 40$ Ⓓ $7 \times 6 = 42$

23. Last week Arabeth read 123 pages in her book. This week she read 136 pages. There are 575 pages in the book. How many pages does she have left to read? ↓ TEKS 3.5.A

Ⓐ 452 Ⓒ 316

Ⓑ 256 Ⓓ Not here

24. Mr. Kane keeps track of ticket sales at The Playhouse. The table shows the tickets sold for afternoon and evening shows on Friday, Saturday, and Sunday.

Playhouse Tickets Sales

	Friday	Saturday	Sunday
Afternoon	53	59	64
Evening	94	83	79

Each show has the same number of seats available. At the Friday evening show, there were 31 empty seats. How many empty seats were there at one of the other shows? Explain how you found your answer. ↓ TEKS 3.5.A

_____

_____

_____

Geometry and Measurement

Show What You Know ✓

Check your understanding of important skills.

Name _____

▶ **Sort Two-Dimensional Figures by Attributes**

1. **Circle the figures with 4 sides and 4 vertices.**

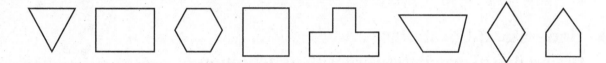

▶ **Model Multiplication with Arrays**

Use the array. Complete the multiplication sentence.

2.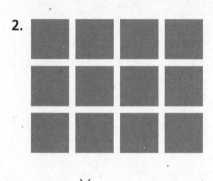

___ × ___ = ___

3.

___ × ___ = ___

▶ **Tell Time to the Minute** **Write the time.**

4.

_____

5.

_____

6.

_____

Assessment Options:
Soar to Success Math

Vocabulary Builder

Complete the tree map by using the words with a ✓.

quadrilateral

▶ **Understand Vocabulary**

Draw a line to match the word with its definition.

1. perimeter •

2. elapsed time •

3. congruent •

4. capacity •

5. area •

6. vertex •

7. mass •

• The time that passes from the start of an activity to the end of an activity

• The measure of the number of unit squares needed to cover a surface

• The distance around a shape

• Figures that have the same size and shape

• The point where three or more edges meet in a solid figure

• The amount a container can hold

• The amount of matter in an object

Preview Words
area
capacity
cone
congruent
cube
cylinder
edge
elapsed time
face
mass
✓ parallelogram
perimeter
quadrilateral
✓ rectangle
rectangular prism
✓ rhombus
sphere
✓ square
✓ trapezoid
triangular prism
vertex
weight

Interactive Student Edition
Multimedia eGlossary

Name _____

Vocabulary

When you find how long or tall something is, you find its **length**. When you find how much matter something has, you find its **mass**.

Use the words in the **Word Bank** to complete the table below.

Word Bank for Metric Measurements

centimeter   meter   kilogram

gram   kilometer

Length	Mass
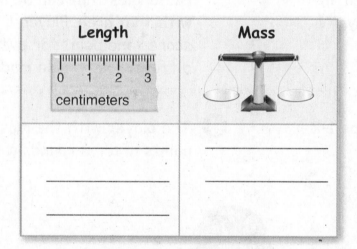	
_____	_____
_____	_____
_____	

Writing Look at the units of mass you listed. Write them in order by size from smallest to largest.

_____

Reading Look for this book in your library.
Counting On Frank, by Rod Clement

Get Ready Game

Area in Action

Object of the Game To make as many rectangles with a given area as possible.

Materials

- 2 number cubes labeled 1–6
- 1-centimeter grid paper
- crayons

Number of Players 2

How to Play

1 Player 1 tosses the number cubes. The sum of the numbers tells the area, in square units, that Player 1 should color.

2 Player 1 uses crayons to show the different rectangles that can be made with that area. Player 1 scores one point for every different rectangle made.

3 Player 2 repeats Steps 1–2.

4 The player with the most points after 3 rounds wins.

480

TEKS **Geometry and Measurement—3.6.A, 3.6.B**
MATHEMATICAL PROCESSES
3.1.D, 3.1.F

15.1 Classify Quadrilaterals

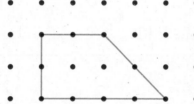

Essential Question

How can you use right angles and parallel sides to help you classify quadrilaterals?

Unlock the Problem

An **angle** is formed by two rays that share an endpoint. Two dimensional figures have angles formed by two line segments that share an endpoint. The shared endpoint is called a **vertex**. The plural of *vertex* is *vertices*.

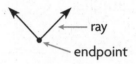

ray
endpoint

Jason drew this polygon on dot paper.

There are _____ angles.

There are _____ sides.

> **Math Idea**
> A polygon is a closed plane figure with straight sides that are line segments.

Jason's polygon has 2 **right angles**. They form square corners. You can use the corner of a sheet of paper to tell if an angle is a right angle. Draw boxes to show the right angles.

Look at Jason's polygon. How many pairs of sides are parallel?

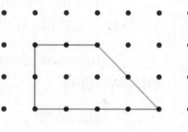

Think: Which sides will never cross or meet?

Lines that appear to never cross or meet and are always the same distance apart are **parallel lines**.

So, Jason's polygon has _____ pair of parallel sides.

Classify Quadrilaterals

Quadrilaterals are named by their sides and their angles.

ERROR Alert

Some quadrilaterals cannot be classified as a trapezoid, parallelogram, rectangle, square, or rhombus.

Describe quadrilaterals.

quadrilateral

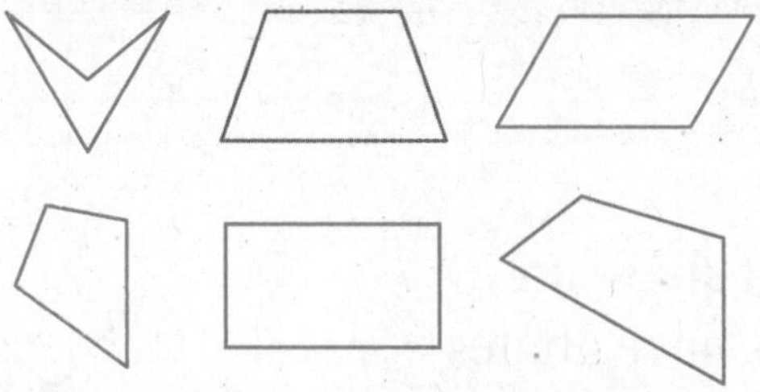

________ sides

________ angles

---

trapezoid

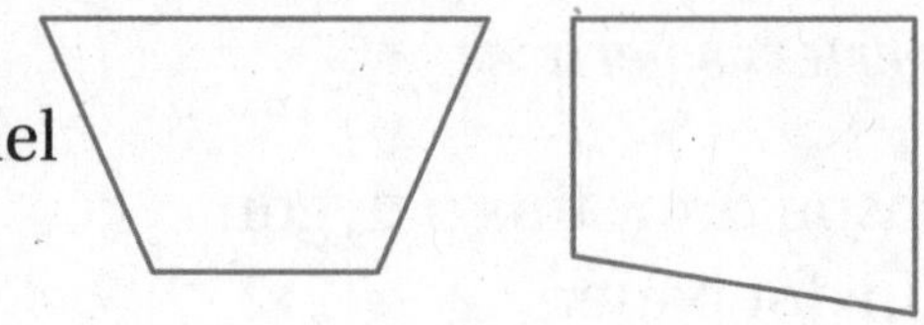

exactly ________ pair of opposite sides that are parallel

lengths of sides could be the same

---

parallelogram

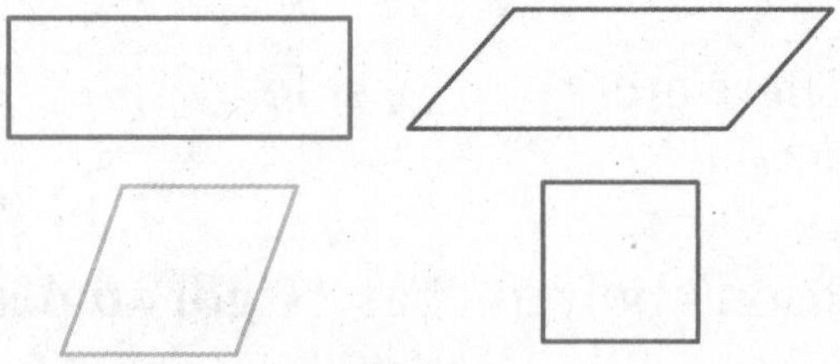

________ pairs of opposite sides that are parallel

________ pairs of sides that are of equal length

---

rectangle

______ pairs of opposite sides that are parallel

______ pairs of sides that are of equal length

______ right angles

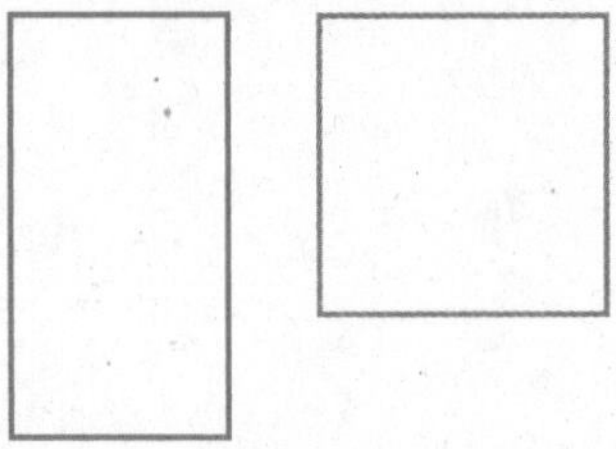

square

______ pairs of opposite sides that are parallel

______ sides that are of equal length

______ right angles

rhombus

______ pairs of opposite sides that are parallel

______ sides that are of equal length

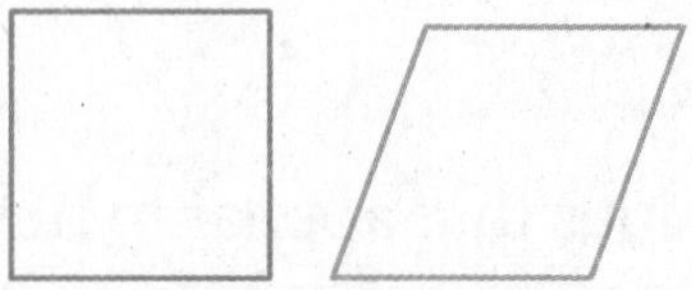

Math Talk

Mathematical Processes

Explain why a square can also be named a rectangle or a rhombus.

Name _____

Look at the quadrilateral at the right.

1. How many right angles are in the quadrilateral?

   _____ right angles

2. Which sides appear to be parallel? _____

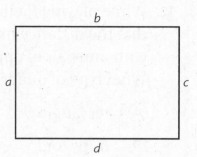

3. Name the quadrilateral. _____

Circle all the words that describe the quadrilateral.

4.

   rectangle

   rhombus

   square

   parallelogram

5.

   rhombus

   parallelogram

   square

   rectangle

Problem Solving

H.O.T. **Analyze** Write *all* or *some* to complete the sentence for 6–9.

6. The opposite sides of _____ rectangles are parallel.

7. _____ sides of a rhombus are the same length.

8. _____ rhombuses are squares.

9. _____ trapezoids have 1 pair of opposite sides that are parallel.

10. **Communicate** I am a quadrilateral that has no right angles and 4 sides that are of equal length. What figure am I?

    _____

11. **H.O.T.** **Multi-Step** I am a polygon that has 4 sides and 4 angles. All of my angles are right angles. Circle all the figures that I could be.

   quadrilateral   rectangle   square   rhombus

   trapezoid   parallelogram

Mathematical Processes
Model • Reason • Communicate

Fill in the bubble for the correct answer choice.

12. While playing football after school, Jesse notices that the distance marker contains a quadrilateral with one pair of opposite sides that are parallel. What type of quadrilateral is it?

Ⓐ rectangle

Ⓑ trapezoid

Ⓒ square

Ⓓ rhombus

13. Dean makes a pattern using 10 square tiles. How many pairs of opposite sides are parallel in the 10 square tiles?

Ⓐ 20　　　　　Ⓒ 40

Ⓑ 10　　　　　Ⓓ 0

14. **Multi-Step** Carina is using scraps of fabric to make a quilt. How many of the fabric scraps are in the shape of rhombuses?

Ⓐ 1　　　　　Ⓒ 0

Ⓑ 2　　　　　Ⓓ 3

 TEXAS Test Prep

15. What is a true statement about the quadrilateral at the right?

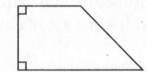

Ⓐ There is 1 right angle.

Ⓑ There are 4 right angles.

Ⓒ There are no right angles.

Ⓓ There are 2 right angles.

TEKS Geometry and Measurement—3.6.A, 3.6.B
MATHEMATICAL PROCESSES 3.1.D, 3.1.F

Name _____

15.1 Classify Quadrilaterals

Circle all the words that describe the quadrilateral.

1. parallelogram

   trapezoid

   rhombus

   rectangle

2. 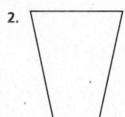 parallelogram

   trapezoid

   rhombus

   rectangle

Problem Solving

Write *all* or *some* to complete the sentence for 3–6.

3. _____ rectangles are squares.

4. _____ angles of a rectangle are right angles.

5. _____ parallelograms have all 4 sides that are equal in length.

6. _____ trapezoids have 2 sides that are equal in length.

7. I am a polygon that has 2 pairs of opposite sides that are parallel. Circle all of the figures that I could be.

   parallelogram   square

   trapezoid   quadrilateral

   rhombus   rectangle

8. I am a quadrilateral that has 4 right angles. My opposite sides are parallel and of equal length. What figure am I?

   _____

Fill in the bubble completely to show your answer.

9. Lily makes an art poster that has exactly one pair of opposite sides that are parallel and 2 sides that are the same length. What figure is Lily's poster?

Ⓐ trapezoid

Ⓑ rectangle

Ⓒ rhombus

Ⓓ parallelogram

10. Desmond draws a polygon that has 4 sides that are the same length and no right angles. How can Desmond classify the polygon he drew?

Ⓐ square

Ⓑ rhombus

Ⓒ rectangle

Ⓓ parallelogram

11. Kara makes the kite shown at the right from 4 triangles. What is the shape of Kara's kite?

Ⓐ square

Ⓑ parallelogram

Ⓒ rhombus

Ⓓ quadrilateral

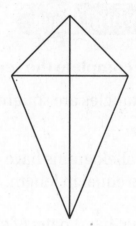

12. **Multi-Step** Ben is making cutouts to use in an art design. How many of the cutouts have the shape of a rectangle?

Ⓐ 5

Ⓑ 2

Ⓒ 4

Ⓓ 3

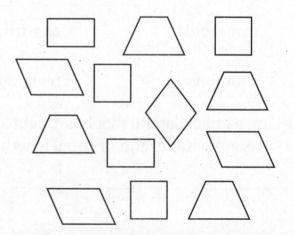

TEKS Geometry and Measurement—3.6.B
Also 3.6.A
MATHEMATICAL PROCESSES
3.1.D, 3.1.G

15.2 Draw Quadrilaterals

? Essential Question

How can you draw quadrilaterals?

Unlock the Problem

Connect You have learned to classify quadrilaterals by the number of pairs of opposite sides that are parallel, by the number of pairs of sides of equal length, and by the number of right angles.

How can you draw quadrilaterals?

Activity 1 Use grid paper to draw quadrilaterals.

Materials ■ ruler

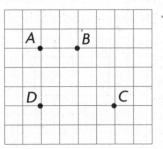

- Use a ruler to draw line segments from points A to B, from B to C, from C to D, and from D to A.

- Write the name of your quadrilateral.

_____

Activity 2 Draw a figure that does not belong.

Materials ■ ruler

A Here are three examples of a parallelogram. Draw an example of a quadrilateral that is not a parallelogram.

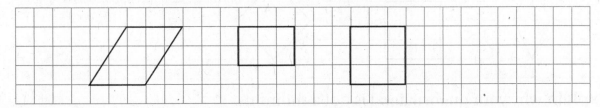

- **Explain** why your quadrilateral is not a parallelogram.

_____

_____

B Here are three examples of a square.
Draw a quadrilateral that is not a square.

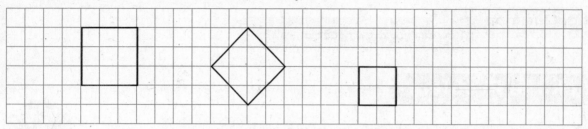

• **Explain** why your quadrilateral is not a square.

_____

_____

C Here are three examples of a rectangle.
Draw a quadrilateral that is not a rectangle.

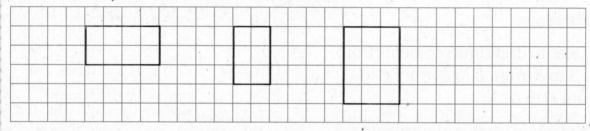

• **Explain** why your quadrilateral is not a rectangle.

_____

_____

D Here are three examples of a rhombus.
Draw a quadrilateral that is not a rhombus.

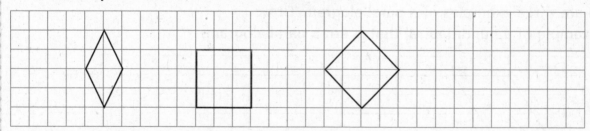

• **Explain** why your quadrilateral is not a rhombus.

_____

_____

_____

Math Talk
Mathematical Processes

Compare your drawings with your classmates. **Explain** how your drawings are alike and how they are different.

Name _____

1. Choose four endpoints that connect to make a rectangle.

   Think: A rectangle has 2 pairs of opposite sides that are parallel, 2 pairs of sides of equal length, and 4 right angles.

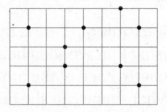

Draw a quadrilateral that is described.
Name the quadrilateral you drew.

✓ 2. 4 right angles

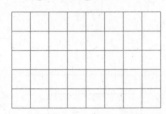

Name _____

3. 2 pairs of opposite sides that are parallel

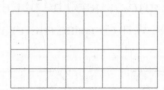

Name _____

Draw a quadrilateral that does not belong. Then explain why.

✓ 4.

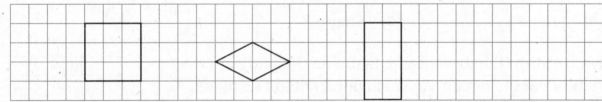

_____

5. **H.O.T.** **Multi-Step** Amy has 4 straws of equal length. Name the quadrilaterals she can make

using these 4 straws. _____

Amy cuts one of the straws in half. She uses the two halves and two of the other straws to make a quadrilateral. Name a quadrilateral she can make using

these 4 straws. _____

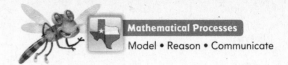
Daily Assessment Task

Fill in the bubble for the correct answer choice.

6. **Reasoning** Clara is building a frame for a doghouse wall using four wooden boards. Two of the boards are the same length. Each of the other two boards is a different length. What shape can she build?

   Ⓐ rectangle   Ⓒ trapezoid

   Ⓑ square   Ⓓ rhombus

7. **Use Diagrams** The pieces of a pattern for a mosaic are drawn on grid paper. The pattern shows four quadrilaterals. Which quadrilateral is not a parallelogram?

   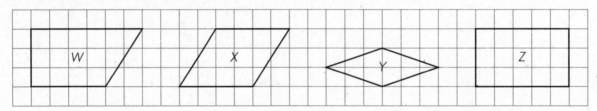

   Ⓐ Shape *W*   Ⓒ Shape *X*

   Ⓑ Shape *Y*   Ⓓ Shape *Z*

8. **Multi-Step** Ethan wants the figure on the grid paper to be a parallelogram. At which point should he place the fourth vertex?

   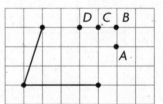

   Ⓐ Point *D*   Ⓒ Point *C*

   Ⓑ Point *B*   Ⓓ Point *A*

 TEXAS Test Prep

9. Jordan drew a quadrilateral with 2 pairs of opposite sides that are parallel. Which figure could NOT be the quadrilateral Jordan drew?

   Ⓐ 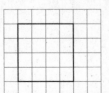   Ⓑ 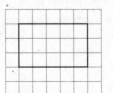   Ⓒ 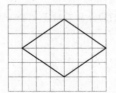   Ⓓ

TEKS Geometry and Measurement—3.6.B
Also 3.6.A
MATHEMATICAL PROCESSES 3.1.D, 3.1.G

Name _____

15.2 Draw Quadrilaterals

Draw a quadrilateral that is described.
Name the quadrilateral you drew.

1. 2 pairs of opposite sides that are parallel and no right angles

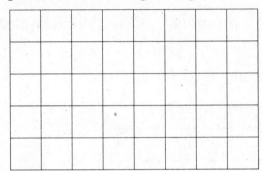

Name _____

2. 1 pair of opposite sides that are parallel

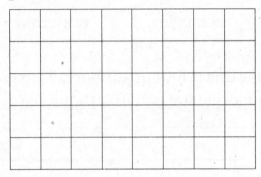

Name _____

3. Draw a quadrilateral that does not belong. Then explain why.

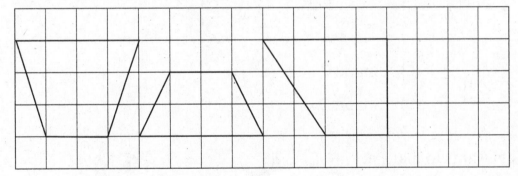

_____

_____

Problem Solving

4. Enrique has the craft sticks shown. Name the possible polygons Enrique can make.

_____

Fill in the bubble completely to show your answer.

5. Midori uses wooden sticks to make a quadrilateral. She has 2 equal-length long sticks and 2 equal-length short sticks. If she places the sticks so there are 4 right angles, which figure does Midori make?

Ⓐ rhombus Ⓒ square

Ⓑ rectangle Ⓓ trapezoid

6. Han has 2 long pencils of equal length and 2 short pencils of equal length. If he arranges them so that the long pencils and short pencils are opposite and parallel, which figure does he make?

Ⓐ trapezoid Ⓒ square

Ⓑ rhombus Ⓓ parallelogram

7. Rex draws four quadrilaterals on grid paper. Which quadrilateral is NOT a rhombus?

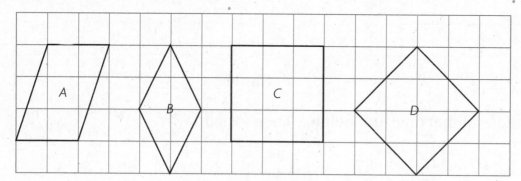

Ⓐ Shape A Ⓒ Shape C

Ⓑ Shape B Ⓓ Shape D

8. **Multi-Step** Gigi wants to make a figure with four craft sticks. She has the three craft sticks shown and needs one more. Which size of craft stick does Gigi need to make the figure?

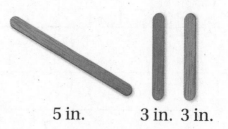

5 in. 3 in. 3 in.

Ⓐ 5-in. craft stick; rectangle Ⓒ 5–in. craft stick; square

Ⓑ 3-in. craft stick; rectangle Ⓓ 6–in. craft stick; square

Name _____

15.3 PROBLEM SOLVING • Classify
Plane Figures

TEKS Geometry and Measurement—3.6.A
Also 3.6.B
MATHEMATICAL PROCESSES
3.1.B, 3.1.D

Essential Question

How can you use the strategy *draw a diagram* to classify plane figures?

? Unlock the Problem Real World

A **Venn diagram** shows how sets of things are related. In the Venn diagram at the right, one circle has figures that are rectangles. Figures that are rhombuses are in the other circle. The figures in the section where the circles overlap are both rectangles and rhombuses.

What type of quadrilateral is in both circles?

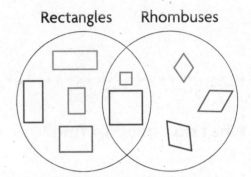

Rectangles   Rhombuses

Read

What do I need to find?

_____

What information am I given?

the circles labeled _____ and

_____

Plan

What is my plan or strategy?

_____

_____

_____

Solve

What is true about all quadrilaterals?

_____

Which quadrilaterals have 2 pairs of opposite sides that are parallel?

_____

Which quadrilaterals have 4 sides of equal length? _____

Which quadrilaterals have 4 right angles?

_____

The quadrilaterals in the section where the circles overlap have _____ pairs of opposite sides that are parallel, _____ sides of equal length, and _____ right angles.

So, _____ are in both circles.

Math Talk
Mathematical Processes

Does a △ fit in the Venn diagram? Explain.

© Houghton Mifflin Harcourt Publishing Company

Module 15   493

Try Another Problem

The Venn diagram at the right shows the figures Abbie used to make a picture. Where would the figure shown below be placed in the Venn diagram?

Quadrilaterals   Polygons with Right Angles

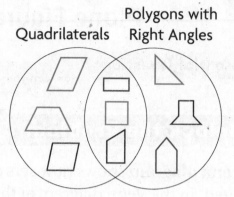

Read	Solve
What do I need to find?	
What information am I given?	
Plan	
What is my plan or strategy?	

1. How many figures do not have right angles?

   _____

2. How many red figures have right angles but are

   not quadrilaterals? _____

3. **Analyze** What is a different way to sort the figures?

   _____

   _____

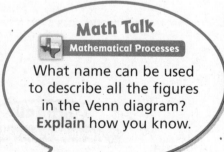

Math Talk

Mathematical Processes

What name can be used to describe all the figures in the Venn diagram? **Explain** how you know.

494

Name _____

Use the Venn diagram for 1–2.

☑ 1. Jordan is sorting the figures at the right in a Venn diagram. Where does the ◇ go?

First, look at the sides and angles of the polygons.

Next, draw the polygons in the Venn diagram below.

The figure above has _____ sides of equal length

and _____ right angles.

So, the figure goes in the circle labeled

_____

☑ 2. Where in the Venn diagram would you place a ⬠?

_____

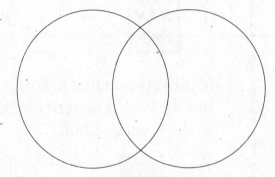

Polygons with Right Angles   Polygons with All Sides Equal in Length

Problem Solving

3. **H.O.T.** **Multi-Step** **Use Math Language**
Eva drew the Venn diagram at the right. What labels could she have used for the diagram? Where would each label go?

_____

_____

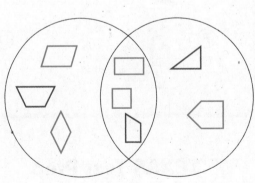

4. **H.O.T.** **Multi-Step** **Display**
Draw and label a Venn diagram to show one way you can sort a parallelogram, a rectangle, a square, a trapezoid, and a rhombus.

Daily Assessment Task

Fill in the bubble for the correct answer choice.

5. Max classifies the street signs he sees by shape, and then sorts them in a Venn diagram. The circles are labeled "Polygons with Right Angles" and "Polygons with All Sides Equal in Length." Which sign is in the section where the two circles overlap?

Ⓐ

Ⓒ

Ⓑ

Ⓓ

6. **Multi-Step** Jenna makes a design using pattern blocks. Which pattern block is placed incorrectly in the Venn diagram?

Ⓐ

Ⓒ

Ⓑ

Ⓓ

Polygons with All Sides Equal in Length   Polygons with Opposite Sides Parallel

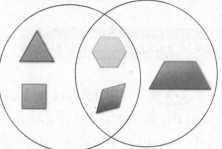

⭐ TEXAS Test Prep

7. What label could describe Circle A?

Ⓐ Polygons with 4 Right Angles

Ⓑ Polygons with 2 Pairs of Opposite Sides That Are Parallel

Ⓒ Polygons with 2 Pairs of Sides of Equal Length

Ⓓ Polygons with All Sides of Equal Length

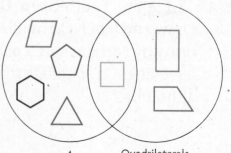

A   Quadrilaterals with Right Angles

15.3 PROBLEM SOLVING • Classify Plane Figures

Use the Venn diagram for 1 and 2.

1. Draw the polygons in the Venn diagram.

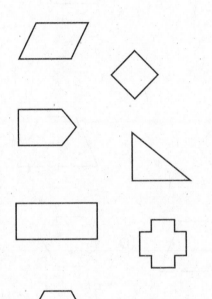
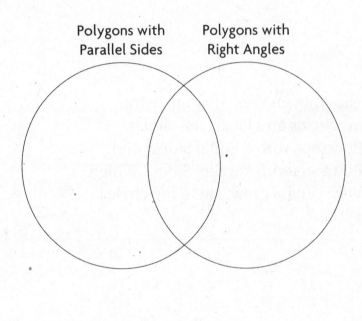

2. Where in the Venn diagram would you place a 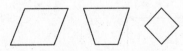 ?

Problem Solving Real World

3. Tia wants to include the figures at the right in one circle of a Venn diagram. What label can she use?

Fill in the bubble completely to show your answer.

4. Fran draws a Venn diagram with two circles and labels the circles "Polygons with Parallel Sides" and "Quadrilaterals with Parallel Sides." Which figure belongs only in the circle labeled "Polygons with Parallel Sides?"

Ⓐ 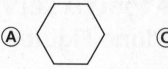   Ⓒ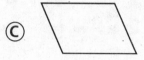

Ⓑ   Ⓓ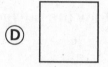

5. Sean draws a Venn diagram with two circles and labels the circles "Polygons with 4 Equal Sides" and "Polygons with Parallel Sides." Which figure can he draw where the circles overlap?

Ⓐ 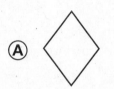   Ⓒ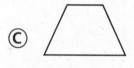

Ⓑ    Ⓓ

6. **Multi-Step** Jessica draws this Venn diagram. Which of the following two figures can she place only in circle A?

Ⓐ

Ⓑ

Ⓒ

Ⓓ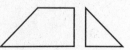

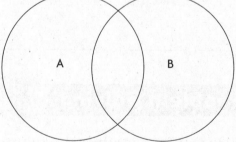

Polygons with Right Angles   Polygons with 2 Pairs of Equal Sides

A   B

Name _____

TEKS Geometry and Measurement—3.6.E

MATHEMATICAL PROCESSES
3.1.C, 3.1.D

15.4 Identify Congruent Figures

? Essential Question

How can you identify two-dimensional figures that are congruent?

🔑 Unlock the Problem

Figures that have the same size and the same shape are **congruent**.

Look at the pattern blocks at the right. Do the shapes appear to be congruent?

🔒 Compare size and shape.

These pairs of shapes appear to be congruent.

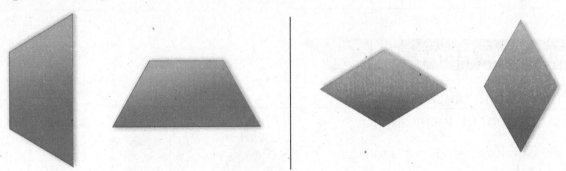

Same size, same shape

These pairs of shapes are not congruent.

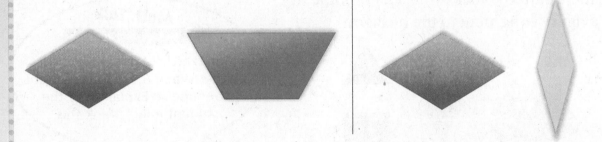

Not the same shape   Not the same size

The yellow pattern blocks appear to be _____ size

and _____ shape. So, they are _____.

🔓 **Activity** Materials ■ pattern blocks ■ paper

Trace pattern blocks to find congruent figures.

STEP 1 Trace a blue rhombus pattern block in the space below.

STEP 2 Trace two pattern blocks to make a figure that is congruent to the rhombus.

STEP 3 Compare the tracings you made. Are the outlines the same size and shape? _____

• Are the figures you traced congruent? **Explain**.

_____

Share and Show

1. Which pattern block appears to be congruent to Shape *A*?

   Think: Which pattern block is the same size and shape?

   _____

Shape *A*   Shape *B*   Shape *C*

✓ 2. Circle the 2 pattern blocks you can combine to make a figure congruent to the hexagon.

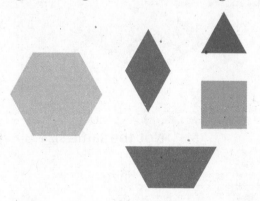

Math Talk
Mathematical Processes

For Exercise 1, a student said neither shape *B* or *C* is congruent to shape *A*. **Explain** why the student might think this.

2 rhombuses   2 squares   2 trapezoids   2 triangles

Name _____

Look at the first figure. Tell if it appears to be congruent to the second figure. Write *yes* or *no*.

 3.

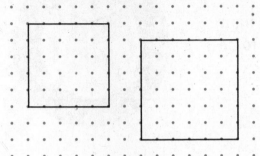

_____

4.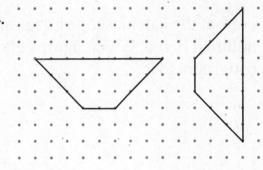

_____

 Problem Solving Real World

5. **H.O.T.** **Multi-Step** List all the ways you can use congruent pattern blocks to make the hexagon shown.

_____

6. **Write Math** ▶ **What's the Error?** Isabel says that all squares are congruent. **Use Math Language** to explain her error.

_____

_____

7. **Use Diagrams** List all the pairs of figures that appear to be congruent.

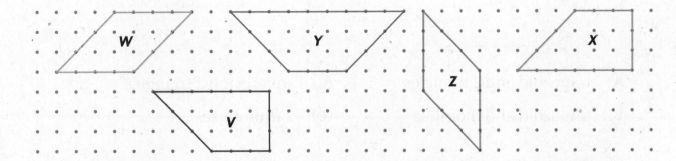

© Houghton Mifflin Harcourt Publishing Company

Daily Assessment Task

Fill in the bubble for the correct answer choice.

8. Look at the kaleidoscope image and find the figure outlined in red. Which figure below appears to be congruent to it?

Ⓐ K Ⓑ L Ⓒ J Ⓓ M

9. **Multi-Step** Israel is making a pattern with quadrilaterals for a wallpaper border. Which figures appear to be congruent?

Ⓐ the two rectangles

Ⓒ the square and one rectangle

Ⓑ the trapezoid and one rectangle

Ⓓ the rhombus and the square

⭐ **TEXAS Test Prep**

10. Which pattern blocks can you combine to make a shape that is congruent to the shape below?

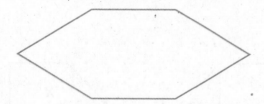

Ⓐ trapezoid and 2 triangles

Ⓒ square and 2 triangles

Ⓑ trapezoid and rhombus

Ⓓ 2 rhombuses

15.4 Identify Congruent Figures

Look at the first figure. Tell if it appears to be congruent to the second figure. Write *yes* or *no*.

1.
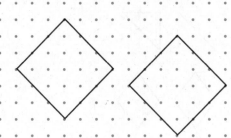

_____

2.
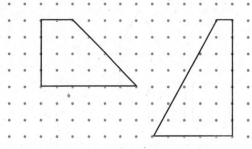

_____

Problem Solving (Real World)

3. List all the ways you can use congruent pattern blocks to make the figure shown.

_____

_____

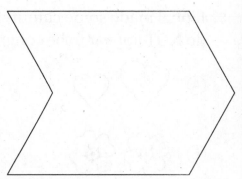

4. List the pairs of figures that appear to be congruent.

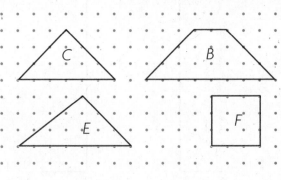

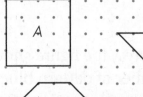

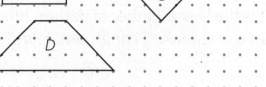

_____

5. Draw a congruent figure on the dot paper for each figure you did not list in exercise 4.

Fill in the bubble completely to show your answer.

6. Ursula drew the congruent figures below. Which 2 pattern blocks can she combine to make a rhombus?

Ⓐ

Ⓑ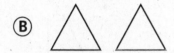

Ⓒ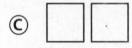

Ⓓ

7. Albert wants to make a parallelogram. Which figures can he add to the ends of a square to make the shape?

Ⓐ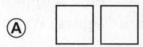

Ⓑ

Ⓒ

Ⓓ

8. Lionel made some cutout shapes. Which figures do NOT appear to be congruent?

Ⓐ    Ⓒ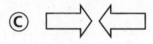

Ⓑ    Ⓓ

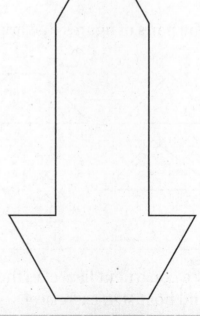

9. **Multi-Step** Manny drew the figure shown. What is the least number of pattern blocks he can use to make a congruent figure?

Ⓐ 2   Ⓒ 4

Ⓑ 5   Ⓓ 3

© Houghton Mifflin Harcourt Publishing Company

Name _____

15.5 Three-Dimensional Solids

? Essential Question

How can you identify, describe, and classify three-dimensional solids?

🔑 Unlock the Problem

Solid figures have length, width, and height. They are also called **three-dimensional figures**.

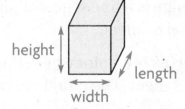

height

length

width

🔒 **Find solid figures.**

Carly has a wooden clown puppet. Which parts of the puppet are shaped like a rectangular prism?

rectangular prism

cube

sphere

cone

cylinder

 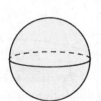

triangular prism

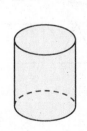 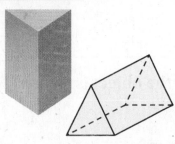

Math Talk
Mathematical Processes

Give an example of an object in the classroom that has both curved and flat surfaces.

So, the _____ are shaped like a rectangular prism.

1. What part of the puppet is shaped like a triangular prism? _____

🔑 Explore solid figures.

Solid figures can be classified by the number of faces, edges, and vertices.

A polygon that is a flat surface of a solid figure is a **face**.

An **edge** is a line segment formed where two faces meet.

A **vertex** is a point where three or more edges meet. The plural of *vertex* is *vertices*.

Try This! Write the word to describe what the arrow is pointing to.

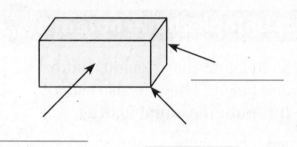

_____

_____   _____

🔑 Activity Name the faces of prisms.

Materials ■ cube, rectangular prism, triangular prism, paper, crayons

- Trace the faces of a cube. Name the plane figures you drew.

- Count the number of faces, edges, and vertices. Record the numbers in the table.

- Repeat the steps for a rectangular prism and a triangular prism.

Name of Figure	Names of Faces	Number of		
		Faces	Edges	Vertices
cube				
rectangular prism				
triangular prism				

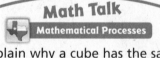

Share and Show

 MATH BOARD

Math Talk
Mathematical Processes
Explain why a cube has the same number of faces, edges, and vertices as a rectangular prism.

1. Name the solid figure that has the faces shown at the right.

_____

Name the solid figure that the object is shaped like.

2.

_____

✓ 3.

_____

4.

_____

5.

_____

Name _____

Name the solid figure. Then write the number of faces, edges, and vertices.

6.

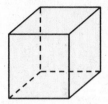

_____ faces

_____ edges

_____ vertices

_____

7. Write one way you can sort a sphere, a cone, and a cylinder.

_____

H.O.T. **Write *All*, *Some*, or *None* to complete the sentence.**

8. _____ of the faces of a cube are squares.

9. _____ of the faces of a triangular prism are triangles.

10. _____ of the faces of a rectangular prism is curved.

Unlock the Problem Real World

11. **H.O.T.** **Multi-Step Analyze**
Fiona drew the Venn diagram at the right to help her sort solid figures. Where would the figure below be placed in the Venn diagram?

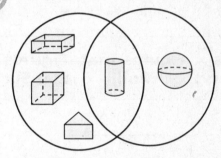

Solid Figures with Flat Surfaces   Solid Figures with Curved Surfaces

Math on the Spot

a. What do you need to find? _____

b. What information are you given? _____

_____

c. How will you solve the problem?

_____

_____

d. Complete the sentences.

I know that a cone has a _____

surface and a _____ surface.

So, a cone goes _____

_____

Daily Assessment Task

For 12 and 14, fill in the bubble completely to show your answer.

12. **Multi-Step** Scarlet and Violet take turns stacking blocks. They start with a cube. Next, Scarlet adds a cylinder. Violet puts a rectangular prism on top. Scarlet takes off the rectangular prism. She adds another cube. What does the structure look like?

Ⓐ Ⓑ Ⓒ Ⓓ

13. **Representations** Joseph wants to sort the solid figures below into five groups. Use what you know about solid figures to complete the table.

Figures That Stack	Figures That Roll	Figures with Flat Surfaces	Figures with Curved Surfaces	Figures with More Than 2 Faces

 TEXAS Test Prep

14. Aaron drew the figure at the right. What solid figure did he draw?

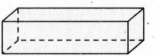

   Ⓐ cube   Ⓒ rectangular prism

   Ⓑ cone   Ⓓ cylinder

Homework and Practice

Name _____

15.5 Three-Dimensional Solids

Name the solid figure that the object is shaped like.

1.

_____

2.

_____

3.
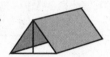

_____

Name the solid figure. Then write the number of faces, edges, and vertices.

4.
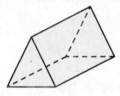

_____

_____ faces

_____ edges

_____ vertices

5.
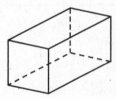

_____

_____ faces

_____ edges

_____ vertices

Problem Solving (Real World)

6. Amber drew this Venn diagram. Can Amber place a cone or a cylinder in the diagram? **Explain.**

   _____

   _____

   _____

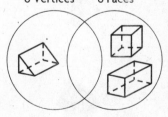

Figures with   Figures with
6 Vertices   6 Faces

7. Mathias says that all of the faces of a triangular prism are triangles. Is his statement correct? **Explain.**

   _____

Fill in the bubble completely to show your answer.

8. Pia is making a rectangular prism from cutouts. She has these figures.

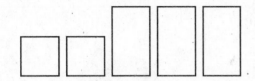

Which flat figure does Pia need to complete the solid figure?

Ⓐ square

Ⓑ rectangle

Ⓒ triangle

Ⓓ circle

9. Trent is making a triangular prism from cutouts. He has 2 triangles and 2 rectangles. Which flat figure does Trent need to complete the solid figure?

Ⓐ    Ⓒ

Ⓑ 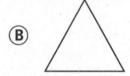   Ⓓ

10. **Multi-Step** Victor stacks some solid figures. He starts with a cylinder. Then he puts a cube on top. He places a triangular prism on top of the cube. Then he takes away the prism and adds a cone. What does Victor's structure look like?

Ⓐ   Ⓒ

Ⓑ   Ⓓ

11. **Multi-Step** Yoshi stacks these figures from bottom to top: cube, cylinder, rectangular prism, cone. He removes the cylinder and replaces it with a cube. What does Yoshi's structure look like?

Ⓐ    Ⓒ

Ⓑ    Ⓓ

Name _____

 Module 15 Assessment

Vocabulary

Choose the best term from the box to complete the sentence.

Vocabulary
congruent
parallel lines
right angle
vertex

1. _____ figures have the same size and shape. (p. 499)

2. A _____ forms a square corner. (p. 481)

3. _____ appear to never cross or meet and are always the same distance apart. (p. 481)

Concepts and Skills

Circle all the words that describe the quadrilateral. ⬇ TEKS 3.6.A, 3.6.B

4.

rectangle

rhombus

parallelogram

square

5.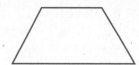

parallelogram

rhombus

trapezoid

rectangle

6.

rhombus

rectangle

square

parallelogram

Look at the first figure. Tell if it appears to be congruent to the second figure. Write *yes* or *no*. ⬇ TEKS 3.6.E

7.

_____

8.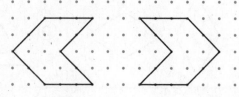

_____

Fill in the bubble for the correct answer choice.

9. What is one way you can sort the figures at the right? TEKS 3.6.A

   Ⓐ   4 sides that are equal in length

   Ⓑ   2 pairs of opposite sides that are parallel

   Ⓒ   4 right angles

   Ⓓ   exactly 1 pair of opposite sides that are parallel

10. Jennifer drew the quadrilaterals below. Which figure is NOT a rhombus? TEKS 3.6.A, 3.6.B

    Ⓐ   Ⓑ   Ⓒ    Ⓓ

11. Which solid figure does NOT have a curved surface? TEKS 3.6.A

    Ⓐ   Ⓑ 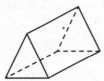   Ⓒ   Ⓓ

12. Alyssa combined which two pattern blocks to make a figure congruent to the one at the right? TEKS 3.6.E

    Ⓐ 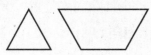   Ⓒ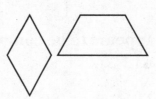

    Ⓑ 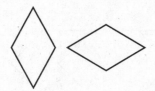   Ⓓ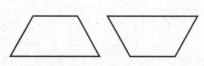

16.1 Measure Area

? Essential Question

How can you find the area of a plane figure?

Investigate

Area is the measure of the number of unit squares needed to cover a flat surface. A **unit square** is a square with a side length of 1 unit. It has an area of 1 **square unit**.

Activity   **Materials** ■ 1-inch grid paper
■ scissors

You can measure the area of the rectangles with 1-inch square tiles.

Cut out eight 1-inch squares. Use the dashed lines as guides to place tiles for *A–C*.

Ⓐ Place 4 tiles on Rectangle *A*.

- Are there any gaps? _____

- Are there any overlaps? _____

- Jaime says that the area is 4 square inches.

  Is Jaime's measurement correct? _____

When you measure area, there can be no space, or gaps, between the tiles.

Ⓑ Place 8 tiles on Rectangle *B*.

- Are there any gaps? _____

- Are there any overlaps? _____

- Jaime says that the area is 8 square inches.

  Is Jaime's measurement correct? _____

When you measure the area, the tiles cannot overlap.

Unit Square

1 unit

1 unit [square] 1 unit

1 unit

Area

Math Idea

You can count the number of unit squares inside a figure to find its area in square units.

1 square unit

1 square inch

Rectangle *A*

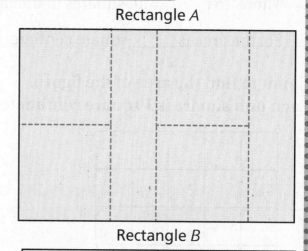

Rectangle *B*

C Place 6 tiles on Rectangle C.

- Are there any gaps? _____

- Are there any overlaps? _____

- Jaime says that the area is 6 square inches.

  Is Jaime's measurement correct? _____

So, the area of the rectangle is

_____ square inches.

Rectangle C

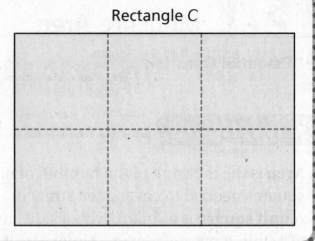

Share and Show

MATH BOARD

1. Count to find the area of the large figure.
   Each unit square is 1 square centimeter.

   Think: I can put the small shapes together if there are no gaps and no overlaps.

   There are _____ unit squares in the figure.

   So, the area is _____ square centimeters.

Count to find the area of the figure. Each unit square is 1 square centimeter.

2.

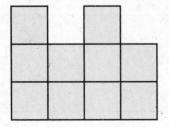

Area = _____ square centimeters

✓ 3.

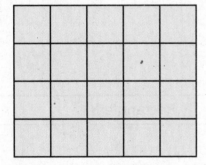

Area = _____ square centimeters

Count to find the area of the figure. Each unit square is 1 square inch.

✓ 4.

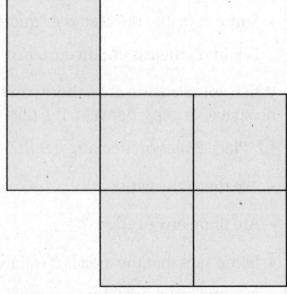

Area = _____ square inches

Name _____

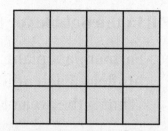

5. Danny is placing tiles on the floor of an office lobby. Each tile is 1 square meter. The diagram at the right shows the lobby. What is the area of the lobby?

_____

6. **Multi-Step** Angie is painting a space shuttle mural on a wall. Each section is one square foot. The diagram shows the unfinished mural. How many more square feet has Angie painted than NOT painted on her mural?

_____

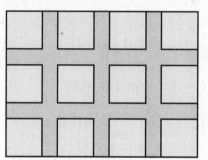

7. **Write Math** ▶ **Sense or Nonsense?** Tom places green square tiles on the figure at the right. He says that the figure has an area of 12 square units. Does his statement make sense? **Explain.**

_____

_____

_____

Rectangle A

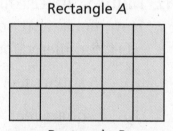

8. **H.O.T.** **Pose a Problem** Write an area problem that can be solved by using Rectangle A and Rectangle B. Then solve your problem.

Rectangle B

_____

_____

_____

9. **H.O.T.** **Reasoning** You measure the area of a table top with blue unit squares and green unit squares. Which unit square will give you a greater number of square units for area? **Explain.**

_____

_____

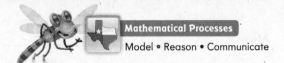

Daily Assessment Task

Fill in the bubble for the correct answer choice.

10. Farmer Paul plants peas. The diagram shows his field. Each unit square is 1 square meter. What is the area of Farmer Paul's field?

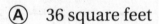

   (A) 28 square meters

   (B) 24 square meters

   (C) 30 square meters

   (D) 11 square meters

11. Sheri is making the quilt shown in the diagram. Each unit square is 1 square foot. The blue squares are completed. What is the area of the quilt that Sheri has completed?

   (A) 36 square feet   (C) 20 square feet

   (B) 17 square feet   (D) 16 square feet

12. **Multi-Step** Use the diagram from Exercise 11. How many more square feet has Sheri completed than NOT completed for her quilt?

   (A) 16 square feet   (C) 12 square feet

   (B) 4 square feet   (D) 14 square feet

 TEXAS Test Prep

13. What is the area of the figure at the right? Each unit square is 1 square foot.

   (A) 3 square feet

   (B) 15 square feet

   (C) 13 square feet

   (D) 10 square feet

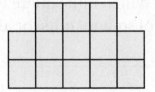

516

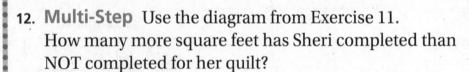

Name _____

16.1 Measure Area

Count to find the area of the figure.
Each unit square is 1 square centimeter.

1.

Area = _____ square centimeters

2.

Area = _____ square centimeters

Problem Solving Real World

3. Kaylee is covering the top of a box with tiles. Each tile is 1 square centimeter. The diagram shows the top of the box. What is the area?

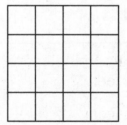

_____

4. Miguel drew this puzzle. He divides the area into one-inch square sections. The diagram shows how much of the puzzle Miguel puts together. What is the area of the puzzle Miguel has completed so far?

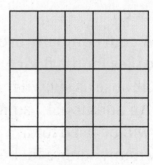

_____

5. Dawn draws a picture that is 12 square inches. She draws another picture that is 12 square centimeters. Which picture is larger? Use centimeter and inch square paper to solve the problem. **Explain** how you solved the problem.

_____

_____

Fill in the bubble completely to show your answer.

6. Angelina is covering a closet floor with 1-foot square tiles. The green squares are completed. What area of the floor has Angelina covered?

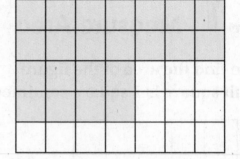

Ⓐ 22 square feet

Ⓑ 35 square feet

Ⓒ 24 square feet

Ⓓ 20 square feet

7. **Multi-Step** Dom is tiling a countertop. Each unit square is 1 square foot. The blue squares are completed. How many more square feet of countertop has Dom NOT completed, compared to what he has completed?

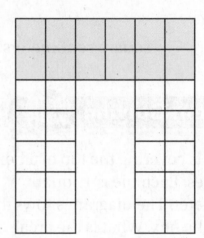

Ⓐ 12 square feet

Ⓑ 20 square feet

Ⓒ 32 square feet

Ⓓ 8 square feet

8. **Multi-Step** A craft company uses 1-inch square tiles for the floor and closet of a dollhouse as shown in the diagram. An additional 7 square inches of tile will be used for a hallway. How many square inches of tile does the craft company need for the dollhouse?

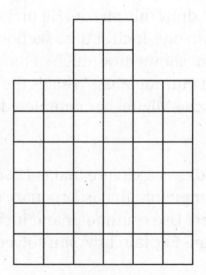

Ⓐ 47 square inches

Ⓑ 51 square inches

Ⓒ 48 square inches

Ⓓ 40 square inches

518

© Houghton Mifflin Harcourt Publishing Company

Name _____

 Use Area Models

? Essential Question

Why can you multiply to find the area of a rectangle?

You can count the number of square units to find the area of a figure. This rectangle has an area of 6 square units. You can also use multiplication.

🔑 Unlock the Problem

Melissa has a garden that is shaped like the rectangle below. Each unit square represents 1 square meter. What is the area of her garden?

Remember

A unit square can be different sizes: 1 square meter, 1 square foot, 1 square centimeter, and so on.

🔒 One Way Use repeated addition.

Count the number of rows.
Count the number of unit squares in each row.

_____ rows of _____ = ■

Write an addition equation.

So, the area is _____ square meters.

_____ unit squares

_____ unit squares

_____ unit squares

_____ + _____ + _____ = _____

🔒 Another Way Use multiplication.

Count the number of rows. Count the number of unit squares in each row.

_____ rows of _____ = ■

This figure is like an array. How do you find the total number of squares in an array?

_____

Write a multiplication equation.

So, the area is _____ square meters.

_____ unit squares in each row

_____ rows

_____ × _____ = _____

Math Talk
Mathematical Processes

Explain when you can use different methods to find the same area.

Share and Show

MATH BOARD

1. Find the area of the rectangle in two ways.

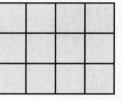

_____ rows of _____ = ⬛

Add. _____ + _____ + _____ = _____

Multiply. _____ × _____ = _____

What is the area of the rectangle?

_____ square units

Math Talk
Mathematical Processes

Which method do you prefer using? **Explain.**

Find the area of the rectangle.
Each unit square is 1 square foot.

2.

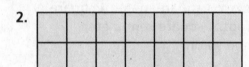

_____

3.

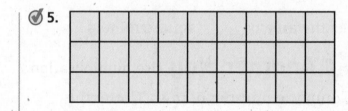

_____

Find the area of the rectangle.
Each unit square is 1 square meter.

4.

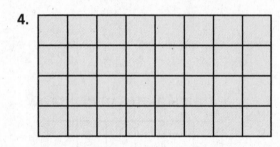

_____

5.

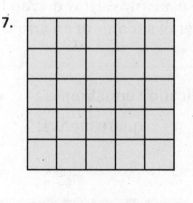

_____

6.

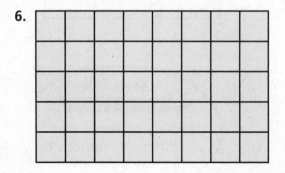

_____

7.

_____

Name _____

 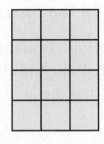
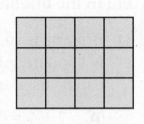

8. **Write Math** ▶ **Use Math Language**
Multi-Step Compare the areas of the two
rugs at the right. Each unit square represents
1 square foot. Which rug has the greater
area? **Explain.**

_____

_____

9. **H.O.T.** **Pose a Problem**
A tile company tiled a wall
using square tiles. A mural is
painted in the center. The
drawing shows the design.
The area of each tile used is
1 square foot.

Write a problem that can be solved by using
the drawing. Then solve your problem.

_____

_____

10. **H.O.T.** Draw and shade three different rectangles
with an area of 24 square units. Then write an addition or
multiplication equation for each area.

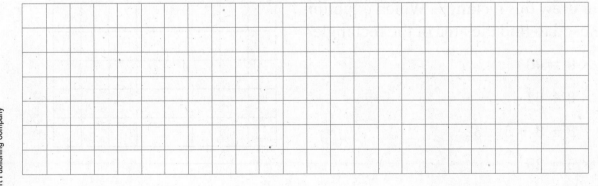

_____

Daily Assessment Task

Fill in the bubble for the correct answer choice.

11. Brianna is coloring a bookmark. Each unit square is 1 square inch. Which multiplication equation can be used to find the area of the bookmark?

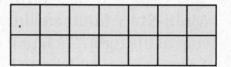

(A) $7 + 7 = 14$

(B) $7 \times 7 = 49$

(C) $2 \times 7 = 14$

(D) $2 \times 2 = 4$

12. Maria is painting a tile design for her porch. Each square tile is 1 square foot. What is the area of the design?

(A) 9 square feet

(B) 18 square feet

(C) 16 square feet

(D) 20 square feet

13. **Multi-Step** Tom and Bill are painting a fence. Tom paints the yellow area. Bill paints the white area. Each unit square is 1 square foot. How many more square feet does Bill paint than Tom?

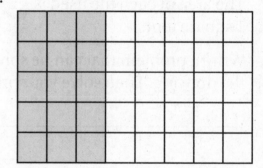

(A) 10 square feet

(B) 40 square feet

(C) 15 square feet

(D) 25 square feet

⭐ TEXAS Test Prep

14. Heather drew this rectangle. Which equation can be used to find the area of the rectangle?

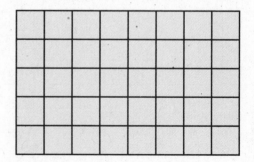

(A) $5 \times 8 = 40$

(B) $8 \times 8 = 64$

(C) $8 + 8 + 8 + 8 = 32$

(D) $5 \times 5 = 25$

522

Name _____

16.2 Use Area Models

Find the area of the rectangle.
Each unit square is 1 square meter.

1.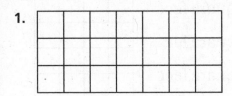

_____

2.

_____

3.

4.

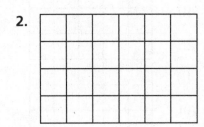

_____   _____

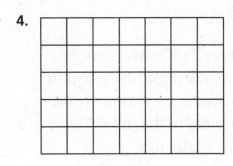

Problem Solving *Real World*

5. Shoshauna is using one-inch tiles to cover a table. She wants to put a green border around the edge of the table. She wants to make the center of the table yellow. How many more yellow tiles does she need than green tiles? **Explain**.

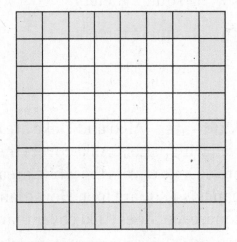

_____

_____

_____

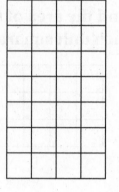
Fill in the bubble completely to show your answer.

6. Nolan draws this diagram for a rug.

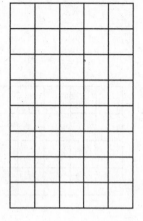

Which equation can be used to find the area?

Ⓐ $5 + 8 = 40$

Ⓑ $5 \times 5 = 25$

Ⓒ $8 \times 5 = 40$

Ⓓ $8 \times 8 = 64$

7. Marisol puts together a floor puzzle. Each puzzle piece is 1 square foot.

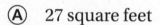

What is the area of the puzzle?

Ⓐ 27 square feet

Ⓑ 28 square feet

Ⓒ 32 square feet

Ⓓ 25 square feet

8. **Multi-Step** Lu Chen draws this diagram of his patio. Each square is 1 square meter. He wants to add 12 square meters to the patio. What will be the size of the new patio?

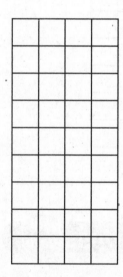

Ⓐ 40 square meters

Ⓑ 36 square meters

Ⓒ 42 square meters

Ⓓ 48 square meters

9. **Multi-Step** Aliki and Deke are covering a wall with panels. Aliki covers the yellow area. Deke covers the white area. Each panel is 1 square foot. How many more square feet does Aliki cover than Deke?

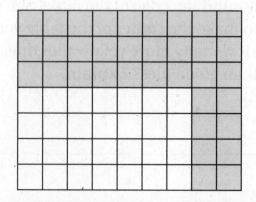

Ⓐ 6 square feet   Ⓒ 9 square feet

Ⓑ 8 square feet   Ⓓ 7 square feet

Name _____

16.3 PROBLEM SOLVING • Area of Rectangles

TEKS Geometry and Measurement—3.6.C
MATHEMATICAL PROCESSES
3.1.A, 3.1.B, 3.1.E

 Essential Question How can you use the strategy *find a pattern* to solve area problems?

Unlock the Problem

The rectangles show Mr Koi's plans for storage sheds. How are the areas of the sheds related? How will the areas of Sheds *A* and *B* change? How will the areas of Sheds *C* and *D* change?

Use the graphic organizer to help you solve the problem.

```
        4 ft            8 ft
3 ft  [ A ]          [ B ]    3 ft
        4 ft            8 ft
6 ft  [ C ]          [ D ]    6 ft
```

Read

What do I need to find?

I need to find how the areas will change from *A* to *B* and from ____ to ____.

What information am I given?

I am given the _____ and _____ of each shed to find its area.

Plan

What is my plan or strategy?

I will record the areas in a table. Then I will look for a pattern to see how the _____ will change.

Solve

I will complete the table to find patterns to solve the problem.

	Length	Width	Area		Length	Width	Area
Shed *A*	3 ft			Shed *C*		4 ft	
Shed *B*	3 ft			Shed *D*		8 ft	

The areas change from _____ to _____ and from _____ to _____. I see that the lengths will be the same and the widths will be doubled.

So, when the lengths are the same and the widths are doubled, the areas will be _____.

Try Another Problem

Mr. Koi is planning more storage sheds. He wants to know how the areas of the sheds are related. How will the areas of Sheds *E* and *F* change? How will the areas of Sheds *G* and *H* change?

Use the graphic organizer to help you solve the problem.

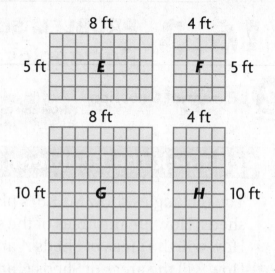

Read	**Plan**

What do I need to find?	**What information am I given?**	**What is my plan or strategy?**

Solve

I will complete the table to find patterns to solve the problem.

	Length	Width	Area		Length	Width	Area
Shed *E*				Shed *G*			
Shed *F*				Shed *H*			

- How did your table help you find a pattern?

_____

_____

- **What if** both the lengths and widths of the sheds are doubled? How would the areas change?

_____

Name _____

Use the table for 1–2.

Swimming Pool Sizes			
Pool	Width (in feet)	Length (in feet)	Area (in square feet)
A	8	20	
B	8	30	
C	8	40	
D	8	50	

1. Many swimming pools are built in rectangular shapes. How do the areas of the pools in the table change when the lengths change?

   The _____ stays the same.

   The lengths _____.

   The areas _____ by _____ square feet.

2. **What if** the width of each pool was 4 feet? **Explain** how the areas would change.

   _____

   _____

Problem Solving

3. **H.O.T.** **Apply** Elizabeth built a sandbox that is 4 feet long and 4 feet wide. She also built a flower garden that is 4 feet long and 6 feet wide. She built a vegetable garden that is 4 feet long and 8 feet wide. **Explain** how the areas change.

   _____

   _____

   _____

4. **H.O.T.** **Reasoning** Jacob has a rectangular garden with an area of 56 square feet. The length of the garden is 8 feet. What is the width of the garden? **Hint:** Use an array of unit squares.

   _____

Daily Assessment Task

Fill in the bubble for the correct answer choice.

5. **Multi-Step** You have a square photo that is 2 inches on each side. You make it larger by doubling each side. Then you double each side again. How do the areas change?

  Ⓐ They stay the same.   Ⓒ They double.

  Ⓑ They are 4 times greater.   Ⓓ They are 3 times greater.

6. Lou makes rugs for an art fair. Each unit square is 1 square foot. Lou continues the pattern shown. What is the area in square feet of his next rug?

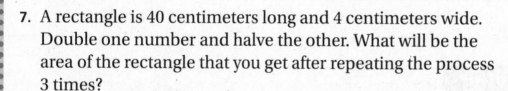

  Ⓐ 25 square feet   Ⓒ 30 square feet

  Ⓑ 8 square feet   Ⓓ 32 square feet

7. A rectangle is 40 centimeters long and 4 centimeters wide. Double one number and halve the other. What will be the area of the rectangle that you get after repeating the process 3 times?

  Ⓐ 120 square centimeters   Ⓒ 320 square centimeters

  Ⓑ 240 square centimeters   Ⓓ 160 square centimeters

 TEXAS Test Prep

8. Caroline mows the three lawns shown in the table. How do the areas change from one row to the next?

Yard	Length	Width
A	4 yards	8 yards
B	8 yards	8 yards
C	12 yards	8 yards

  Ⓐ The areas double.

  Ⓑ The areas do not change.

  Ⓒ The areas increase by 4 square yards.

  Ⓓ The areas increase by 32 square yards.

16.3 PROBLEM SOLVING • Area of Rectangles

Use the table for 1–2.

1. A company builds wooden porches. The porches are built in rectangular shapes. How do the areas of the porches change when the lengths change?

   The _____ stays the same.

   The lengths _____.

   The areas _____ by _____ square feet.

Porch Sizes			
Porch	Length (in feet)	Width (in feet)	Area (in square feet)
A	10	6	
B	15	6	
C	20	6	
D	25	6	

2. What if 2 feet were added to each width? **Explain** how the area of each porch would change.

   _____

   _____

Problem Solving Real World

3. An artist paints a mural that is 3 feet long and 5 feet wide. She paints a second mural that is 5 feet long and 5 feet wide. A third mural is 7 feet long and 5 feet wide. **Explain** how the areas of the murals change.

   _____

   _____

   _____

4. A flag has a total area of 42 square feet. A second flag has an area of 48 square feet. If the widths of both flags are each 6 feet, what are the lengths? **Explain**.

   _____

   _____

   _____

Fill in the bubble completely to show your answer.

5. **Multi-Step** Hideki makes a quilt that has a length of 6 feet and an area of 36 feet. If he increases the length to 8 feet, and the width stays the same how much will the area increase?

Ⓐ 6 square feet

Ⓑ 12 square feet

Ⓒ 48 square feet

Ⓓ 20 square feet

6. Marina makes tablecloths. Each unit square is 1 square meter. She continues the pattern shown below.

What is the area of the next tablecloth?

Ⓐ 9 square meters

Ⓑ 15 square meters

Ⓒ 12 square meters

Ⓓ 18 square meters

7. A company makes tarps in the sizes shown in the table. How do the areas change?

Ⓐ They do not change.

Ⓑ They increase by 4 square meters.

Ⓒ They increase by 6 square meters.

Ⓓ They increase by 8 square meters.

Length	Width
3 meters	6 meters
4 meters	6 meters
5 meters	6 meters

8. **Multi-Step** Maya has a paint canvas that is 2 feet long and 4 feet wide. Another canvas is double the length and width of the first canvas. How does the area change?

Ⓐ It is doubled.

Ⓑ It is 3 times greater.

Ⓒ It is tripled.

Ⓓ It is 4 times greater.

9. **Multi-Step** A rectangle is 20 centimeters long and 6 centimeters wide. Double the width and halve the length. What is the area of the new rectangle?

Ⓐ 70 square centimeters

Ⓑ 120 square centimeters

Ⓒ 90 square centimeters

Ⓓ 100 square centimeters

Name _____

16.4 Relate Figures, Fractions, and Area

Essential Question

How can you divide figures into parts with equal areas and write the area as a unit fraction of the whole?

Investigate

Materials ■ pattern blocks ■ color pencils ■ ruler

Connect Use what you know about combining and separating pattern blocks to explore the relationship between fractions and area.

A. Trace a hexagon pattern block.

B. Divide your hexagon into two parts with equal area. What new figures have you drawn?

_____

C. Write the fraction that names each part of the

whole you divided. _____
Each part is $\frac{1}{2}$ of the whole figure's area.

D. Write the fraction that names the whole area. _____

Math Idea
Equal parts of a whole have equal area.

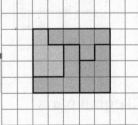

Make Connections

The rectangle at the right is divided into four parts with equal area.

- Write the unit fraction that names each part of the divided whole. _____

- What is the area of each part? _____

- How many equal shares does it take to make one whole? _____

- Does each equal share of the whole have the same shape? _____

- Is the area of each equal share the same? **Explain** how you know.

_____

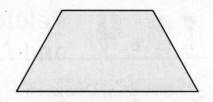

Share and Show

1. Divide the trapezoid into 3 parts with equal area. Write the names of the new shapes. Then write the fraction that names the area of each part of the whole.

_____

Math Talk
Mathematical Processes
Explain how you know the areas of all the parts are equal.

Draw lines to divide the figure into equal parts that show the fraction given.

2.

$\frac{1}{6}$

3.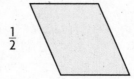

$\frac{1}{2}$

✓ 4.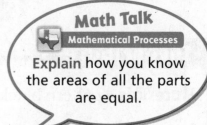

$\frac{1}{8}$

Draw lines to divide the figure into parts with equal area. Write the area of each part as a unit fraction.

5.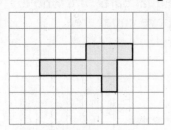

3 equal parts _____

✓ 6.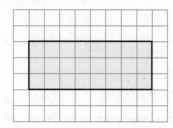

6 equal parts _____

7.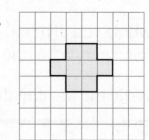

4 equal parts _____

Problem Solving

8. **H.O.T.** **Write Math** ▶ If the area of three ◇ is equal to the area of one ⬡, the area of how many ◇ equals four ⬡? **Explain** your answer.

_____

9. **H.O.T.** **Apply** Show how you can divide the hexagon into four shapes with equal area.

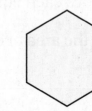

Each part is _____ of the whole shape's area.

10. **H.O.T.** Multi-Step Sense or Nonsense?

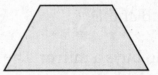

Divide the hexagon into six equal parts.

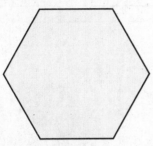

Which pattern block represents $\frac{1}{6}$ of the whole area?

_____

Divide the trapezoid into three equal parts.

Which pattern block represents $\frac{1}{3}$ of the whole area?

_____

Alexis said the area of $\frac{1}{3}$ of the trapezoid is greater than the area of $\frac{1}{6}$ of the hexagon because $\frac{1}{3} > \frac{1}{6}$. Does her statement make sense? **Explain** your answer.

_____

_____

_____

Write a statement that makes sense.

_____

_____

11. **What if** you divide the hexagon into 3 equal parts?
Use Math Language to write a sentence that compares the area of each equal part of the hexagon to each equal part of the trapezoid.

_____

_____

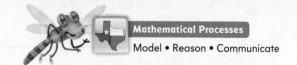
Daily Assessment Task

Fill in the bubble for the correct answer choice.

12. Inez made a stained glass design with the rectangles shown at the right. Which rectangles have the same shape and the same area?

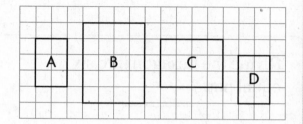

(A) A and C

(C) A and D

(B) B and D

(D) B and C

13. Paulo buys a mirror. The frame is made of 6 same-size trapezoids. What unit fraction of the frame is each trapezoid?

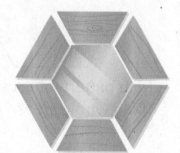

(A) $\frac{1}{3}$

(C) $\frac{1}{8}$

(B) $\frac{1}{6}$

(D) $\frac{1}{2}$

14. **Multi-Step** Anastasia is painting one wall of her room. She divides the wall into 8 squares with the same area. She paints half of the squares light green and half of the squares dark green. What fraction of the wall is one dark green square?

(A) $\frac{1}{2}$

(C) $\frac{1}{4}$

(B) $\frac{1}{8}$

(D) $\frac{1}{1}$

 TEXAS Test Prep

15. Rav divided the rectangle at the right into six parts with equal area. What is the area of each part?

(A) 6 square units

(B) 24 square units

(C) 4 square units

(D) 10 square units

16.4 Relate Figures, Fractions, and Area

Draw lines to divide the figure into equal parts that show the fraction given.

1.

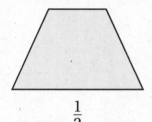

$\frac{1}{2}$

2.

$\frac{1}{4}$

3.

$\frac{1}{6}$

Draw lines to divide the figure into parts with equal area. Write the area of each part as a unit fraction.

4.

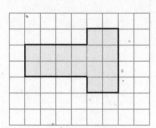

4 equal parts

_____

5.

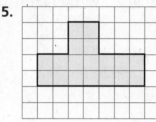

3 equal parts

_____

Problem Solving Real World

6. Sanchez puts a window in his house made of 2 same-size triangles. What unit fraction of the window is each triangle?

_____

Fill in the bubble completely to show your answer.

7. Georgie has a rectangular window that is divided into 6 same-size squares. What fraction of the window is 1 square?

Ⓐ $\frac{1}{2}$

Ⓑ $\frac{1}{4}$

Ⓒ $\frac{1}{3}$

Ⓓ $\frac{1}{6}$

8. Marcy has a square window that is divided into 8 same-size squares. What fraction of the window is 1 square?

Ⓐ $\frac{1}{3}$

Ⓑ $\frac{1}{4}$

Ⓒ $\frac{1}{8}$

Ⓓ $\frac{1}{2}$

9. Rory divides the rectangle into 7 parts with equal area. What is the area of each part?

Ⓐ 4 square units

Ⓑ 5 square units

Ⓒ 7 square units

Ⓓ 6 square units

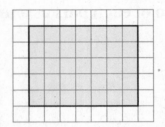

10. **Multi-Step** Perry makes a quilt with same-size squares. He makes 2 red squares, 2 blue squares, 2 yellow squares, and 2 green squares. What fraction of the quilt are the red squares?

Ⓐ $\frac{1}{4}$

Ⓑ $\frac{1}{2}$

Ⓒ $\frac{1}{8}$

Ⓓ $\frac{1}{3}$

11. **Multi-Step** Doreen makes a painting with 12 same-size squares. She has painted one-half of the squares with a design. How many squares has Doreen painted?

Ⓐ 1

Ⓑ 4

Ⓒ 3

Ⓓ 6

16.5

Area of Combined Rectangles

TEKS Geometry and Measurement—3.6.C, 3.6.D
MATHEMATICAL PROCESSES 3.1.C, 3.1.E

 Essential Question How can you break apart a figure to find the area?

Unlock the Problem

Anna's rug has side lengths of 4 feet and 9 feet. What is the area of Anna's rug?

Remember

You can use the Distributive Property to break apart an array.

$3 \times 3 = 3 \times (2 + 1)$

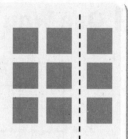

Activity Materials ■ square tiles

STEP 1 Use square tiles to model 4×9.

STEP 2 Draw a rectangle on grid paper to show your model.

STEP 3 Draw a vertical line to break apart the model to make two smaller rectangles.

The side length 9 is broken into _____ plus _____.

STEP 4 Find the area of each of the two smaller rectangles.

Rectangle 1: _____ × _____ = _____

Rectangle 2: _____ × _____ = _____

STEP 5 Add the products to find the total area.

_____ + _____ = _____ square feet

STEP 6 Check your answer by counting the number of square feet.

_____ square feet

So, the area of Anna's rug is _____ square feet.

Math Talk
Mathematical Processes

Did you draw a line in the same place as your classmates? Explain why you found the same total area.

Connect Using the Distributive Property, you found that you could break apart a rectangle into smaller rectangles, and combine the area of each smaller rectangle to find the total area.

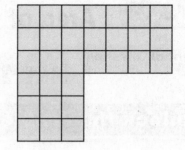

How can you break apart this figure into rectangles to find its area?

🔓 **One Way** Use a horizontal line.

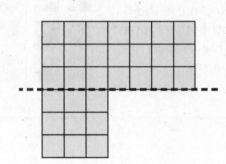

🔓 **Another Way** Use a vertical line.

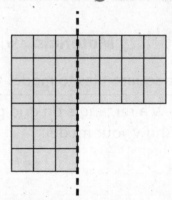

STEP 1 Write a multiplication equation for each rectangle.

Rectangle 1: ____ × ____ = ____

Rectangle 2: ____ × ____ = ____

STEP 2 Add the products to find the total area.

____ + ____ = ____ square units

So, the area is _____ square units.

STEP 1 Write a multiplication equation for each rectangle.

Rectangle 1: ____ × ____ = ____

Rectangle 2: ____ × ____ = ____

STEP 2 Add the products to find the total area.

____ + ____ = ____ square units

Math Talk
Mathematical Processes

Explain how you can check your answer.

Share and Show

MATH BOARD

1. Draw a line to break apart the figure into rectangles. Find the total area of the figure.

Think: I can draw vertical or horizontal lines to break apart the figure to make rectangles.

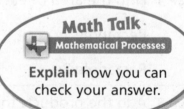

Rectangle 1: ___ × ___ = ___

Rectangle 2: ___ × ___ = ___

___ + ___ = ___ square units

538

Name _____

Draw a line to break apart the figure into rectangles. Then find the area. Show your multiplication and addition equations.

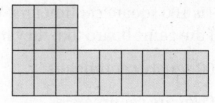
✓ **2.**

Rectangle 1: ____ × ____ = ____

Rectangle 2: ____ × ____ = ____

____ + ____ = ____ square units

✓ **3.**

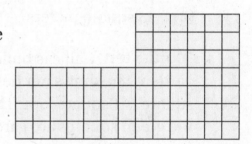

Rectangle 1: ____ × ____ = ____

Rectangle 2: ____ × ____ = ____

____ + ____ = ____ square units

Problem Solving Real World

4. **Multi-Step Connect** A model of Lee School's Media Center is shown at the right. Each unit square is 1 square yard. Draw a line to break apart the figure into rectangles. What is the total area of the media center?

_____

5. **H.O.T** **Multi-Step Apply** A builder uses glass bricks shaped like cubes for a playroom wall. Draw a line to break apart the figure into rectangles. Find the area of the wall. **What if** the height of the wall is 8 feet and the glass area must be a rectangle? How many bricks will be left over?

_____

6. **H.O.T** **Multi-Step Explain** how to break apart the figure to find the area.

_____

_____

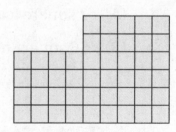

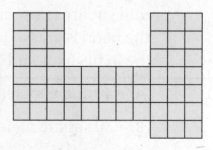

Math on the Spot

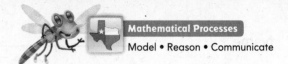
Daily Assessment Task

Fill in the bubble for the correct answer choice.

7. Max and Josh are playing Tic-Tac-Toe. Each unit square is 100 square centimeters. What is the area of the game board that they have used so far?

   Ⓐ 100 square centimeters

   Ⓑ 10 square centimeters

   Ⓒ 500 square centimeters

   Ⓓ 50 square centimeters

8. **Multi-Step** Mike is helping his uncle pave a parking lot. Each unit square is 1 square meter. How many square meters do they need to pave?

   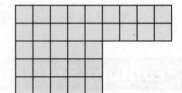

   Ⓐ 45 square meters   Ⓒ 35 square meters

   Ⓑ 33 square meters   Ⓓ 28 square meters

9. **Multi-Step** Callie is building a backyard pond and garden. She draws her design on grid paper. Each unit square is 1 square foot. The blue squares are pond and the green squares are garden. How many more square feet of garden are there than square feet of pond?

   Ⓐ 2 square feet   Ⓒ 8 square feet

   Ⓑ 16 square feet   Ⓓ 24 square feet

TEXAS Test Prep

10. Pete drew a diagram of his backyard on grid paper. Each unit square is 1 square meter. The area surrounding the patio is grass. How many square meters of grass are in his backyard?

    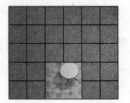

    Ⓐ 4 square meters   Ⓒ 26 square meters

    Ⓑ 30 square meters   Ⓓ 18 square meters

Homework and Practice

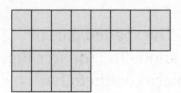

Name _____

16.5 Area of Combined Rectangles

Use the Distributive Property to find the area, or draw a line to break apart the figure into rectangles. Show your multiplication and addition equations.

1.

2.

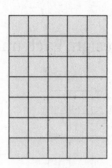

Rectangle 1: ____ × ____ = ____

Rectangle 2: ____ × ____ = ____

____ + ____ = ____ square units

_____

_____ square units

 Problem Solving Real World

3. Mr. Franklin's patio is shown at the right. Each unit square is 1 square foot. Draw a line to break apart the shape into rectangles. What is the total area of Mr. Franklin's patio?

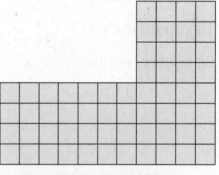

_____

4. Ms. Ferrara has a rectangular kitchen with a pantry closet. Each unit square is 1 square foot. Draw a line to break apart the shape into rectangles. What is the total area of Ms. Ferrara's kitchen?

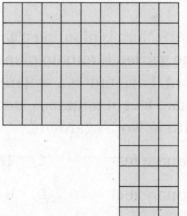

_____

Fill in the bubble completely to show your answer.

5. Anya is building a wooden deck. The diagram shows the plan. Each unit square is 1 square meter. How many square meters is Anya's deck?

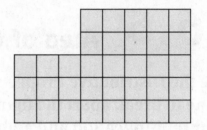

Ⓐ 40 square meters Ⓒ 25 square meters

Ⓑ 34 square meters Ⓓ 30 square meters

6. Opal creates a tile design. Each unit is 1 square inch.

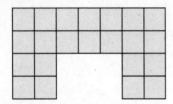

How many square inches is Opal's design?

Ⓐ 22 square inches

Ⓑ 16 square inches

Ⓒ 18 square inches

Ⓓ 28 square inches

7. **Multi-Step** The shaded part of the diagram shows the squares that have game pieces on them for Team A. The board for Team B has 4 fewer game pieces on the board. Each unit is 1 square inch.

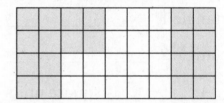

How much of Team B's board is covered?

Ⓐ 24 square inches

Ⓑ 16 square inches

Ⓒ 20 square inches

Ⓓ 36 square inches

8. **Multi-Step** Nora is planting a garden. The shaded area of the garden is tomato plants and the white area is corn. Each unit is 1 square foot. How many more square feet of tomatoes are there than square feet of corn in Nora's garden?

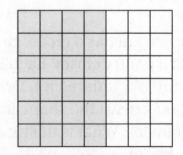

Ⓐ 24 square feet Ⓒ 18 square feet

Ⓑ 12 square feet Ⓓ 6 square feet

Name _____

 Module 16 Assessment

Vocabulary

Choose the best term from the box.

Vocabulary
area
length
unit squares

1. You can find the _____ of a rectangle by multiplying the number of unit squares in each row by the number of rows. (p. 513)

2. You can count _____ to find the area of a shape. (p. 513)

Concepts and Skills

Find the area of the figure. Each unit square is 1 square meter. ⬇ TEKS 3.6.C, 3.6.D

3.

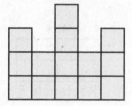

_____ square meters

4.

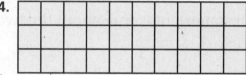

_____ square meters

Draw a line to break apart the figure into rectangles. Find the area of the figure. ⬇ TEKS 3.6.C, 3.6.D

5.

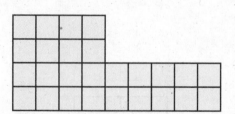

Rectangle 1: _____ × _____ = _____

Rectangle 2: _____ × _____ = _____

_____ + _____ = _____ square units

6.

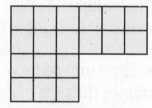

Rectangle 1: _____ × _____ = _____

Rectangle 2: _____ × _____ = _____

_____ + _____ = _____ square units

7. Peter drew this rectangle. Which equation can be used to find the area?

   ↳ TEKS 3.6.C

   (A) $4 \times 4 = 16$

   (C) $4 + 7 + 4 + 7 = 22$

   (B) $7 + 7 + 7 = 21$

   (D) $4 \times 7 = 28$

8. Alfredo used the Distributive Property to find the area of this rectangle. Which set of multiplication and addition equations could he have used? ↳ TEKS 3.6.C, 3.6.D

   (A) $4 + 5 = 9; 4 + 5 = 9; 9 + 9 = 18$

   (B) $4 + 5 = 9; 4 + 5 = 9; 9 \times 9 = 81$

   (C) $4 \times 5 = 20; 4 \times 5 = 20; 20 + 20 = 40$

   (D) $4 \times 10 = 40; 4 \times 10 = 40; 40 + 40 = 80$

9. Which statement is true about the two rectangles? ↳ TEKS 3.6.C

   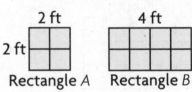

   2 ft   4 ft

   2 ft   2 ft

   Rectangle A   Rectangle B

   (A) The area of Rectangle B is double the area of Rectangle A.

   (B) The area of Rectangle A is double the area of Rectangle B.

   (C) The area of Rectangle B is half of the area of Rectangle A.

   (D) The area of Rectangle A is the same as the area of Rectangle B.

10. Sam divided the figure into parts with equal area. Which fraction names the area of each part of the divided figure? ↳ TEKS 3.6.E

    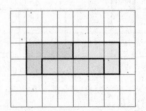

    (A) $\frac{1}{2}$

    (C) $\frac{1}{4}$

    (B) $\frac{1}{3}$

    (D) $\frac{1}{6}$

TEKS Geometry and Measurement—3.7.B
MATHEMATICAL PROCESSES
3.1.C, 3.1.E, 3.1.G

17.1 Model Perimeter

? Essential Question

How can you find perimeter?

Investigate

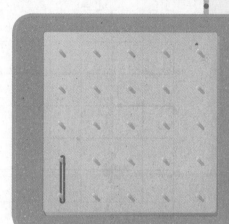

Perimeter is the distance around a figure.

Materials ▪ geoboard ▪ rubber bands

You can find the perimeter of a rectangle on a geoboard or on dot paper by counting the number of units on each side.

A. Make a rectangle on the geoboard that is 3 units on two sides and 2 units on the other two sides.

B. Draw your rectangle on the dot paper below.

← 1 Unit

C. Write the length next to each side of your rectangle.

D. Add the number of units on each side.

_____ + _____ + _____ + _____ = _____

E. So, the perimeter of the rectangle is _____ units.

- How would the perimeter of the rectangle change if the length of two of the sides was 4 units instead of 3 units?

_____

_____

Make Connections

You can also use grid paper to find the perimeter of figures by counting the number of units on each side.

Start at the arrow and trace the perimeter. Begin counting with 1. Continue counting each unit around the figure until you have counted each unit.

Math Talk
Mathematical Processes

If a rectangle has a perimeter of 12 units, how many units wide and how many units long could it be? **Explain**.

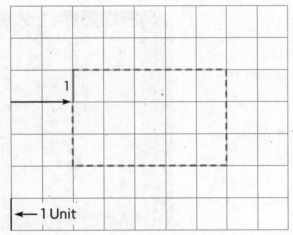

A

1

← 1 Unit

Perimeter = _____ units

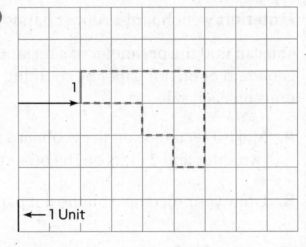

B

1

← 1 Unit

Perimeter = _____ units

Share and Show

 MATH BOARD

Find the perimeter of the figure. Each unit is 1 centimeter.

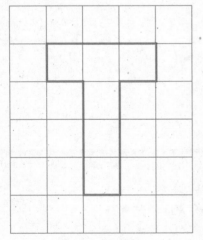

1.

_____ centimeters

2.

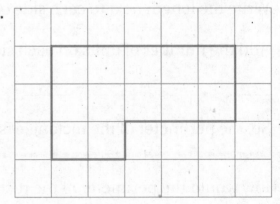

_____ centimeters

546

Problem Solving Real World

H.O.T. Multi-Step What's the Error?

3. Kevin is solving perimeter problems. He counts the units and says that the perimeter of this figure is 18 units.

Look at Kevin's solution.   **Find Kevin's error.**

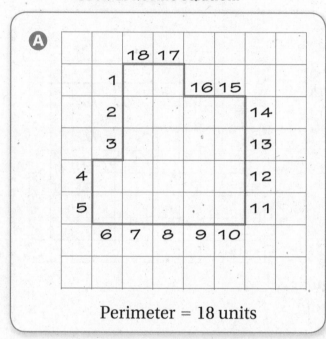

Perimeter = 18 units   Perimeter = _____ units

- Use the grid on the right to find the correct perimeter of the figure above. _____

4. **Apply** Describe the error Kevin made.

_____

5. **Use Diagrams** Circle the places in the drawing of Kevin's solution where he made an error.

6. **H.O.T.** **Write Math** ▶ **Explain** how to find the length of each side of a triangle with sides of equal length, and a perimeter of 27 inches.

_____

_____

Fill in the bubble completely to show your answer.

7. Joseph drew a game court on grid paper. Each unit is 1 meter. What is the perimeter of the game court?

   Ⓐ 18 meters   Ⓒ 16 meters

   Ⓑ 15 meters   Ⓓ 8 meters

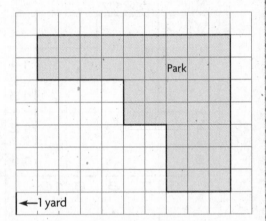

8. Val is designing a dog park. She needs to find the length for a fence around the park. Each unit is 1 yard. What is the perimeter of the park?

   Ⓐ 29 yards   Ⓒ 47 yards

   Ⓑ 32 yards   Ⓓ 34 yards

9. **Multi-Step** Greg is framing two rectangular paintings. One painting has side lengths of 3 inches and 9 inches. The other painting has side lengths of 4 inches and 6 inches. How many inches of framing material will Greg need for the two paintings?

   Ⓐ 48 inches   Ⓒ 22 inches

   Ⓑ 51 inches   Ⓓ 44 inches

⭐ TEXAS Test Prep

10. Naomi drew this design for a quilt block. What is the perimeter of the design?

    Ⓐ 12 units   Ⓒ 14 units

    Ⓑ 16 units   Ⓓ 18 units

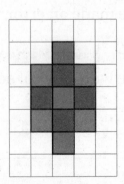

17.1 Model Perimeter

Find the perimeter of the figure. Each unit is 1 centimeter.

1.

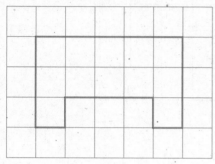

_____ centimeters

2.

_____ centimeters

Problem Solving Real World

3. Alyssa says the perimeter of this figure is 13 units. Describe the error Alyssa made.

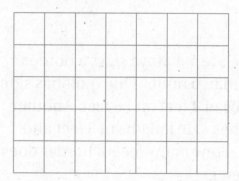

_____

_____

_____

_____

4. Draw your own figure on the grid. Find the perimeter.

Perimeter = _____ units

Fill in the bubble completely to show your answer.

5. Paula drew this plan for a new backyard shed. Each unit is 1 foot. What is the perimeter of the shed?

Ⓐ 24 feet

Ⓑ 20 feet

Ⓒ 18 feet

Ⓓ 42 feet

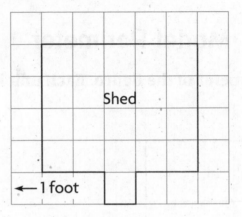

Shed

← 1 foot

6. Andy drew this plan for a fence in his yard. Each unit is 1 meter. What is the perimeter of the fence?

Ⓐ 18 meter

Ⓑ 24 meter

Ⓒ 22 meter

Ⓓ 36 meter

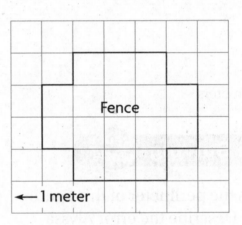

Fence

← 1 meter

7. **Multi-Step** Latoya sews a border around two quilts. One quilt has side lengths of 4 feet and 6 feet. Another quilt has side lengths of 8 feet and 6 feet. How many feet of border does she sew?

Ⓐ 28 feet

Ⓑ 20 feet

Ⓒ 48 feet

Ⓓ 42 feet

8. **Multi-Step** Roland buys baseboards for two rectangular rooms. One room has side lengths of 5 meters and 7 meters. The second room has side lengths of 6 meters and 9 meters. How many meters of baseboard does Roland buy?

Ⓐ 50 meters

Ⓑ 30 meters

Ⓒ 24 meters

Ⓓ 54 meters

Name _____

17.2 Find Perimeter

 Essential Question

How can you measure perimeter?

You can estimate and measure perimeter in standard units, such as inches and centimeters.

🔑 Unlock the Problem ⟨Real World⟩

Find the perimeter of the cover of a notebook.

🔒 Activity Materials ■ inch ruler

STEP 1 Estimate the perimeter of a notebook in inches. Record your estimate. _____ inches

STEP 2 Use an inch ruler to measure the length of each side of the notebook to the nearest inch.

STEP 3 Record and add the lengths of the sides measured to the nearest inch.

_____ + _____ + _____ + _____ = _____

So, the perimeter of the notebook cover measured

to the nearest inch is _____ inches.

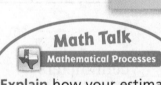

Math Talk
Mathematical Processes

Explain how your estimate compares with your measurement.

Try This! **Find the perimeter.**

Use an inch ruler to find the length of each side.

Use a centimeter ruler to find the length of each side.

Add the lengths of the sides:

_____ + _____ + _____ + _____ = _____

The perimeter is _____ inches.

Add the lengths of the sides:

_____ + _____ + _____ + _____ = _____

The perimeter is _____ centimeters.

1. Use an inch ruler to find the perimeter of the triangle.

_____ in. 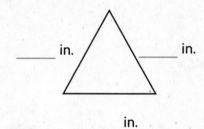 _____ in.

_____ in.

_____ inches

Think: How long is each side?

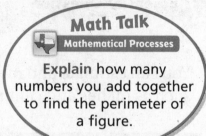

Math Talk

Mathematical Processes

Explain how many numbers you add together to find the perimeter of a figure.

Use a centimeter ruler to find the perimeter.

2.

_____ cm

_____ cm   _____ cm

_____ cm

_____ centimeters

3.

_____ cm   _____ cm

_____ cm

_____ cm

_____ cm

_____ centimeters

4. Use the grid paper to draw a figure that has a perimeter of 24 centimeters. Label the length of each side.

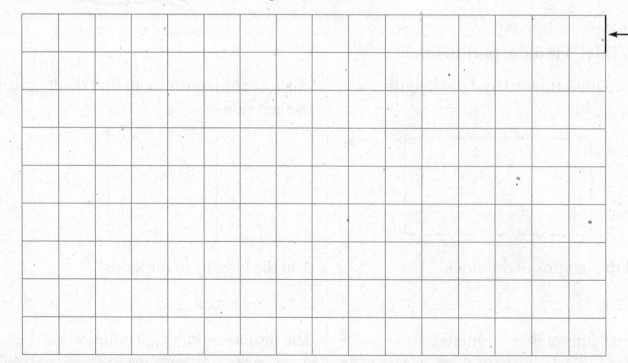

← 1 cm

Name _____

Use the photos for 5–6.

5 in.

8 in.

5 in.

7 in.

8 in. 4 in.

4 in.

7 in.

5. Which of the animal photos has a perimeter of 26 inches?

   _____

6. **Multi-Step Analyze** How much greater is the perimeter of the bird photo than the perimeter of the cat photo?

   _____

Math on the Spot

Write Math ▶

Show Your Work

7. **H.O.T. Multi-Step** Erin is putting a fence around her square garden. Each side of her garden is 3 meters long. The fence costs $5 for each meter. How much will the fence cost?

   _____

8. **H.O.T. Write Math ▶** Gary's garden is shaped like a rectangle with two pairs of sides of equal length, and it has a perimeter of 28 feet. **Explain** how to find the lengths of the other sides if one side measures 10 feet.

   _____

   _____

   _____

9. **Evaluate** Jill says that finding the perimeter of a figure with all sides of equal length is easier than finding the perimeter of other figures. Do you agree? **Explain**.

   _____

   _____

   _____

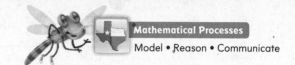

Daily Assessment Task

Fill in the bubble completely to show your answer.

10. Sally is putting frosting around the edges of the roof of a gingerbread house. What is the perimeter of the roof?

Ⓐ 18 cm   Ⓒ 8 cm

Ⓑ 16 cm   Ⓓ 20 cm

11. Kyle is adding a border to his triangular flag. What is the perimeter of the flag?

Ⓐ 2 inches   Ⓒ 3 inches

Ⓑ 6 inches   Ⓓ 1 inch

12. **Multi-Step** Pete glues a rope around his rectangular rodeo sign. His sign has side lengths of 2 feet and 3 feet. The rope costs $4 for each foot. How much does Pete pay for rope?

Ⓐ $24   Ⓒ $10

Ⓑ $20   Ⓓ $40

⭐ TEXAS Test Prep

13. Austin's class is making a poster for Earth Day. What is the perimeter of the poster?

Ⓐ 24 feet

Ⓑ 21 feet

Ⓒ 15 feet

Ⓓ 30 feet

9 ft

6 ft   6 ft

9 ft

Name _____

17.2 Find Perimeter

Use a centimeter ruler to find the perimeter.

1.

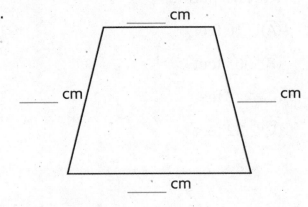

_____ cm

_____ cm   _____ cm

_____ cm

_____ centimeters

2.

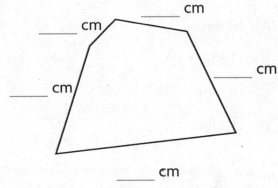

_____ cm

_____ cm   _____ cm

_____ cm

_____ cm

_____ centimeters

Problem Solving Real World

Use the drawings for 3–4.

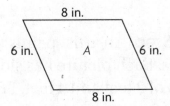

8 in.

6 in.   A   6 in.

8 in.

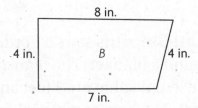

8 in.

4 in.   B   4 in.

7 in.

3. Carly drew quadrilaterals A and B. Which quadrilateral has a perimeter of 28 inches?

4. How much greater is the perimeter of quadrilateral A than the perimeter of quadrilateral B?

_____   _____

Fill in the bubble completely to show your answer.

5. Benjamin builds a fence in the shape of a triangle. Each side of the fence is the same length. If the perimeter is 36 feet, how long is each side of the fence?

   Ⓐ 6 feet

   Ⓑ 12 feet

   Ⓒ 9 feet

   Ⓓ 18 feet

6. Anton puts a rail around his patio. The patio is in the shape of a rectangle with side lengths of 7 feet and 9 feet. What is the perimeter of Anton's patio?

   Ⓐ 16 feet

   Ⓑ 63 feet

   Ⓒ 22 feet

   Ⓓ 32 feet

7. Alexander makes this name plate from wood in art class. What is the perimeter of the name plate?

   Ⓐ 18 cm

   Ⓑ 9 cm

   Ⓒ 3 cm

   Ⓓ 6 cm

8. **Multi-Step** Iris sews a border around a blanket. The blanket has side lengths that are 4 feet and 6 feet. The border material costs $2 for each foot. How much does Iris pay for the border?

   Ⓐ $20

   Ⓑ $12

   Ⓒ $40

   Ⓓ $16

9. **Multi-Step** An artist paints two pictures. Each picture has side lengths of 2 feet and 4 feet. Framing costs $3 for each foot. How much will the artist pay to put a frame around both paintings?

   Ⓐ $18

   Ⓑ $72

   Ⓒ $36

   Ⓓ $24

17.3 Find Unknown Side Lengths

ALGEBRA

 Essential Question

How can you find the unknown length of a side in a polygon when you know its perimeter?

Unlock the Problem

Chen has 27 feet of fencing to put around his garden. He has already used the lengths of fencing shown. How much fencing does he have left for the last side?

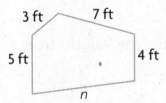

3 ft   7 ft

5 ft   4 ft

n

Find the unknown side length.

Write an equation for the perimeter.

Think: If I knew the length of n, I would add all the side lengths to find the perimeter.

Add the lengths of the sides you know.

Think: Addition and subtraction are inverse operations.

Write a related equation.

So, Chen has _____ feet of fencing left.

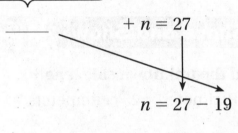

$5 + 3 + $ _____ $+$ _____ $+ n = 27$

$5 + 3 + \;\;7\;\; + \;\;4\;\; + n = 27$

_____ $+ n = 27$

$n = 27 - 19$

_____ $= 27 - 19$

Math Idea

A symbol or letter can stand for an unknown side length.

Example Find unknown side lengths of a square.

The square has a perimeter of 20 inches. What is the length of each side of the square?

Think: A square has four sides that are equal in length.

You can multiply to find the perimeter.

• Write a multiplication equation for the perimeter.

• Use a multiplication fact you know to solve.

So, the length of each side of the square is _____ inches.

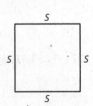

s

s   s

s

$4 \times \;\;s\;\; = 20$

$4 \times$ _____ $= 20$

🔑 **Example** Find unknown side lengths of a rectangle.

Lauren has a rectangular blanket. The perimeter is 28 feet. The width of the blanket is 5 feet. What is the length of the blanket?

5 ft

Hint: A rectangle has two pairs of opposite sides that are equal in length.

l l

- Add the lengths of the sides you know.

  _____ + _____ = _____

- Subtract the lengths from the perimeter.

  28 − _____ = _____

- Divide the difference by 2.

  _____ ÷ 2 = _____

So, the length of the blanket is _____ feet.

5 ft

Share and Show

Find the unknown side lengths.

1. Perimeter = 25 centimeters

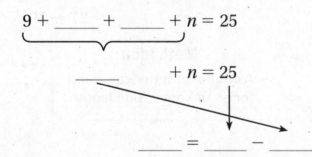

$$9 + \underline{\quad} + \underline{\quad} + n = 25$$

$$\underline{\quad} + n = 25$$

$$\underline{\quad} = \underline{\quad} - \underline{\quad}$$

9 cm

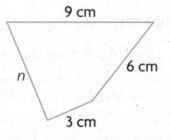

n 6 cm

3 cm

$n = \underline{\quad}$ centimeters

✓ 2. Perimeter = 34 meters

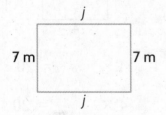

j

7 m   7 m

j

$j = \underline{\quad}$ meters

✓ 3. Perimeter = 12 feet

r

r r

r

$r = \underline{\quad}$ feet

Math Talk
Mathematical Processes

Explain how you can use division to find the length of a side of a square.

Name _____

4. **Multi-Step Use Diagrams** Latesha wants to make a border with ribbon around a figure she made and sketched at the right. She will use 44 centimeters of ribbon for the border. What is the unknown side length?

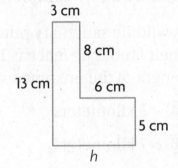

3 cm
8 cm
13 cm
6 cm
5 cm
h

(A) 3 centimeters   (C) 9 centimeters

(B) 13 centimeters   (D) 6 centimeters

a. What do you need to find? _____

b. How will you use what you know about perimeter to help you

solve the problem? _____

_____

c. Write an equation to solve the problem.

d. Complete the sentences.

The perimeter is _____ centimeters.

The sum of the sides I know is

_____ centimeters.

A related subtraction equation is

_____ = _____ − _____.

So, the length of side h is

_____ centimeters.

e. Fill in the bubble for the correct answer choice above.

5. **H.O.T.** **Multi-Step** A rectangle has a perimeter of 34 inches. The left side is 6 inches long. What is the length of the top side?

_____

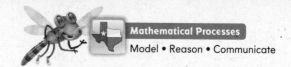
Daily Assessment Task

Fill in the bubble completely to show your answer.

6. A wildlife sanctuary puts a fence around a section of their land. The fence is 19 kilometers long. What is the length of the unknown side?

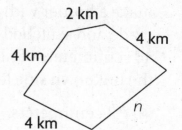

   Ⓐ 5 kilometers   Ⓒ 33 kilometers

   Ⓑ 7 kilometers   Ⓓ 14 kilometers

7. Ciara buys a piece of ribbon to sew around the edges of a square blanket. She uses 36 inches of ribbon. How long is each side of the blanket?

   Ⓐ 18 inches   Ⓒ 4 inches

   Ⓑ 9 inches   Ⓓ 32 inches

8. **Multi-Step** Kenny puts a fence around his 5-sided garden. He starts with 35 feet of fencing. After he is done, he has 5 feet of fencing left over. How long is each side of his garden?

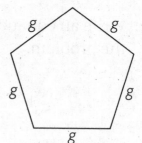

   Ⓐ 7 feet   Ⓒ 6 feet

   Ⓑ 5 feet   Ⓓ 3 feet

TEXAS Test Prep

9. Eleni wants to put a fence around her square garden. The garden has a perimeter of 28 meters. How long will each side of the fence be?

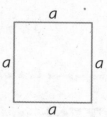

   Ⓐ 8 meters

   Ⓑ 7 meters

   Ⓒ 14 meters

   Ⓓ 6 meters

17.3 Find Unknown Side Lengths

ALGEBRA

Find the unknown side lengths.

1. Perimeter = 28 centimeters

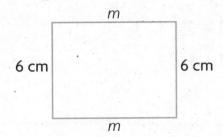

$m =$ _____ centimeters

2. Perimeter = 40 feet

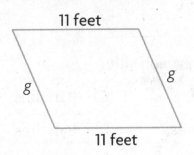

$g =$ _____ feet

Problem Solving

Use the diagram for 3–4.

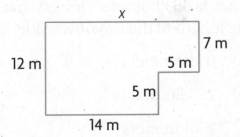

3. Mitch needs to replace the fence in his backyard. The diagram shows the lengths of the borders of the fence. The length of the fence is 62 meters. What is the unknown side length? **Explain** how you will solve the problem. Then write an equation to solve the problem.

_____

_____

_____

_____

4. What if Mitch changes the shape of his fence to a rectangle? How much fencing will Mitch need? **Explain**.

_____

_____

_____

_____

Fill in the bubble completely to show your answer.

5. Nagi has a mirror in the shape of a hexagon. He puts a frame around it that has a perimeter of 42 inches.

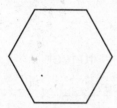

How long is each side?

(A) 7 inches   (C) 8 inches

(B) 6 inches   (D) 9 inches

6. Zena has a square picture frame with a perimeter of 28 inches. Which equation can she use to find the length of each side?

(A) $4 \times s = 28$

(B) $4 + s = 28$

(C) $28 \times 4 = s$

(D) $28 + 4 = s$

7. A farmer is putting a new fence around a section of his ranch. The fence is 35 kilometers long. What is the length of the unknown side?

(A) 6 kilometers

(B) 29 kilometers

(C) 7 kilometers

(D) 35 kilometers

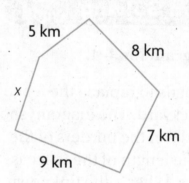

8. **Multi-Step** Glenda puts a border of wallpaper around her bedroom wall. The room is a rectangle with side lengths of 3 meters and 4 meters. If she has 20 meters of wallpaper, how much wallpaper is left over?

(A) 13 meters   (C) 27 meters

(B) 6 meters   (D) 14 meters

9. **Multi-Step** Jorge sews a trim around the edge of a tablecloth with 8 sides. He has 32 feet of trim. If each side of the tablecloth is 2 feet long, how much trim will Jorge have left?

(A) 10 feet   (C) 42 feet

(B) 8 feet   (D) 16 feet

Name _____

Module 17 Assessment

Vocabulary

Choose the best term from the box.

Vocabulary
area
perimeter

1. The distance around a figure is the _____. (p. 545)

Concepts and Skills

Find the perimeter of the figure. Each unit is 1 centimeter. ⬆ TEKS 3.7.B

2.

_____ centimeters

3.

_____ centimeters

Find the unknown side lengths. ⬆ TEKS 3.7.B

4. Perimeter = 33 centimeters

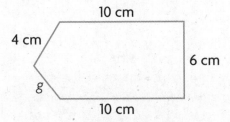

g = _____ centimeters

5. Perimeter = 32 feet

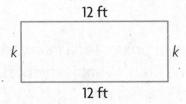

k = _____ centimeters

6. Use a centimeter ruler to find the perimeter. ⬆ TEKS 3.7.B

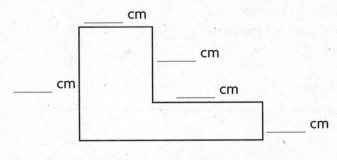

_____ centimeters

Fill in the bubble for the correct answer choice.

7. Jacob built a toolbox with a perimeter of 70 inches. What is the length of side *m*? ⚑ TEKS 3.7.B

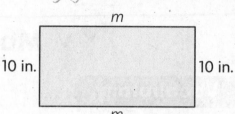

Ⓐ 50 inches

Ⓑ 20 inches

Ⓒ 25 inches

Ⓓ 10 inches

8. Adrienne is decorating a square picture frame. She glued 32 inches of ribbon around the edge of the frame. What is the length of each side of the picture frame? ⚑ TEKS 3.7.B

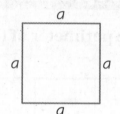

Ⓐ 4 inches Ⓒ 28 inches

Ⓑ 8 inches Ⓓ 16 inches

9. What is the perimeter of the figure? Each unit is 1 centimeter. ⚑ TEKS 3.7.B

Ⓐ 20 centimeters Ⓒ 23 centimeters

Ⓑ 18 centimeters Ⓓ 9 centimeters

10. Jeff is making a poster for a car wash for the Campout Club. What is the perimeter of the poster? ⚑ TEKS 3.7.B

Ⓐ 8 feet Ⓒ 6 feet

Ⓑ 3 feet Ⓓ 4 feet

11. A rectangle has side lengths of 8 inches and 10 inches. What is the perimeter of the rectangle? ⚑ TEKS 3.7.B

Ⓐ 28 inches Ⓒ 32 inches

Ⓑ 18 inches Ⓓ 36 inches

Name _____

18.1 Measure Time Intervals

? Essential Question How can you measure elapsed time in minutes?

🔑 Unlock the Problem

Ava and her family visited Space Center Houston. They watched a movie that began at 4:10 P.M. and ended at 4:53 P.M. How long did the movie last?

To find **elapsed time**, find the amount of time that passes from the start of an activity to the end of the activity.

- What time did the movie begin?

  _____

- What time did the movie end?

  _____

- Underline the question.

🔑 One Way Use a number line.

STEP 1 Find the time on the number line that the movie began.

_____

STEP 2 Count on to the ending time, 4:53. Count on by tens for each 10 minutes. Count on by ones for each minute. Write the times below the number line.

_____

STEP 3 Draw the jumps on the number line to show the minutes from 4:10 to 4:53. Record the minutes.

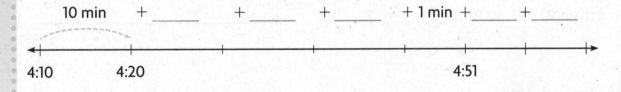

10 min   + _____   + _____   + _____   + 1 min + _____ + _____

4:10   4:20   4:51

_____

STEP 4 Add to find the total minutes.

$10 + 10 + 10 + 10 + 1 + 1 + 1 =$ _____

The elapsed time from 4:10 P.M. to 4:53 P.M. is _____ minutes.

So, the movie lasted _____ minutes.

Math Talk

Mathematical Processes
Describe another way you can use jumps on the number line to find the elapsed time from 4:10 P.M. to 4:53 P.M.

🔑 Other Ways

Start time: 4:10 P.M. End time: 4:53 P.M.

🅐 Use an analog clock.

STEP 1 Find the starting time on the clock.

STEP 2 Count the minutes by counting on by fives and ones to 4:53 P.M. Write the missing counting numbers next to the clock.

So, the elapsed time is _____ minutes.

🅑 Use subtraction.

STEP 1 Write the ending time. Then write the starting time so that the hours and minutes line up.

STEP 2 The hours are the same, so subtract the minutes.

  ← end time

  ← start time

← elapsed time

Share and Show MATH BOARD Hands On

1. Use the number line to find the elapsed time from 1:15 P.M. to 1:40 P.M. _____

1:15

Find the elapsed time.

✓ 2. Start: 11:35 A.M. End: 11:54 A.M.

✓ 3. Start: 4:20 P.M. End: 5:00 P.M.

Problem Solving

4. **Apply** Connor started reading his book about outer space at quarter after nine in the morning. He read until quarter to ten in the morning. How long did Connor read his book?

_____

Write Math ▶ Show Your Work . . . .

5. **H.O.T.** **Multi-Step** Aiden arrived at the rocket display at 3:35 P.M. and left at 3:49 P.M. Ava arrived at the rocket display at 3:30 P.M. and left at 3:56 P.M. Ava spent how many more minutes at the rocket display than Aiden?

_____

6. **H.O.T.** **Multi-Step** At the space center, Hannah bought a model of a lunar rover. She started working on the model the next day at 11:13 A.M. She worked until leaving for lunch at 11:51 A.M. After lunch, she worked on the model again from 1:29 P.M. until 1:48 P.M. How long did Hannah work on the model?

_____

7. **Write Math** ▶ Aiden's family took the NASA Tram tour from 2:05 P.M. to 2:45 P.M. **Explain** how you know that the tour was more than 30 minutes.

_____

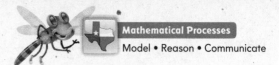

Daily Assessment Task

Fill in the bubble for the correct answer choice.

8. Samantha practices for a kayak race from 8:02 A.M. to 8:49 A.M. How long does Samantha practice?

   Ⓐ 41 minutes   Ⓒ 69 minutes

   Ⓑ 47 minutes   Ⓓ 51 minutes

9. Amy reads a book from 9:15 A.M. to 9:29 A.M. before she goes to class. During lunch, she reads the same book from 1:18 P.M. to 1:35 P.M. How long does Amy read the book?

   Ⓐ 14 minutes   Ⓒ 31 minutes

   Ⓑ 22 minutes   Ⓓ 17 minutes

10. **Multi-Step** Lucas does his science homework from 5:12 P.M. to 5:43 P.M. It takes him 5 more minutes to do his history project than it does to finish his science homework. How long does it take Lucas to finish his history project?

    Ⓐ 31 minutes   Ⓒ 41 minutes

    Ⓑ 26 minutes   Ⓓ 36 minutes

 TEXAS Test Prep

11. Kira got on the tour bus at 5:15 P.M. She got off the bus at 5:37 P.M. How long was Kira on the bus?

    Ⓐ 37 minutes

    Ⓑ 22 minutes

    Ⓒ 15 minutes

    Ⓓ 52 minutes

18.1 Measure Time Intervals

Find the elapsed time.

1. Start: 1:10 A.M.   End: 1:55 A.M.

_____

2. Start: 3:40 P.M.   End: 4:15 P.M.

_____

3. Start: 12:25 A.M.   End: 12:51 A.M.

_____

4. Start: 10:05 A.M.   End: 10:55 A.M.

_____

Problem Solving Real World

5. Dane started running at half past three in the afternoon. He stopped running at ten minutes after four. How long did Dane run?

_____

6. Multi-Step Myoshi began making dinner at 5:25 P.M. He finished making dinner at 6:07 P.M. He served dinner to his guests from 7:10 P.M. until 7:33 P.M. How long did it take Myoshi to make and serve dinner?

_____

Fill in the bubble completely to show your answer.

7. Mr. Divak leaves for work at 8:15 A.M. He gets to work at 8:33 A.M. How long does it take Mr. Divak to get to work?

(A) 18 minutes

(B) 23 minutes

(C) 15 minutes

(D) 28 minutes

8. Cara started her homework at 6:10 P.M. She finished at 6:49 P.M. How long did it take Cara to do her homework?

(A) 49 minutes

(B) 40 minutes

(C) 39 minutes

(D) 59 minutes

9. Art class begins at 1:30 P.M. It ends at 2:13 P.M. How long does art class last?

(A) 53 minutes

(B) 33 minutes

(C) 30 minutes

(D) 43 minutes

10. A TV shows starts at 5:03 P.M. It lasts 55 minutes. What time does the show end?

(A) 6:00 P.M.

(B) 4:58 P.M.

(C) 5:58 P.M.

(D) 4:47 P.M.

11. **Multi-Step** Ben gets on a bus at Main Street at 10:13 A.M. The bus arrives at Elm Street at 10:27 A.M. It waits for 10 minutes. Then it arrives at Broadway at 10:50 A.M. How long is Ben on the bus if he rides from Main Street to Broadway?

(A) 37 minutes

(B) 14 minutes

(C) 27 minutes

(D) 42 minutes

12. **Multi-Step** Marcella works on her art project from 4:10 P.M. to 4:35 P.M. Then she takes a break. She continues to work on her project from 6:25 P.M. to 6:43 P.M. How long does Marcella work on her art project?

(A) 43 minutes

(B) 33 minutes

(C) 55 minutes

(D) 25 minutes

Name _____

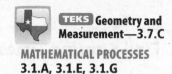

18.2 Use Time Intervals

 Essential Question

How can you find a starting time or an ending time when you know the elapsed time?

Unlock the Problem Real World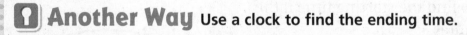

Jacob begins working on his oceans project at 1:30 P.M. He spends 30 minutes painting a model of Earth and 12 minutes labeling the continents and oceans. At what time does Jacob finish working on his project?

• What time is given?

_____

_____

• What time do you need to find?

_____

_____

One Way Use a number line to find the ending time.

STEP 1 Find the time on the number line when Jacob started working on the project.

STEP 2 Count forward on the number line to add the elapsed times. Draw and label the jumps to show the minutes.

> **Think:** I can break apart 12 minutes into shorter amounts of time.

STEP 3 Write the times below the number line.

Math Talk
Mathematical Processes
Explain how you decided what size jumps to make on the number line.

←—|————————————————————→

1:30 P.M.

The jumps end at _____

So, Jacob finishes working on his project at _____

Another Way Use a clock to find the ending time.

STEP 1 Find the starting time on the clock.

STEP 2 Count on by fives and ones for the elapsed time of 42 minutes. Write the missing counting numbers next to the clock.

So, the ending time is _____

Find Starting Times

Whitney swam laps in the pool for 25 minutes. She finished swimming at 11:15 A.M. At what time did Whitney start swimming?

🔑 One Way Use a number line to find the starting time.

STEP 1 Find the time on the number line when Whitney finished swimming laps in the pool.

_____

STEP 2 Count back on the number line to subtract the elapsed time. Draw and label the jumps to show the minutes.

_____

STEP 3 Write the times below the number line.

←————————————————————————————|————→
                                                    11:15 A.M.

You jumped back to _____

So, Whitney started swimming at _____

🔑 Another Way Use a clock to find the starting time.

STEP 1 Find the ending time on the clock.

_____

STEP 2 Count back by fives for the elapsed time of 25 minutes. Write the missing counting numbers next to the clock.

So, the starting time is _____

  Share and Show

1. Use the number line to find the starting time if the elapsed time is 35 minutes. _____

←————————————————————————————|————→
                                                    5:10 P.M.

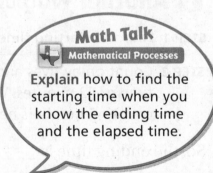

Math Talk
Mathematical Processes

Explain how to find the starting time when you know the ending time and the elapsed time.

Name _____

Find the ending time.

2. Starting time: 1:40 P.M.
   Elapsed time: Lunch: 20 minutes
                   Walk dog: 13 minutes

_____

3. Starting time: 9:55 A.M.
   Elapsed time: Ride bike: 15 minutes
                   Homework: 12 minutes

_____

Problem Solving Real World

Use the table for 4–5.

4. **Multi-Step Analyze** The first morning, Courtney walked on the beach for 10 minutes and swam for 10 minutes. She finished her walk and swim 30 minutes before high tide. At what time did Courtney start her walk?

_____

5. The third afternoon, Courtney started collecting shells at low tide. She collected shells for 35 minutes. At what time did Courtney finish collecting shells?

_____

Tide Times Atlantic City, NJ		
	Low Tide	High Tide
Day 1	2:12 A.M.	9:00 A.M.
	2:54 P.M.	9:00 P.M.
Day 2	3:06 A.M.	9:36 A.M.
	3:36 P.M.	9:54 P.M.
Day 3	4:00 A.M.	10:12 A.M.
	4:30 P.M.	10:36 P.M.

▲ Ocean tides are mostly caused by the pull of the moon and the sun's gravity. High tide is when the water is at its highest level. Low tide is when the water is at its lowest level.

6. **H.O.T. Multi-Step** Suzi began fishing at 10:30 A.M. and fished until 11:10 A.M. James finished fishing at 11:45 A.M. He fished for the same length of time as Suzi. At what time did James start fishing? **Explain.**

_____

_____

_____

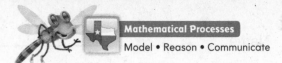

Daily Assessment Task

Fill in the bubble for the correct answer choice.

7. Fiona practices for her piano recital 30 minutes before lunch each day. If she has lunch at 12:15 P.M., what time does Fiona start practicing each day?

   Ⓐ 12:00 P.M.   Ⓒ 11:30 A.M.

   Ⓑ 11:45 A.M.   Ⓓ 12:45 P.M.

8. This morning, Damon woke up at 7:45 A.M. His brother Sam woke up 45 minutes later. At what time did Sam wake up?

   Ⓐ 7:45 P.M.   Ⓒ 8:30 A.M.

   Ⓑ 8:45 A.M.   Ⓓ 7:00 A.M.

9. **Multi-Step** Jessica starts cleaning her room at 5:50 P.M. and finishes at 6:44 P.M. Her sister Norah finishes cleaning her room at 7:12 P.M. She cleans for the same amount of time as Jessica. At what time does Norah start cleaning?

   Ⓐ 6:12 P.M.   Ⓒ 7: 22 P.M.

   Ⓑ 7:38 P.M.   Ⓓ 6:18 P.M.

 TEXAS Test Prep

10. Dante's paddleboarding lesson began at 2:35 P.M. His lesson lasted 45 minutes. At what time did Dante's lesson end?

   Ⓐ 1:50 P.M.

   Ⓑ 3:45 P.M.

   Ⓒ 3:20 P.M.

   Ⓓ 2:45 P.M.

Name _____

18.2 Use Time Intervals

Find the ending time.

1. Starting time: 5:10 P.M.
   Elapsed time: Read: 15 minutes
   Homework: 23 minutes

_____

2. Starting time: 10:50 A.M.
   Elapsed time: Swim: 20 minutes
   Snack: 14 minutes

_____

Problem Solving Real World

Use the table for 3–5.

Bus Schedule	
Town	**Time**
Bear Falls	9:20 A.M.
Little Creek	9:45 A.M.
New Bridge	10:15 A.M.
Ellenville	10:37 A.M.
Newton	11:05 A.M.

3. **Multi-Step** Serena gets off the bus at New Bridge. From there she walks for 15 minutes to the grocery store. She shops for 23 minutes. What time does Serena finish shopping?

   _____

4. **Multi-Step** Terrence rides the bus from Little Creek to New Bridge. Janey rides the bus from Ellenville to Newton. Who has a longer ride on the bus? **Explain**.

   _____

   _____

   _____

5. **Multi-Step** It takes Niles 15 minutes to walk from his house to the bus stop at Little Creek. He waits for 12 minutes before the bus picks him up. What time did Niles leave his house?

   _____

Fill in the bubble completely to show your answer.

6. Sara has soccer practice at 4:15 P.M. It takes her 35 minutes to get to soccer practice from her house. At what time does Sara leave for soccer practice?

   Ⓐ 3:40 P.M.

   Ⓑ 4:50 P.M.

   Ⓒ 3:45 P.M.

   Ⓓ 4:00 P.M.

7. Alana starts her homework at 5:23 P.M. It takes her 40 minutes to complete her homework. At what time does Alana finish doing her homework?

   Ⓐ 5:53 P.M.

   Ⓑ 5:40 P.M.

   Ⓒ 4:43 P.M.

   Ⓓ 6:03 P.M.

8. Sissy starts practicing her violin at 3:30 P.M. She practices for 45 minutes. At what time does Sissy finish practicing her violin?

   Ⓐ 2:45 P.M.

   Ⓑ 4:15 P.M.

   Ⓒ 4:30 P.M.

   Ⓓ 3:45 P.M.

9. Oswald gets on the bus for school at 8:25 A.M. It takes him 13 minutes to walk to the bus stop. What time does Oswald leave his house for the bus?

   Ⓐ 8:38 A.M.

   Ⓑ 8:12 A.M.

   Ⓒ 8:13 A.M.

   Ⓓ 8:30 A.M.

10. **Multi-Step** Vera starts reading her book at 11:15 A.M. She finishes reading at 11:43 A.M. Wade finishes reading his book at 11:30 A.M. Both children read for the same amount of time. At what time did Wade start reading his book?

    Ⓐ 11:12 A.M.

    Ⓑ 11:28 A.M.

    Ⓒ 11:02 A.M.

    Ⓓ 11:20 A.M.

11. **Multi-Step** Paco gets on the bus at 7:45 A.M. He arrives at school at 8:10 A.M. Milos gets on the bus at 8:05 A.M. and arrives at school at 8:18 A.M. For how many more minutes does Paco ride the bus than Milos?

    Ⓐ 13 minutes

    Ⓑ 25 minutes

    Ⓒ 12 minutes

    Ⓓ 20 minutes

18.3 PROBLEM SOLVING • Time Intervals

? Essential Question How can you use the strategy *draw a diagram* to solve problems about time?

🔑 Unlock the Problem (Real World)

Alec and his family are going to New York City. Their airplane leaves at 9:15 A.M. They need to arrive at the airport 60 minutes before their flight. It takes 15 minutes to get to the airport. The family needs 30 minutes to get ready to leave. At what time should Alec's family start getting ready?

Read

What do I need to find?

I need to find

what _____

Alec's family should start

_____ .

What information am I given?

the time the airplane _____ ; the

time the family needs to _____

at the airport; the time it takes to

_____ the airport; and the time

the family needs to _____

Plan

What is my plan or strategy?

I will use a

_____

to find the answer.

Solve

• Find 9:15 A.M. on the number line. Draw the jumps to show the time.

• Count back ____ minutes for the time they need to arrive at the airport.

⟵————————————|⟶
9:15 A.M.

• Count back ____ minutes for the time to get to the airport.

• Count back ____ minutes for the time to get ready.

So, Alec's family should start getting ready at ____ ____ .M.

Math Talk
Mathematical Processes
How can you check your answer by starting with the time the family starts getting ready?

Try Another Problem

Cory gets out of school at 2:45 P.M. It takes him 10 minutes to walk home. Then he spends 10 minutes eating a snack. He spends 8 minutes putting on his soccer uniform. It takes 20 minutes for Cory's father to drive him to soccer practice. At what time does Cory arrive at soccer practice?

Read

What do I need to find?

What information am I given?

Plan

What is my plan or strategy?

Solve

Draw a diagram to help you explain your answer.

$\longleftrightarrow$

1. At what time does Cory arrive at soccer practice? _____

2. How do you know your answer is reasonable? _____

_____

Math Talk

Mathematical Processes

Do you need to draw jumps on the number line in the same order as the times in the problem? **Explain.**

Name _____

🔑 **Unlock the Problem** Tips

✓ Circle the question.
✓ Underline important facts.
✓ Choose a strategy you know.

✅ **1.** Isabella went to the shopping mall at 11:30 A.M. She shopped for 25 minutes. She spent 40 minutes eating lunch. Then she met a friend at a movie. At what time did Isabella meet her friend?

First, begin with _____ on the number line.

Then, count forward _____.

Next, count forward _____.

Think: I can break apart the times into shorter amounts of time that make sense.

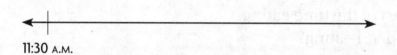

11:30 A.M.

So, Isabella met her friend at _____ _____M.

✅ **2.** **What if** Isabella goes to the mall at 11:30 A.M. and meets a friend at a movie at 1:15 P.M.? Isabella wants to shop and have 45 minutes for lunch before meeting her friend. How much time can Isabella spend shopping?

_____

Problem Solving Real World

3. **H.O.T.** **Multi-Step** When Ethan got home from school, he studied for a test for 30 minutes. Then he spent 10 fewer minutes working on his science project than he did studying for the test. He finished at 4:35 P.M. At what time did Ethan get home from school?

Math on the Spot

_____

4. **Multi-Step Apply** Emma got on the bus at 1:10 P.M. The trip took 90 minutes. Then she walked for 32 minutes to get home. At what time did Emma arrive at home?

_____

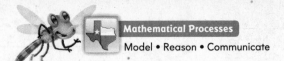

Daily Assessment Task

Fill in the bubble completely to show your answer.

5. Nathalie leaves work at 5:15 P.M. It takes her 7 minutes to walk to the train station. The train ride takes 21 minutes. Then she walks for 11 minutes to get home. At what time does Nathalie arrive home?

   Ⓐ 5:22 P.M.   Ⓒ 5:54 P.M.

   Ⓑ 6:01 P.M.   Ⓓ 5:43 P.M.

6. Liam has a lunch break from 1:05 P.M. to 1:50 P.M. He reads a book for 10 minutes and plays soccer for 19 minutes. He spends the rest of the time eating. How much time does Liam spend eating?

   Ⓐ 29 minutes   Ⓒ 35 minutes

   Ⓑ 16 minutes   Ⓓ 26 minutes

7. **Multi-Step** Kate and Victor film four scenes for a movie. They take a break between each scene. The start time and end time of each scene is shown in the table. How long is the movie?

Scene	Start	End
1	4:30 P.M.	4:40 P.M.
2	5:05 P.M.	5:14 P.M.
3	5:27 P.M.	5:33 P.M.
4	5:56 P.M.	6:00 P.M.

   Ⓐ 29 minutes   Ⓒ 26 minutes

   Ⓑ 30 minutes   Ⓓ 37 minutes

⭐ TEXAS Test Prep

8. When Naomi arrived at the library, she spent 40 minutes reading a book. Then she spent 15 minutes reading a magazine. She left the library at 4:15 P.M. At what time did Naomi arrive at the library?

   Ⓐ 3:20 P.M.

   Ⓑ 4:00 P.M.

   Ⓒ 5:10 P.M.

   Ⓓ 3:35 P.M.

Name _____

18.3 PROBLEM SOLVING • Time Intervals

1. Mr. Tani gets out of work at 4:30 P.M. It takes him 20 minutes to drive home. Then he spends 15 minutes walking his dog. He spends 7 minutes opening the mail. Then he cooks dinner for 23 minutes. At what time does Mr. Tani finish cooking dinner?

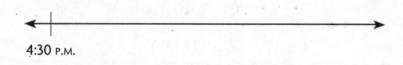

4:30 P.M.

2. Kachina is going to a concert that begins at 7:30 P.M. She needs to arrive at the ticket window 15 minutes before the concert to get her ticket. It takes Kachina 35 minutes to ride to the concert, then 10 minutes to park the car. At what time should Kachina leave for the concert?

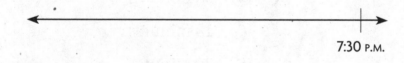

7:30 P.M.

Problem Solving (Real World)

3. **Multi-Step** When Elston got to day camp, he played kickball for 15 minutes. Then he went to play rehearsal for 33 minutes. He finished the rehearsal at 10:18 A.M. What time did Elston get to day camp?

_____

4. **Multi-Step** Danielle gets on the subway at 1:40 P.M. She rides for 17 minutes. Then she walks to her apartment for 18 minutes. At what time does Danielle arrive at her apartment?

_____

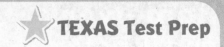
Fill in the bubble completely to show your answer.

5. **Multi-Step** Reading group begins at 10:15 A.M. and lasts for 25 minutes. Math class begins 8 minutes after reading group ends. What time does Math class begin?

Ⓐ 10:40 A.M.

Ⓑ 10:58 A.M.

Ⓒ 10:48 A.M.

Ⓓ 10:45 A.M.

6. **Multi-Step** A ballgame starts at 7:10 P.M. The Lewis family needs 45 minutes to get to the stadium and 12 minutes to walk to their seats. At what time should the Lewis family leave for the ballgame?

Ⓐ 6:10 P.M.

Ⓑ 6:10 P.M.

Ⓒ 6:10 P.M.

Ⓓ 6:13 P.M.

7. **Multi-Step** Martin is at the playground from 3:20 P.M. to 4:10 P.M. He plays on the swings for 14 minutes and then on the monkey bars for 12 minutes. Then he plays tag with friends. How much time does Martin play tag?

Ⓐ 36 minutes

Ⓑ 24 minutes

Ⓒ 28 minutes

Ⓓ 34 minutes

8. **Multi-Step** Theresa is in her yard from 2:10 P.M. to 3:05 P.M. She plants flowers for 15 minutes and waters them for 22 minutes. Then she trims some bushes. How much time does she spend trimming bushes?

Ⓐ 40 minutes

Ⓑ 33 minutes

Ⓒ 18 minutes

Ⓓ 28 minutes

9. **Multi-Step** Evan begins homework at 4:05 P.M. He works on math for 16 minutes and spelling for 15 minutes. Then he works on an art project for 21 minutes. What time does Evan finish his homework?

Ⓐ 4:57 P.M.

Ⓒ 4:52 P.M.

Ⓑ 4:36 P.M.

Ⓓ 4:41 P.M.

10. **Multi-Step** When Basil arrived at the gym, he spent 28 minutes lifting weights and 20 minutes running. Then he had a juice drink for 10 minutes. He left the gym at 11:35 A.M. What time did Basil get to the gym?

Ⓐ 10:27 A.M.

Ⓒ 10:37 A.M.

Ⓑ 10:35 A.M.

Ⓓ 10:45 A.M.

Name _____

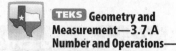
18.4 Fractions in Measurements

 Essential Question

How can you represent fractions of halves, fourths, and eighths, as distances from zero on a number line?

Unlock the Problem 🌎 Real World

Steve ran $\frac{3}{4}$ mile and Jenna ran $\frac{4}{4}$ of a mile. Did Steve and Jenna run the same distance?

🔑 Locate $\frac{3}{4}$ and $\frac{4}{4}$ on a number line.

- Label the number line.

- Draw a point at $\frac{3}{4}$ and $\frac{4}{4}$.

> **Math Idea**
> If two numbers are located at the same point on a number line, then they are equal and represent the same distance from zero.

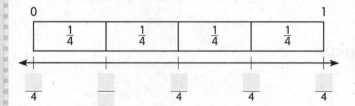

0   1

| $\frac{1}{4}$ | $\frac{1}{4}$ | $\frac{1}{4}$ | $\frac{1}{4}$ |

$\frac{}{4}$ $\frac{}{}$ $\frac{}{4}$ $\frac{}{4}$ $\frac{}{4}$

Since the distance _____ and _____ are not at the same point, they are not the same distance from zero.

_____, Steve and Jenna did not run the same distance.

Try This! Complete the number line. Locate and draw points at $\frac{1}{2}$ and $\frac{2}{2}$.

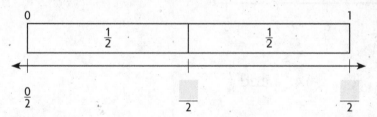

0   1

| $\frac{1}{2}$ | $\frac{1}{2}$ |

$\frac{0}{2}$ $\frac{}{2}$ $\frac{}{2}$

Think: Do the distances end at the same point?

Ⓐ Are $\frac{1}{2}$ and 1 the same distance from zero? **Explain.**

_____

_____

_____

Ⓑ Are $\frac{2}{2}$ and 1 the same distance from zero? **Explain.**

_____

_____

_____

Beth walked $\frac{5}{8}$ mile. Jodi walked $\frac{7}{8}$ mile. Austin watched the girls walk. Did Beth, Jodi, and Austin walk the same distance?

🔑 **Complete the number line. Locate and draw points that Beth, Jodi, and Austin walked.**

Think: Do the distances end at the same point?

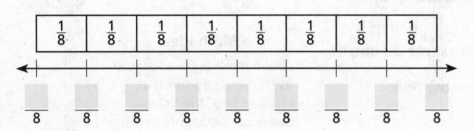

1. How far did Austin walk?

_____

2. Who walked the farthest distance? **Explain**.

_____

_____

Use the number line to find which fraction is farther from zero or if the fractions are the same distance from zero.

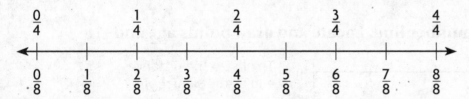

✅ 3. $\frac{1}{8}$ and $\frac{3}{4}$ ✅ 4. $\frac{1}{4}$ and $\frac{2}{8}$

_____   _____

5. $\frac{2}{4}$ and $\frac{4}{8}$ 6. $\frac{5}{8}$ and $\frac{7}{8}$

_____   _____

Name _____

H.O.T. What's the Error?

7. Andrea and Elaina were making material bags. Andrea bought $\frac{4}{8}$ of a yard of material and Elaina bought $\frac{1}{2}$ yard of material. Elaina said she bought more material than Andrea did.

Analyze Look at how Elaina solved the problem. Find her error.

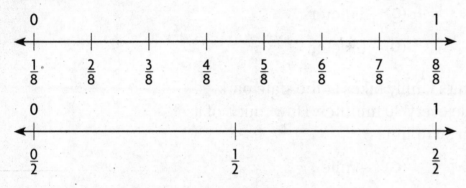

• **Use Math Language** Describe Elaina's error.

_____

_____

8. **H.O.T.** **Multi-Step** Jeff rode his bike around a bike trail that was $\frac{1}{4}$ mile long. He rode around the trail 4 times. Dexter rode around the trail 2 times. Complete the number line to show the distances that Jeff and Dexter rode.

• **Use Tools** Did Dexter ride the same distance as Jeff? **Explain** how you know.

_____

_____

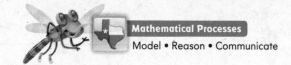

Daily Assessment Task

Fill in the bubble for the correct answer choice.

Use a number line to help solve the problem.

9. A sloth moves $\frac{1}{4}$ meter each second on the ground. How far does the sloth move in 4 seconds?

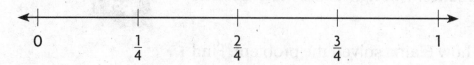

(A) 1 meter   (C) 2 meters

(B) $\frac{1}{2}$ meter   (D) $\frac{1}{4}$ meter

10. On weekends, Salma's family hikes at the state park. They hike $\frac{1}{4}$ of a mile every 30 minutes. How much of a mile do they hike in 90 minutes?

(A) $\frac{1}{2}$ mile   (C) $\frac{3}{4}$ mile

(B) $\frac{1}{4}$ mile   (D) 1 mile

11. **Multi-Step** A football team runs $\frac{1}{8}$ lap around a track in 1 minute. How much of a lap did the team run in 5 minutes?

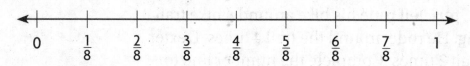

(A) $\frac{2}{8}$ (C) $\frac{8}{8}$

(B) $\frac{5}{8}$ (D) $\frac{3}{8}$

⭐ TEXAS Test Prep

12. Which fraction is the farthest distance from zero?

(A) $\frac{1}{4}$ (C) $\frac{2}{4}$

(B) $\frac{1}{2}$ (D) $\frac{6}{8}$

TEKS Geometry and Measurement—3.7.A
Number and Operations—3.3.B *Also 3.3.A*
MATHEMATICAL PROCESSES 3.1.A, 3.1.C, 3.1.F

Name _____

18.4 Fractions in Measurements

Use the number line to find which fraction is farthest from zero or the same distance.

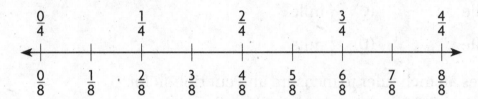

1. $\frac{2}{8}$ and $\frac{1}{4}$ _____

2. $\frac{3}{8}$ and $\frac{2}{4}$ _____

3. $\frac{3}{4}$ and $\frac{5}{8}$ _____

4. $\frac{7}{8}$ and $\frac{3}{4}$ _____

5. $\frac{5}{8}$ and $\frac{1}{4}$ _____

6. $\frac{3}{4}$ and $\frac{6}{8}$ _____

Problem Solving

7. Harley and Noreen were making kites. Harley has $\frac{3}{4}$ of a yard of yellow kite string. Noreen has $\frac{6}{8}$ of a yard of green kite string. She says that she has more kite string than Harley. How can Harley draw a number line to show that Noreen is incorrect? Write a sentence to explain how you solved the problem.

⟵――――――――――――――――⟶

_____

8. Harley gets another $\frac{1}{8}$ yard of kite string. How much string does he have now?

_____

Fill in the bubble completely to show your answer.

9. A flock of geese fly $\frac{1}{4}$ mile every 20 minutes. How far do the geese travel in 1 hour?

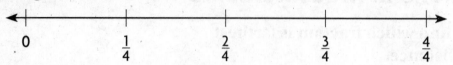

$$0 \qquad \frac{1}{4} \qquad \frac{2}{4} \qquad \frac{3}{4} \qquad \frac{4}{4}$$

Ⓐ $\frac{3}{4}$ mile   Ⓒ $\frac{2}{4}$ mile

Ⓑ $\frac{1}{4}$ mile   Ⓓ $\frac{4}{4}$ mile

10. Adam uses an inch ruler to measure and cut ribbon for an art project. Which statement best describes the pieces that are $\frac{3}{4}$ inch and $\frac{7}{8}$ inch?

Ⓐ the $\frac{3}{4}$ inch piece is farther from zero on the ruler

Ⓑ the pieces are the same distance from zero on the ruler

Ⓒ the $\frac{7}{8}$ inch piece is farther from zero on the ruler

Ⓓ the $\frac{7}{8}$ inch piece is closer to zero on the ruler

11. **Multi-Step** An ant travels $\frac{1}{8}$ yard to an anthill every second. How far does the ant go in 6 seconds?

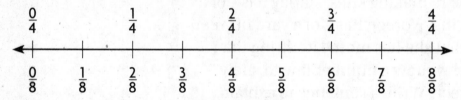

Ⓐ $\frac{3}{4}$ yard   Ⓒ $\frac{2}{4}$ yard

Ⓑ $\frac{1}{4}$ yard   Ⓓ $\frac{7}{8}$ yard

12. **Multi-Step** Edwin runs $\frac{1}{8}$ mile around a track in 2 minutes. He runs for 4 minutes. Then he walks for another $\frac{3}{8}$ mile. How far does Edwin go around the track?

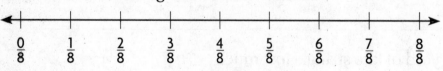

Ⓐ $\frac{3}{8}$ mile   Ⓒ $\frac{2}{8}$ mile

Ⓑ $\frac{4}{8}$ mile   Ⓓ $\frac{5}{8}$ mile

Name _____

18.5 Customary Units for Capacity

© Houghton Mifflin Harcourt Publishing Company • Image Credits: (milk pint) ©D. Hurst/Alamy Images

? Essential Question

How are cups, pints, quarts, and gallons related?

Investigate

Hands On

Capacity is the amount a container will hold. Customary units used to measure capacity are **cup (c)**, **pint (pt)**, **quart (qt)**, and **gallon (gal)**.

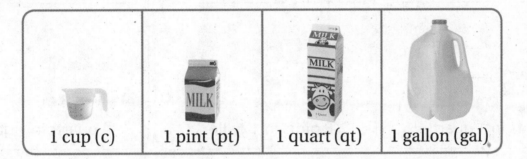

| 1 cup (c) | 1 pint (pt) | 1 quart (qt) | 1 gallon (gal) |

Materials ▪ cup, pint, quart, and gallon containers; water

	Number of Cups		
	Number of Cups in a Pint	Number of Cups in a Quart	Number of Cups in a Gallon
Estimate			
Capacity			

Math Idea

The smallest of these customary units of capacity is a cup.

A. Estimate the number of cups it will take to fill the pint container. Record your estimate.

B. Fill a cup and pour it into the pint container. Repeat until the pint container is full.

C. Record the number of cups it took to fill the pint container.

D. Repeat Steps A to C for the quart and gallon containers.

• How many cups are in a pint? _____ in a quart? _____

  in a gallon? _____

Make Connections

These drawings show how cups, pints, quarts, and gallons are related.

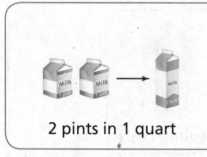

2 cups in 1 pint

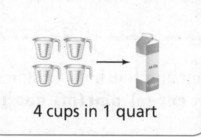

4 cups in 1 quart

16 cups in 1 gallon

2 pints in 1 quart

8 pints in 1 gallon

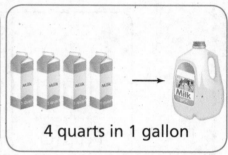

4 quarts in 1 gallon

Share and Show

Choose the unit you would most likely use to measure the capacity. Write *cup*, *pint*, *quart*, or *gallon*.

1.

2.

3.

✓ 4.

_____

_____

_____

_____

Circle the groups that equal the unit named.
Then, rename the capacity using the unit shown.

5.

6 pints in ____ quarts

✓ 6.

8 cups in ____ pints

590

Name _____

Problem Solving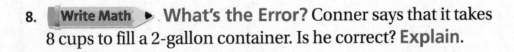

7. **Multi-Step** Janet is serving lemonade. Each glass contains 1 pint. If Janet serves 16 glasses, how many gallons will she serve?

_____

8. **Write Math** ▶ **What's the Error?** Conner says that it takes 8 cups to fill a 2-gallon container. Is he correct? **Explain.**

_____

_____

9. **H.O.T.** **Multi-Step** Mr. Velez has 8 pints of orange juice and 1 gallon of grape juice. How many quarts of juice does he have? **Explain.**

_____

_____

Write Math ▶ ....
Show Your Work

10. **Reasoning** What unit of capacity would you use to measure the amount of water in a bathtub?

_____

_____

11. **H.O.T.** Which is the greater capacity, 2 gallons or 7 quarts? **Justify** by drawing a picture.

_____

12. **What's the Question?** Angela used the drawing below to help answer a question. The answer is 1 quart.

_____

© Houghton Mifflin Harcourt Publishing Company

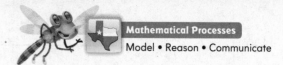

Mathematical Processes

Daily Assessment Task

Fill in the bubble for the correct answer choice.

13. Tiger asks Shakira for 1 quart of milk for his tea. How many pints of milk does Shakira need to give Tiger?

Ⓐ 2 pints

Ⓑ 4 pints

Ⓒ 3 pints

Ⓓ 8 pints

14. Steve buys a 2-quart container of orange juice. How many cups of orange juice does he buy?

Ⓐ 3 cups   Ⓒ 4 cups

Ⓑ 8 cups   Ⓓ 2 cups

15. **Multi-Step** Mr. Armstrong is serving 8 quarts of cranberry juice and 3 gallons of apple juice at a party. Each glass contains 2 cups. How many glasses will Mr. Armstrong serve?

Ⓐ 80 glasses   Ⓒ 16 glasses

Ⓑ 40 glasses   Ⓓ 24 glasses

 TEXAS Test Prep

16. Emily enjoys drinking cocoa before she goes to bed at night. Choose the amount that her mug could hold?

Ⓐ 4 quarts

Ⓑ 2 gallons

Ⓒ 2 cups

Ⓓ 4 pints

18.5 Customary Units for Capacity

Choose the unit you would use to measure the capacity.
Write *cup*, *pint*, *quart*, or *gallon*.

1.

_____

2.

_____

3.

_____

Circle the groups that equal the unit named.
Then, rename the capacity using the unit shown.

4.

8 quarts in ____ gallons

5.

4 pints in ____ quarts

6.

6 cups in ____ pints

Problem Solving Real World

7. Jacey's fish tank holds 12 quarts of water. How many gallons of water should Jacey use to fill his fish tank?

_____

8. Selena has a cooking pot that holds 3 quarts of water. How many cups of water does she need to fill the pot?

_____

Fill in the bubble completely to show your answer.

9. Zuri wants to fill a 1-gallon jug with pints of juice. How many pints of juice does Zuri need to fill the jug?

Ⓐ 8 pints

Ⓑ 4 pints

Ⓒ 2 pints

Ⓓ 6 pints

10. Tanner buys a 1-gallon jug of milk. How many cups of milk can Tanner pour from the gallon?

Ⓐ 10 cups

Ⓑ 8 cups

Ⓒ 16 cups

Ⓓ 12 cups

11. Henley needs $2\frac{1}{2}$ quarts of water to make a batch of chicken soup. How many pints of soup will Henley make?

Ⓐ 4 pints

Ⓑ 3 pints

Ⓒ 5 pints

Ⓓ 6 pints

12. Chen places a large pot on the stove to cook spaghetti. Choose the amount that Chen's pot could hold if it were full.

Ⓐ 8 gallons

Ⓑ 3 quarts

Ⓒ 2 cups

Ⓓ 1 pint

13. **Multi-Step** Mr. Tome uses 5 quarts of pineapple juice and 2 gallons of orange juice to make punch. How many 1-cup servings of punch will Mr. Tome make?

Ⓐ 20 cups

Ⓑ 16 cups

Ⓒ 40 cups

Ⓓ 52 cups

14. **Multi-Step** Garcia has a 5-gallon fish tank and a 3-gallon fish tank. How many more pints of water are in the 5-gallon tank than in the 3-gallon tank?

Ⓐ 16 pints

Ⓑ 40 pints

Ⓒ 24 pints

Ⓓ 30 pints

Name _____

18.6 Metric Units for Liquid Volume

Essential Question How can you measure liquid volume in metric units?

Unlock the Problem (Real World)

Hands On

Liquid volume is the amount of liquid in a container. The **liter (L)** is the basic metric unit for measuring liquid volume. A **milliliter (mL)** is the metric unit to measure liquid in very small containers.

Activity

Materials ▪ 1-L beaker ▪ a bottle cap ▪ 1-mL dropper
▪ 2 containers ▪ water ▪ tape

STEP 1 Fill a 1-liter beaker with water to the 1-liter mark.

STEP 2 Pour 1 liter of water to fill a container. Mark the level of the water with a piece of tape. Draw the container below and name the container. Write if the container holds less than a liter, a liter, or more than a liter.

STEP 3 Repeat Steps 1 and 2 with a different-sized container.

Container 1 | Container 2

_____ | _____

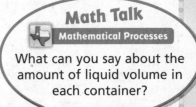
Math Talk
Mathematical Processes
What can you say about the amount of liquid volume in each container?

STEP 4 Use the 1–mL dropper filled with water to fill the bottle cap. How many times did you fill the dropper? _____

Explain if the bottle cap is less than a milliliter, a milliliter, or more than

a milliliter? _____

• Name a container that will hold a liter of water. _____

Will the container hold 50 bottle caps of water? Justify.

_____

_____

A dropper holds about 1 mL.

A full glass holds about 250 mL.

A sports bottle holds about 1,000 mL or 1 L.

- Suppose you drank a glass of orange juice. Did you drink about 4 mL or 300 mL of orange juice? **Explain.**

_____

_____

Share and Show

MATH BOARD

Choose the unit you would use to measure each container's capacity. Write *milliliter* or *liter*.

1.

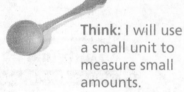

Think: I will use a small unit to measure small amounts.

_____

2.

_____

3.

_____

4.

_____

5.

_____

6.

_____

Ginger pours punch into three 1-L bottles. Choose the metric unit to measure the liquid volume in each bottle. Write *milliliter* or *liter*.

7.

_____

8.

_____

9.

_____

© Houghton Mifflin Harcourt Publishing Company • Image Credits:(teapot) ©Stockbyte/Getty Images

Name _____

Problem Solving  Real World

Use the containers for 10–13. Container A is full when 1 liter of water is poured into it.

10. **Write Math** ▶ **What if** you poured 1 liter of water into Container B? Describe the way the water fills the container. **Explain** how you know.

_____

_____

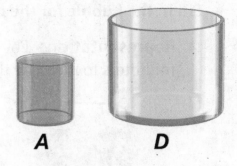

A   D

11. **H.O.T.** **Reasoning** Bryson filled 2 containers full with water. One container held 2 liters and the other container held 250 milliliters. Which two containers did he fill?

_____

_____

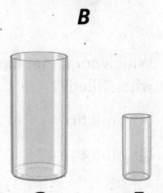

B

12. **H.O.T.** **Evaluate** Name two containers that will be filled with about the same number of liters of water. **Explain.**

_____

_____

_____

C   E

13. **H.O.T.** **What's the Error?** Samuel says that you can pour more liters of water into Container B than into Container D. Is he correct? **Explain.**

_____

_____

_____

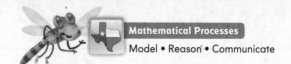
Daily Assessment Task

Fill in the bubble for the correct answer choice.

14. **Representations** For which container would you use milliliters to measure the amount of liquid?

Ⓐ

Ⓒ

Ⓑ

Ⓓ

15. Which container has the greatest liquid volume when filled?

Ⓐ pitcher   Ⓒ bucket

Ⓑ mug   Ⓓ bottle cap

16. **Multi-Step** If the liquid in two of the bottles are poured into another container, which two will have the least combined liquid volume?

Ⓐ C and D   Ⓒ A and C

Ⓑ A and B   Ⓓ B and D

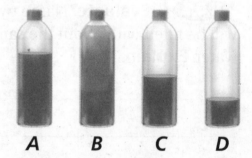

A   B   C   D

 TEXAS Test Prep

17. The bottles of tea are all liter bottles. Which bottle has a liter of tea?

Ⓐ Bottle *J*   Ⓒ Bottle *M*

Ⓑ Bottle *K*   Ⓓ Bottle *L*

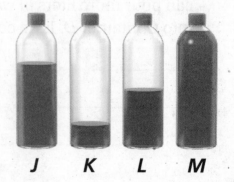

J   K   L   M

18.6 Metric Units for Liquid Volume

**Choose the unit you would use to measure the capacity.
Write *milliliter* or *liter*.**

1.

_____

2.

_____

3.

_____

4.

_____

5.

_____

6.

_____

Problem Solving Real World

**Use the containers for 7–9. Container A is full when
1 liter of water is poured into it.**

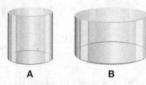
A   B   C

D   E

7. What if you poured 1 liter of water into container C?
   Describe the way the water fills the container.

   _____

   _____

8. Which container would hold about
   half of the water as in container D?
   Explain.

   _____

   _____

   _____

9. For which containers would you
   use milliliters to measure the liquid
   volume? **Explain.**

   _____

   _____

   _____

Fill in the bubble completely to show your answer.

10. Which container has the least liquid volume when filled?

   Ⓐ water glass   Ⓒ soup bowl

   Ⓑ tablespoon   Ⓓ fish bowl

11. Which container would you use a liter to measure the amount of liquid?

   Ⓐ   Ⓒ

   Ⓑ   Ⓓ

12. The bottles of liquid are all liter bottles. Which amount of liquid would fill a juice glass?

   Ⓐ   Ⓑ   Ⓒ   Ⓓ

13. **Multi-Step** If the liquid in two of the containers is poured into another container, which two will have the greatest combined liquid volume?

   Ⓐ E and H
   Ⓑ F and H
   Ⓒ E and F
   Ⓓ G and H

   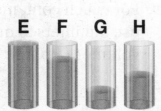

14. **Multi-Step** Each of the containers has a capacity of 1 liter. If the liquid in two of the containers is poured into another container, which two will have a combined volume of 1 liter?

   Ⓐ C and D
   Ⓑ B and C
   Ⓒ A and D
   Ⓓ B and D

   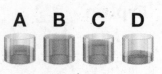

Name _____

18.7 Customary Units for Weight

TEKS Geometry and Measurement—3.7.D, 3.7.E

MATHEMATICAL PROCESSES 3.1.C, 3.1.G

? Essential Question

How are ounces and pounds related?

🔑 Unlock the Problem

Real World

Hands On

Weight is the measure of how heavy an object is. Customary units for weight include **ounce (oz)** and **pound (lb)**.

Circle the correct word to complete the sentences.

One slice of bread weighs

about 1   ounce.
             pound.

One loaf of bread weighs

about 1   ounce.
             pound.

Math Talk

Mathematical Processes

Suppose you weigh a bag of potatoes in pounds, and then in ounces. Which number would be greater, the number of ounces or the number of pounds? Explain.

Try This!

Sixteen ounces and one pound equal the same weight. Finish the drawing of slices of bread to show how ounces and pounds are related.

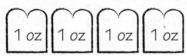

1 oz | 1 oz | 1 oz | 1 oz

→

____ ounces in ____ pound

© Houghton Mifflin Harcourt Publishing Company

 Activity

Materials ■ scale, classroom objects

Weight of Objects		
Objects	Unit	Weight
apple		
book		
pencil box		
tape dispenser		

STEP 1 Use a scale to measure to the nearest ounce or pound. Record the weight.

STEP 2 Repeat for each object.

Share and Show

1. A strawberry weighs about 1 _____ ounce. pound.

Choose the unit you would use to measure the weight.
Write *ounce* or *pound*.

2. _____

3.  _____

4. _____

⊘ 5.  _____

Find an object in the classroom to match the description.
Draw and label the object.

6. greater than 1 pound

⊘ 7. less than 1 pound

⚷ Unlock the Problem

8. **H.O.T.** **Multi-Step** Jared has a canister that has 48 ounces of home-made trail mix. He wants to package the mix in bags that each hold 1 pound of mix. How many bags can Jared fill?

a. What do you need to find? _____

b. What are two ways to describe the amount the bags can hold?

_____

c. **Representations** Show the steps you used to solve the problem.

d. Complete the sentences.

Sixteen ounces is the same weight

as _____.

Each bag holds _____ ounces of mix.

48 ounces can be separated

into _____ groups of _____ ounces

each.

So, Jared can fill _____ bags with 1 pound of trail mix each.

9. **H.O.T.** **Use Math Language** Hank says that 32 ounces is the same as 3 pounds. Does this statement make sense? **Explain.**

_____

_____

Daily Assessment Task

Fill in the bubble for the correct answer choice.

10. A watermelon weighs 6 pounds. Which item would be about the same weight as the watermelon?

   Ⓐ 10-ounce package of straws

   Ⓑ 8 slices of cheese pizza

   Ⓒ 6 erasers

   Ⓓ 480 quarters

11. Brianna is building a doghouse. Each board weighs about 10 ounces. She lifts 8 boards at a time. About how much does Brianna lift?

   Ⓐ 3 ounces   Ⓒ 5 pounds

   Ⓑ 4 ounces   Ⓓ 2 pounds

12. **Multi-Step** Sandra and Richelle baked 2 cakes. They cut both cakes into 8 equal slices. Each slice weights about 2 ounces. Which is the combined weight of the cakes?

   Ⓐ 4 ounces   Ⓒ 16 ounces

   Ⓑ 2 pounds   Ⓓ 1 pound

TEXAS Test Prep

13. There are 4 baseball caps at a store. Each cap weighs 8 ounces. How much do the caps weigh in all?

   Ⓐ 8 ounces

   Ⓑ 10 ounces

   Ⓒ 2 pounds

   Ⓓ 4 pounds

Name _____

18.7 Customary Units for Weight

**Choose the unit you would use to measure the weight.
Write *ounce* or *pound*.**

1.

_____

2.

_____

3.

_____

4.

_____

5.

_____

6.

_____

Problem Solving

7. **Multi-Step** Janet buys 6 bags of potatoes. Each bag holds 8 ounces. How many pounds of potatoes does Janet buy?

_____

8. **Multi-Step** Pedro buys 2 pounds 8 ounces of tomatoes. How many ounces of tomatoes does Pedro buy?

_____

9. Sonny has a bag that holds 32 ounces of rice. He wants to divide the rice into boxes that hold 1 pound each. How many boxes can Jared fill? Draw a picture to solve the problem. **Explain** how you solved the problem.

_____

_____

_____

Fill in the bubble completely to show your answer.

10. A small paperback book weighs about 10 ounces. Which item would be about the same weight as the paperback book?

   Ⓐ   a slice of pizza

   Ⓑ   a pound of potatoes

   Ⓒ   a quart of milk

   Ⓓ   a radio

11. A bag of onions weighs about 3 pounds. Which items would be about the same weight as the bag of onions?

   Ⓐ   20 balloons

   Ⓑ   5 turkeys

   Ⓒ   10 tomatoes

   Ⓓ   15 feathers

12. **Multi-Step** A worker loads boxes of sugar. Each box weighs 16 ounces. The worker loads 20 boxes at one time. How many pounds of sugar does the worker load?

   Ⓐ   36 pounds

   Ⓑ   20 pounds

   Ⓒ   16 pounds

   Ⓓ   10 pounds

13. **Multi-Step** Otis bakes 8 mini loaves of bread. Each loaf weighs about 8 ounces. About how many pounds of bread does Otis bake?

   Ⓐ   4 pounds

   Ⓑ   6 pounds

   Ⓒ   5 pounds

   Ⓓ   3 pounds

14. **Multi-Step** Yogurt comes in containers that weigh 4 ounces. Each pack contain 6 yogurt containers. If Otis buys 2 packs of yogurt, how many pounds of yogurt does he buy?

   Ⓐ   4 pounds

   Ⓑ   2 pounds

   Ⓒ   3 pounds

   Ⓓ   5 pounds

15. **Multi-Step** There are 5 bananas in a bunch. Each banana weighs about 8 ounces. How many pounds and ounces does the bunch of bananas weigh?

   Ⓐ   2 pounds 8 ounces

   Ⓑ   1 pound 8 ounces

   Ⓒ   2 pounds 5 ounces

   Ⓓ   1 pound 5 ounces

18.8 Metric Units for Mass

TEKS Geometry and Measurement—3.7.D, 3.7.E
MATHEMATICAL PROCESSES 3.1.C, 3.1.E

? Essential Question

How can you measure mass in metric units?

? Unlock the Problem Real World

Hands On

🔑 Peter has a dollar bill in his pocket. Should Peter measure the mass of the dollar bill in grams or kilograms?

The **gram (g)** is the basic metric unit for measuring **mass**, or the amount of matter in an object. Mass can also be measured by using the metric unit **kilogram (kg)**.

A small paper clip has a mass of about 1 gram.	A box of 1,000 paper clips has a mass of about 1 kilogram.

Think: The mass of a dollar bill is closer to the mass of a small paper clip than it is to a box of 1,000 paper clips.

So, Peter should measure the mass of the dollar bill in _____.

🔑 Activity 1

Materials ■ pan balance ■ gram and kilogram masses

You can use a pan balance to measure mass.

Do 10 grams have the same mass as 1 kilogram?

• Place 10 gram masses on one side of the balance.

• Place a 1-kilogram mass on the other side of the balance.

Think: If it is balanced, then the objects have the same mass. If it is not balanced, the objects do not have the same mass.

• Complete the picture of the pan balance above by drawing in the masses.

The pan balance is _____.

So, 10 grams and 1 kilogram _____ the same mass.

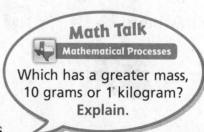

Math Talk
Mathematical Processes

Which has a greater mass, 10 grams or 1 kilogram? Explain.

🔒 Activity 2

Materials ■ pan balance ■ gram and kilogram masses ■ classroom objects

STEP 1 Use the objects in the table. Decide if the object should be measured in grams or kilograms.

STEP 2 Find the mass of each object to the nearest gram or kilogram. Place the object on one side of the balance. Place gram or kilogram masses on the other side until both sides are balanced.

STEP 3 Add the measures of the gram or kilogram masses. This is the mass of the object. Record the mass in the table.

Mass		
Object	**Unit**	**Mass**
crayon		
stapler		
marker		
scissors		

- Write the objects in order from greatest mass to least mass.

_____, _____, _____, _____

Share and Show

1. Five bananas have a mass of about _____.

   Think: The pan balance is balanced, so the objects on both sides have the same mass.

**Choose the unit you would use to measure the mass.
Write *gram* or *kilogram*.**

✓ 2. strawberry

_____

✓ 3. dog

_____

4. sunglasses

_____

Name _____

5. Put the sports balls shown at the right in order from greatest mass to least mass.

_____

_____

Golf ball

6. **H.O.T.** **Multi-Step** One golf ball has a mass of about 46 grams. Mrs. Downs bought a box of 2 golf balls for her first round of golf and bought another box of 2 golf balls for the second round of golf. What is the total mass of the golf balls that Mrs. Downs bought? **Represent** your steps to solve the problem.

Table tennis ball

Bowling ball

Baseball

Tennis ball

_____

_____

_____

7. **H.O.T.** Our dog, Dexter, weighs 72 kilograms. He is 8 times heavier than our cat. What does our cat weigh? **Explain.**

_____

_____

8. **Use Diagrams** Choose two objects that have different masses. Draw a balance with one of these objects on each side.

9. **H.O.T.** **Sense or Nonsense?**
Amber is buying produce at the grocery store. She says that a Fuji apple and a green bell pepper would have the same mass because they are the same size. Does her statement make sense? **Explain.**

_____

_____

Daily Assessment Task

Fill in the bubble for the correct answer choice.

10. A turkey vulture weighs about as much as a laptop computer. Which is the best unit of measure to find the mass of a turkey vulture?

(A) liter

(C) ounce

(B) kilogram

(D) gram

11. Which item's mass should be measured in grams?

(A)

(C)

(B)

(D)

12. **Multi-Step** The third grade classes are making three salt maps on a thin piece of plywood. Together the three maps will have a total mass of 6 kilograms. If the salt mass is about half the mass of each map, which is the mass of salt needed for each map?

(A) 1 kilogram

(C) 3 liters

(B) 5 cups

(D) 5 grams

 TEXAS Test Prep

13. Dan wants to find the mass of a large pumpkin. Which unit should he use?

(A) inch

(C) kilogram

(B) gram

(D) liter

18.8 Metric Units for Mass

Choose the unit you would use to measure the mass.
Write *gram* or *kilogram*.

1.

_____

2.

_____

3.

_____

4.

_____

5.

_____

6.

_____

Problem Solving Real World

7. A bag of peanuts weighs about 36 grams. A bag of walnuts weighs about 42 grams. Yola buys 2 bags of each. How many grams of nuts does Yola have? Represent your steps to solve the problem.

_____

_____

_____

_____

8. Look at the balance scale below. Draw an object on one side of the scale to make the scale balanced.

Fill in the bubble completely to show your answer.

9. A juice box weighs about as much as a softball. Which is the best unit to use to measure the mass of a juice box?

   Ⓐ gram

   Ⓑ pound

   Ⓒ kilogram

   Ⓓ milliliter

10. Antonio wants to find the mass of his backpack filled with books. Which unit should he use?

   Ⓐ ounce

   Ⓑ gram

   Ⓒ kilogram

   Ⓓ quart

11. Which item's mass should be measured in kilograms?

   Ⓐ

   Ⓑ

   Ⓒ

   Ⓓ

12. Which item's mass should be measured in grams?

   Ⓐ

   Ⓑ

   Ⓒ

   Ⓓ

13. **Multi-Step** Sarah is making fruit salad for a picnic. She slices 3 kilograms of apples, 5 kilograms of peaches, and 2 kilograms of strawberries. She divides the fruit into 5 large bowls. About how many kilograms of fruit are in each bowl?

   Ⓐ 12 kilograms

   Ⓑ 2 kilograms

   Ⓒ 7 kilograms

   Ⓓ 10 kilograms

14. **Multi-Step** Desiree is baking cakes. She needs 9 grams of baking powder and 12 grams of baking soda. She divides the baking powder and baking soda equally among 3 pies. How many combined grams of baking powder and baking soda will each pie get?

   Ⓐ 21 grams

   Ⓑ 7 grams

   Ⓒ 24 grams

   Ⓓ 8 grams

Name _____

 Module 18 Assessment

Vocabulary

Vocabulary
capacity
kilograms
liquid volume
liters

Choose the best term from the box.

1. _____ is the amount a container can hold. (p. 589)

2. Mass can be measured in _____ . (p. 607)

Concepts and Skills

Locate and draw points at $\frac{1}{4}$, $\frac{3}{4}$, and $\frac{2}{2}$. Write the fraction that is closest to zero and farthest from zero. TEKS 3.3.B, 3.7.A

3. $\frac{0}{4}$ $\frac{1}{4}$ $\frac{2}{4}$ $\frac{3}{4}$ $\frac{4}{4}$ closest _____

$\frac{0}{2}$ $\frac{1}{2}$ $\frac{2}{2}$ farthest _____

Choose the best unit to measure each capacity. Write *cup*, *pint*, *quart*, or *gallon*. TEKS 3.7.D, 3.7.E

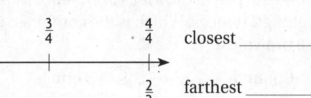

4. bathtub _____   5. pitcher _____   6. a dog bowl _____

Choose the unit you would use to measure the mass. Write *gram* or *kilogram*. TEKS 3.7.D, 3.7.E

7. earphones _____   8. lamp _____   9. boots _____

10. At soccer practice, Valerie ran for 13 minutes and practiced drills for 20 minutes. She left practice at 2:15 P.M. At what time did Valerie arrive at soccer practice? TEKS 3.7.C

Ⓐ 1:33 P.M.   Ⓒ 2:03 P.M.

Ⓑ 1:42 P.M.   Ⓓ 2:48 P.M.

11. Dora placed a pencil on one side of a balance. Which is the mass of the pencil? TEKS 3.7.D, 3.7.E

Ⓐ 1 gram   Ⓒ 1 kilogram

Ⓑ 6 grams   Ⓓ 6 kilograms

12. Arielle and Vienna baked a pan of brownies. Then they divided the pan of brownies into 8 equal squares, each weighing 2 ounces. Which is the combined weight of the the 8 brownies? TEKS 3.7.D, 3.7.E

Ⓐ 1 pound   Ⓒ 8 ounces

Ⓑ 2 ounces   Ⓓ 2 pounds

13. Which measurement unit would you use to find the total liquid volume of this container? TEKS 3.7.D, 3.7.E

Ⓐ pounds

Ⓑ milliliter

Ⓒ liters

Ⓓ grams

14. Allen started his homework at 8:10 P.M. and worked for 45 minutes. Then he phoned a friend and talked for 20 minutes. Allen went to bed at 9:15 P.M. How much time elapsed from Allen starting his homework till he went to bed? TEKS 3.7.C

Ⓐ 15 minutes   Ⓒ 65 minutes

Ⓑ 45 minutes   Ⓓ 20 minutes

Name _____

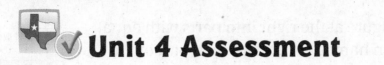

Unit 4 Assessment

Vocabulary

Choose the best term from the box to complete the sentence.

Vocabulary
elapsed time
liquid volume
parallelogram
trapezoid

1. _____ is the amount of liquid in a container. (p. 595)

2. A _____ is a quadrilateral with exactly one pair of parallel sides. (p. 482)

Concepts and Skills

Find the starting time or the ending time. ✦ TEKS 3.7.C

3. Starting time: _____

   Elapsed time: Walk dog:
   20 minutes
   Wash car:
   20 minutes

   Ending time: 10:30 A.M.

   ⟵——————————⟶

   10:30 A.M.

4. Starting time: 3:27 P.M.

   Elapsed time: Practice piano:
   15 minutes
   Play soccer:
   10 minutes

   Ending time: _____

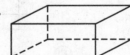

Name the solid figure. Then write the number of faces, edges, and vertices. ✦ TEKS 3.6.A

5. 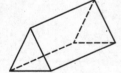   _____

   ___ faces ___ edges ___ vertices

6.   _____

   ___ faces ___ edges ___ vertices

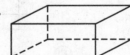

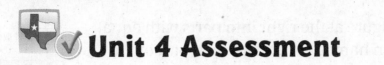

Fill in the bubble for the correct answer choice.

 TEXAS Test Prep

7. Blake divided the figure at the right into parts with equal area. Which fraction names the area of each part of the divided figure? TEKS 3.6.E

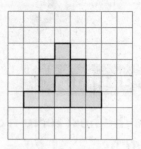

Ⓐ $\frac{1}{6}$ Ⓒ $\frac{1}{4}$

Ⓑ $\frac{1}{8}$ Ⓓ $\frac{1}{3}$

8. What is the area of the figure at the right? Each unit square is 1 square foot. TEKS 3.6.D

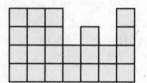

Ⓐ 28 square feet   Ⓒ 27 square feet

Ⓑ 23 square feet   Ⓓ 20 square feet

9. Valentina is pouring water into a freshwater fish tank. What customary unit would be best to measure the capacity of the tank? TEKS 3.7.D

Ⓐ cup   Ⓒ gallon

Ⓑ quart   Ⓓ pint

10. The perimeter of the figure at the right is 24 centimeters. What is the length of side w? TEKS 3.7.B

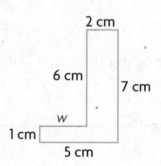

Ⓐ 3 centimeters   Ⓒ 4 centimeters

Ⓑ 21 centimeters   Ⓓ 2 centimeters

11. Spencer drew quadrilaterals with 2 pairs of sides of equal length. Which figure does NOT belong? TEKS 3.6.B

Ⓐ 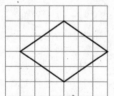   Ⓒ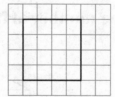

Ⓑ 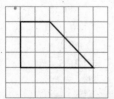   Ⓓ

616

12. Jasmine is making a smoothie with the fruits at the right. How can she put the fruits in order from least to greatest mass? ↳ TEKS 3.7.E

Ⓐ watermelon, banana, strawberry

Ⓑ banana, strawberry, watermelon

Ⓒ strawberry, banana, watermelon

Ⓓ Not here

13. Which fraction shown names the point closest to 0 on the number line? ↳ TEKS 3.7.A

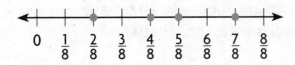

Ⓐ $\frac{7}{8}$ Ⓒ $\frac{4}{8}$

Ⓑ $\frac{2}{8}$ Ⓓ $\frac{5}{8}$

14. Bella is putting a puzzle together. She started at 2:20 P.M. and finished 35 minutes later. At what time did Bella finish the puzzle? ↳ TEKS 3.7.C

Ⓐ 1:45 P.M.   Ⓒ 2:35 P.M.

Ⓑ 2:50 P.M.   Ⓓ 2:55 P.M.

15. A rectangular garden has a width of 6 feet and a perimeter of 32 feet. What is the length? ↳ TEKS 3.7.B

Ⓐ 26 feet   Ⓒ 20 feet

Ⓑ 10 feet   Ⓓ 38 feet

Fill in the bubble for the correct answer choice.

16. Liam is sorting three-dimensional figures into those that have curved surfaces. Which figure would NOT be included? ↯ TEKS 3.6.A

    Ⓐ

    Ⓒ

    Ⓑ

    Ⓓ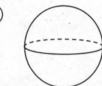

17. Mr. Weber designs houses. He is using grid paper to plan a new house design . The kitchen will have an area between 70 square feet and 85 square feet. The pantry will have an area between 4 square feet and 15 square feet.

    Draw and label a diagram to show what Mr. Weber could design. Find the area of the kitchen. Find the area of the pantry. Then find the total area of the kitchen and pantry combined. ↯ TEKS 3.6.D

    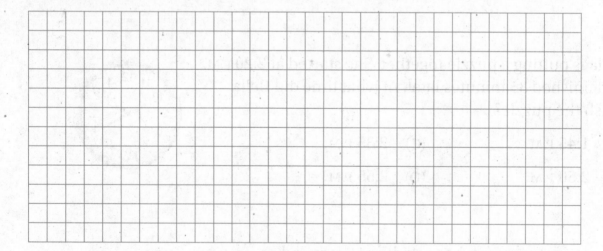

    Area of kitchen = _____ square feet

    Area of pantry = _____ square feet

    Total area of kitchen and pantry combined

    = _____ square feet

Unit 5 Data Analysis

Show What You Know ✓

Check your understanding of important skills.

Name _____

▶ **Skip Count** **Skip count to find the missing numbers.**

1. Count by twos. 2, 4, _____, _____, 10, _____, _____, 16

2. Count by fives. 5, 10, _____, _____, _____, 30, _____

▶ **Read a Pictograph** **For 3, use the pictograph.**

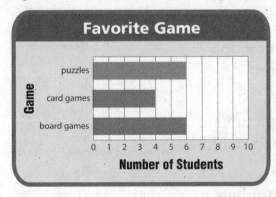

Favorite Vegetable	
carrots	○ ○ ○ ○ ○
corn	○ ○ ○ ○ ○
green beans	○ ○ ○

Key: Each ○ stands for 1 student.

3. Which vegetable did the most students choose? _____

▶ **Read a Bar Graph** **For 4–5, use the bar graph.**

Favorite Game

Number of Students (0–10), Game: puzzles, card games, board games

4. How many students chose puzzles? _____ students

5. How many students answered the question? _____ students

GO DIGITAL Assessment Options:
Soar to Success Math

▶ **Visualize It** ••••••••••••••••••••••••••••

Complete the bubble map by using the words with a ✓.

Review Words

compare

data

fewer

more

survey

✓ tally table

Preview Words

✓ frequency table

✓ horizontal bar graph

key

✓ dot plot

✓ pictograph

scale

✓ vertical bar graph

Organize Data

▶ **Understand Vocabulary** •••••••••••••••••••

Write the preview word that answers the riddle.

1. I am a graph that records each piece of data above a number line. _____

2. I am the numbers that are placed at fixed distances on a graph to help label the graph. _____

3. I am the part of a map or graph that explains the symbols. _____

4. I am a graph that uses pictures to show and compare information. _____

5. I am a table that uses numbers to record data. _____

• Interactive Student Edition
• Multimedia eGlossary

Name _____

Vocabulary

To organize and display information, you can use
a **bar graph** or a **pictograph**.

The teachers at Park Elementary surveyed their students
to find out how much time they spent on homework.
The bar graph shows their data. Use the bar graph to
complete the pictograph.

Bar Graph

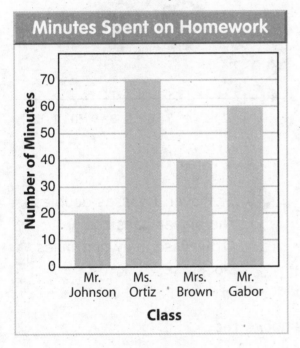

Pictograph

Minutes Spent on Homework	
Mr. Johnson's class	
Ms. Ortiz' class	🕐🕐🕐🕐🕐🕐🕐
Mrs. Brown's class	🕐🕐🕐🕐
Mr. Gabor's class	

Key: Each 🕐 **=10 minutes.**

Writing Survey 5 students about how much
time they spent doing homework last night. You
can use this information to make a bar graph
or a pictograph.

Reading Look for this book in the library.
Tiger Math: Learning to Graph From a Baby Tiger,
by Ann Whitehead Nagda and Cindy Bickel.

Dot Plot Sums

Object of the Game Make a dot plot of the sums you roll.

Materials

- 2 number cubes labeled 1–6
- number lines labeled 2–12
- pencil or marker

Set Up

Each player gets one number line.

Number of Players 2, 3, or 4

How to Play

1 Player 1 tosses the two number cubes. The sum of the numbers tossed is a data value on the dot plot.

2 Player 1 draws a dot above the number line for the sum.

3 If Player 1 tosses doubles, the player goes again. Otherwise, play continues clockwise.

4 The first player who has five dots above the same sum wins the game.

Name _____

19.1 PROBLEM SOLVING • Frequency Tables

TEKS Data Analysis—
3.8.A, 3.8.B
MATHEMATICAL PROCESSES
3.1.A, 3.1.B, 3.1.D, 3.1.E

? Essential Question How can you use the strategy *make a table* to organize data and solve problems?

Unlock the Problem Real World

The students in Alicia's class voted for their favorite ice cream flavor. They organized the data in this tally table. How many more students chose chocolate than strawberry?

Another way to show the data is in a frequency table. A **frequency table** uses numbers to record data.

Favorite Ice Cream Flavor

Flavor	Tally
Vanilla	卌 II
Chocolate	卌 III
Strawberry	IIII

Read

What do I need to find?

How many more students chose

_____ than _____ ice cream
as their favorite?

What information am I given?

the data about favorite _____
in the tally table

Plan

What is my plan or strategy?

I will count the _____. Then I will
put the numbers in a frequency table
and compare the number of students

who chose _____ to the number

of students who chose _____.

Solve

Favorite Ice Cream Flavor

Flavor	Number
Vanilla	

Count the tally marks. Record ____
for vanilla. Write the other flavors and
record the number of tally marks.

To compare the number of students
who chose strawberry and the number
of students who chose chocolate,
subtract.

____ − ____ = ____

So, ____ more students chose
chocolate as their favorite flavor.

Two classes in Carter's school grew bean plants for a science project. The heights of the plants after six weeks are shown in the tally table. The plants were measured to the nearest inch. How many fewer bean plants were 9 inches tall than 7 inches and 8 inches combined?

Bean Plant Heights	
Height in Inches	Tally
7	卌 IIII
8	卌 III
9	卌 卌 II
10	卌 IIII

Read

What do I need to find?

What information am I given?

Plan

What is my plan or strategy?

Solve

Record the steps you used to solve the problem.

• Suppose the number of 3-inch plants was half the number of 8-inch plants. How many 3-inch bean plants were there?

_____

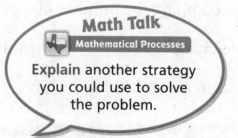

Math Talk
Mathematical Processes

Explain another strategy you could use to solve the problem.

Name _____

Use the Shoe Lengths table for 1–4.

1. The students in three third-grade classes recorded the lengths of their shoes to the nearest centimeter. The data are in the tally table. Count the tally marks and put the data in a frequency table. How many more shoes were 18 or 22 centimeters long combined than 20 centimeters long?

   To find the number of shoes that were 18 or 22 centimeters long, add

   6 + _____ + _____ + _____ = _____.

   To find the number of shoes that were 20

   centimeters long, add _____ + _____ = _____.

   To find the difference between the shoes that were 18 or 22 centimeters long and the shoes that were 20 centimeters long, subtract the sums.

   _____ – _____ = _____.

   So, _____ more shoes were 18 or 22 centimeters long than 20 centimeters long.

Shoe Lengths		
Length in Centimeters	Tally	
	Boys	Girls
18	卌 I	IIII
19	卌	IIII
20	卌 III	卌 IIII
21	卌 II	卌
22	卌 IIII	卌 II

Shoe Lengths		
Length in Centimeters	Number	
	Boys	Girls
18		
19		
20		
21		
22		

2. How many fewer boys' shoes were 19 cm long than 22 cm long?

   _____

Problem Solving

3. **H.O.T.** **What if** the length of 5 more boys' shoes measured 21 centimeters? **Explain** how the table would change.

   _____

4. **H.O.T.** **Multi-Step** How many fewer girls' shoes than boys' shoes were measured?

   _____

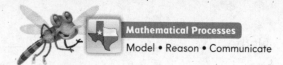
Daily Assessment Task

Fill in the bubble for the correct answer choice. Use the Favorite Outdoor Game frequency table for 5–7.

5. **Analyze** Raj asked his classmates to choose their favorite outdoor game. His results are shown in the frequency table at the right. How many more students choose hide-and-seek than scavenger hunt?

   Ⓐ 8   Ⓒ 14

   Ⓑ 20   Ⓓ 9

Favorite Outdoor Game	
Game Type	**Number**
Hide-and-Seek	14
Jump Rope	9
Scavenger Hunt	6
Tag	16

6. **Multi-Step** How many students in all chose tag, jump rope, or hide-and-seek?

   Ⓐ 31   Ⓒ 25

   Ⓑ 39   Ⓓ 23

7. **Multi-Step** How many more students chose tag than jump rope and scavenger hunt combined?

   Ⓐ 2   Ⓒ 15

   Ⓑ 1   Ⓓ 7

 TEXAS Test Prep

8. **Representations** Jade made a tally table to record how many people have different types of pets. Her table shows

   Dog 卌 卌 ||||

   How many people have dogs?

   Ⓐ 9   Ⓒ 14

   Ⓑ 4   Ⓓ 15

Homework and Practice

Name _____

19.1 PROBLEM SOLVING • Frequency Tables

Problem Solving Real World

Use the Favorite Pet table for 1–7.

1. The students in third grade were asked to choose their favorite pet. The data are in the tally table. Count the tally marks and put the data in a frequency table.

Favorite Pet		
Pet Type	Tally	
	Boys	Girls
Dog	ЖЖ ЖЖ II	ЖЖ II
Cat	ЖЖ I	ЖЖ ЖЖ I
Parakeet	III	ЖЖ
Hamster	ЖЖ III	IIII
Fish	ЖЖ II	ЖЖ I

2. How many more boys than girls chose dog as the favorite pet?

_____

Favorite Pet		
Pet Type	Number	
	Boys	Girls
Dog		
Cat		
Parakeet		
Hamster		
Fish		

3. How many students chose cat as the favorite pet?

_____

4. How many more students chose fish than parakeets?

_____

5. Which pet got the least number of votes?

_____

6. How many more students chose cat or dog combined than parakeet or hamster combined?

7. Did more boys or girls choose a favorite pet? Explain.

_____

_____

Fill in the bubble completely to show your answer.
Use the Favorite Book table for 8–10.

Favorite Book	
Book Type	Tally
Mystery	ЖΙ IIII
Adventure	ЖΙ ЖΙ ЖΙ I
Science Fiction	ЖΙ ЖΙ II
Fairy Tale	IIII
Historical	ЖΙ ЖΙ I

8. Ernie asked the third-grade classes in his school to choose their favorite type of book. How many more students chose adventure books than fairy tale books?

Ⓐ 12 Ⓒ 4

Ⓑ 16 Ⓓ 20

9. How many students in all chose mystery or science fiction?

Ⓐ 9 Ⓒ 21

Ⓑ 12 Ⓓ 3

10. **Multi-Step** How many more students chose historical and science fiction combined than adventure?

Ⓐ 23 Ⓒ 7

Ⓑ 16 Ⓓ 8

Use the Books Read During Summer table for 11–13.

Books Read During Summer	
Books Read	Tally
5	ЖΙ ЖΙ I
6	ЖΙ III
7	ЖΙ ЖΙ ЖΙ I
8	ЖΙ II
9	III

11. Halle recorded in a tally table the number of books that students read during summer vacation. How many more students read 7 books than 5 books during summer vacation?

Ⓐ 2 Ⓒ 12

Ⓑ 5 Ⓓ 27

12. How many students read 8 books during summer vacation?

Ⓐ 15 Ⓒ 16

Ⓑ 4 Ⓓ 7

13. **Multi-Step** How many more students read 7 books than 6 and 9 books combined?

Ⓐ 11 Ⓒ 4

Ⓑ 13 Ⓓ 5

Name _____

19.2 Pictographs

TEKS Data Analysis—
3.8.A, 3.8.B
MATHEMATICAL PROCESSES
3.1.D, 3.1.E, 3.1.F, 3.1.G

? **Essential Question**

How can you display and interpret data in a pictograph?

🔑 Unlock the Problem

A **pictograph** is a graph that uses pictures or symbols to show and compare information.

Delia made the table at the right. She used it to record the places the third grade classes would like to go during a field trip. How can you show the data in a pictograph?

Field Trip Choices

Place	Number
Museum	8
Science Center	20
Aquarium	14
Zoo	12

🔑 **Make a pictograph.**

STEP 1

Write the title. Write the name of a place in each row.

STEP 2

Choose a picture for the key, and let each picture represent 4 students.

STEP 3

Draw the correct number of pictures for each field trip choice.

Museum	

Key: Each ____ = ____ students.

Math Idea

A **key** is a part of a graph that explains the symbols.
In this graph,
= 4 students,
so = 2 students.

• How did you decide how many pictures to draw for Aquarium?

_____

_____

Try This! Make a pictograph from data you collect. Take a survey or observe a subject that interests you. Collect and record the data in a frequency table. Then make a pictograph. Decide on a symbol and a key. Include a title and labels.

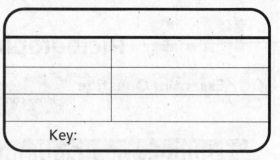

Key:

 Share and Show

Jeremy pulled marbles from a bag one at a time, recorded their color, and then put them back in the bag. Make a pictograph of the data. Use this key:

Each ◯ = 2 marbles.

Jeremy's Marble Experiment

Color	Number
Blue	4
Green	11
Red	8

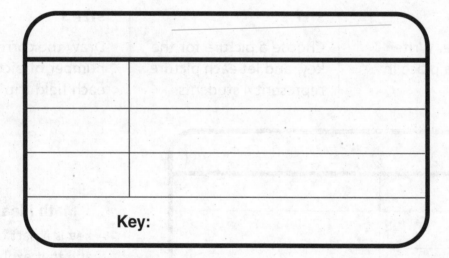

Key:

Use your pictograph above for 1–2.

✓ 1. How many more times did Jeremy pull out a red marble than a blue marble?

_____

✓ 2. How many fewer times did Jeremy pull out green marbles than blue and red marbles combined?

_____

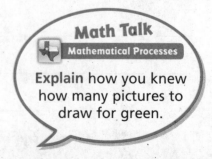

Math Talk
Mathematical Processes

Explain how you knew how many pictures to draw for green.

630

Name _____

Teeth in Mammals	
Animal	**Number**
Hamster	16
Cat	30
Dog	42
Cow	32

3. **Representations** While at the Science Center, Delia's classmates learned how many teeth some mammals have. Use the data in the table to make a pictograph. Use this key: Each △ = 4 teeth.

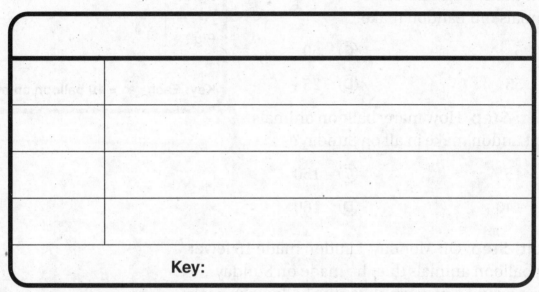

Key: _____

Use your pictograph above for 4–7.

4. **Analyze** How many more teeth do cows have than hamsters?

_____

5. **H.O.T.** **Pose a Problem** Write a problem that can be solved by using the data in your pictograph. Then solve the problem.

_____

_____

6. **H.O.T.** **Multi-Step** How many fewer teeth do cats and hamsters have combined than dogs and cows combined?

_____

7. **Use Symbols** How many pictures would you draw for Cat if each △ = 5 teeth?

_____

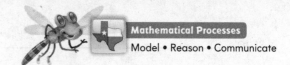

Mathematical Processes
Model • Reason • Communicate

Daily Assessment Task

Fill in the bubble for the correct answer choice. Use the Balloon Animals Made on Sunday pictograph for 8–11.

Balloon Animals Made on Sunday					
Cat	🎈	🎈	🎈	🎈	
Dog	🎈	🎈	🎈	🎈	🎈
Horse	🎈	🎈	🎈		
Pig	🎈	🎈	🎈		

Key: Each 🎈 = 10 balloon animals.

8. **Analyze** Landon made balloon animals in the park on Sunday. How many dog balloon animals did Landon make?

   (A) 5   (C) 50

   (B) 55   (D) 25

9. **Multi-Step** How many balloon animals did Landon make in all on Sunday?

   (A) 15   (C) 150

   (B) 140   (D) 160

10. **Multi-Step** On Monday, Landon made 15 fewer pig balloon animals than he made on Sunday. What would a pictograph for the balloon animals made on Monday show for pig balloon animals?

    (A)

    (B)

    (C) 🎈 🎈 🎈

    (D) 🎈 🎈

TEXAS Test Prep

11. **Representations** How many pictures would you draw for Cat if each = 5 balloon animals?

    (A) 6

    (B) 8

    (C) 5

    (D) 2

632

Name _____

19.2 Pictographs

Problem Solving (Real World)

1. During recycling day, teams of students collected the materials shown in the table. Use the data in the table to make a pictograph. Use this key:

Each ☐ = 4 materials

Recycling Day Collections

Material	Number
Glass bottles	20
Plastic bottles	32
Aluminum cans	26
Newspapers	36
Magazines	24

Recycling Day Collections

Key: _____

Use your pictograph for 2–5.

2. How many more plastic bottles were collected than glass bottles?

_____

3. How many more newspapers were collected than magazines?

_____

4. How many newspapers and magazines were collected?

5. How many plastic and glass bottles were collected?

Fill in the bubble completely to show your answer.
Use the Animals on the Farm pictograph for 6–8.

6. **Multi-Step** The pictograph shows the number of animals at Mr. DiPiero's farm. How many more chickens than ducks does Mr. DiPiero have?

   (A) 3   (C) 10

   (B) 15   (D) 16

Animals on the Farm

Cows	☆☆☆
Horses	☆☆
Chickens	☆☆☆☆☆☆☆
Ducks	☆☆☆☆☆☆

Each ☆ = 5 animals

7. Suppose Mr. DiPiero gets 30 pigs. How many star symbols would he use to show them on the pictograph?

   (A) 6   (C) 5

   (B) 15   (D) 30

8. **Multi-Step** How many animals does Mr. DiPiero have on his farm?

   (A) 21   (C) 105

   (B) 26   (D) 130

Use the Karen's Jewelry pictograph for 9–11.

9. Karen has a table at a craft fair to sell jewelry. How many earrings does Karen have to sell?

   (A) 27   (C) 3

   (B) 18   (D) 6

Karen's Jewelry

Necklaces	◇ ◇ ◇ ◇ ◇
Bracelets	◇ ◇ ◇
Rings	◇ ◇ ◇ ◇ ◇ ◇ ◇ ◇ ◇
Earrings	◇ ◇ ◇ ◇ ◇ ◇

Each ◇ = 3 pieces of jewelry

10. **Multi-Step** Karen sells all of the rings and bracelets. How many pieces of jewelry is this?

    (A) 18   (C) 27

    (B) 36   (D) 69

11. **Multi-Step** Karen pairs up sets of necklaces and bracelets. How many necklaces will she have left that do not have matching bracelets?

    (A) 6   (C) 5

    (B) 2   (D) 12

Name _____

19.3 Bar Graphs

? Essential Question How can you read and interpret data in a bar graph?

🔑 Unlock the Problem

A **bar graph** uses bars to show data. A **scale** of equally spaced numbers helps you read the number each bar shows.

The students in the reading group made a bar graph to record the number of books they read in October. How many books did Seth read?

- Underline the words that tell you where to find the information to answer the question.

> The title tells what the bar graph is about.

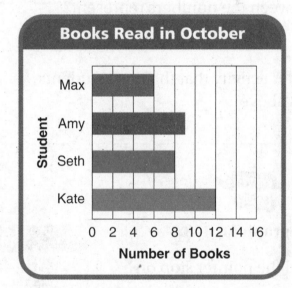

Books Read in October

Student / Number of Books

> The length of a bar tells how many books each student read.

> The scale is 0–16 by twos.

> Each bar is labeled with a student's name.

Math Talk
Mathematical Processes
Explain how to read the bar that tells how many books Amy read.

🔓 Find the bar for Seth. It ends at _____.

So, Seth read _____ books in October.

1. How many books did Max read?   _____

2. Who read 4 fewer books than Kate?   _____

3. **What if** Amy read 5 more books? How many books did Amy read?   _____
   Shade the graph to show how many she read.

Examples These bar graphs show the same data.

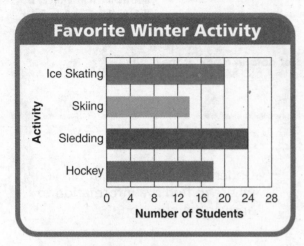

Favorite Winter Activity

In a **horizontal bar graph**, the bars go across from left to right. The length of the bar shows the number.

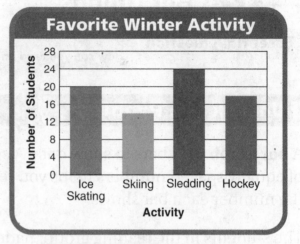

Favorite Winter Activity

In a **vertical bar graph**, the bars go up from the bottom. The height of the bar shows the number.

4. What does each space between the numbers represent?

_____

5. How can you find the winter activity that the most students voted for using the graphs above?

_____

_____

Share and Show

MATH BOARD

Use the Spinner Results bar graph for 1–3.

1. How many more times did the pointer stop on green than on purple?

   _____ more times

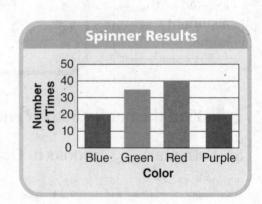

Spinner Results

2. How many fewer times did the pointer stop on blue than on red and green combined?

   _____ fewer times

3. **What if** there were 15 more spins and the pointer stopped 10 more times on green and 5 more times on blue? How many more times did the pointer stop on green than blue?

_____

636

© Houghton Mifflin Harcourt Publishing Company

Name _____

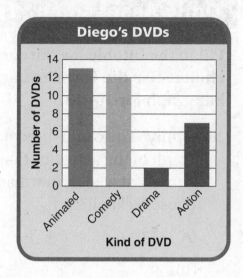

Diego's DVDs

Use the Diego's DVDs bar graph for 4–6.

4. **Analyze** Diego has 5 fewer of this kind of DVD than comedy. Which kind of DVD is this?

   _____

5. **Multi-Step** Is the number of comedy and action DVDs greater than or less than the number of animated and drama DVDs? **Explain**.

   _____

   _____

   _____

6. **H.O.T.** **Multi-Step** How many DVDs does Diego have that are *not* comedy DVDs?

   _____

Use the Science Fair Projects bar graph for 7–9.

7. **Representations** How many more students would have to do a project on plants to equal the number of projects on space?

   _____

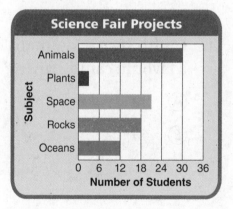

Science Fair Projects

8. **Write Math** ▸ **What's the Question?** The answer is animals, space, rocks, oceans, and plants.

   _____

   _____

9. **H.O.T.** **What if** 3 fewer students did a project on weather than did a project on rocks? Describe what the bar graph would look like.

   _____

   _____

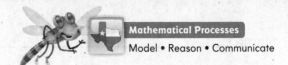
Daily Assessment Task

Fill in the bubble for the correct answer choice. Use the Favorite Camp Activity bar graph for 10–13.

Favorite Camp Activity

Number of Campers / Kind of Activity (Art, Boating, Kickball, Swimming)

10. **Apply** The camp director made a bar graph of the activities that campers chose last week. How many campers chose kickball?

(A) 13

(B) 9

(C) 12

(D) 8

11. **Multi-Step** How many fewer campers chose boating and kickball combined than chose art and swimming combined?

(A) 8

(B) 3

(C) 2

(D) 17

12. **Multi-Step** How many campers in all chose a favorite camp activity?

(A) 30

(B) 40

(C) 29

(D) 42

 TEXAS Test Prep

13. **Analyze** How many campers chose a water activity?

(A) 12

(B) 18

(C) 20

(D) 8

638

Homework and Practice

Name _____

19.3 Bar Graphs

Problem Solving Real World

Use the Roxanne's Bird Feeder bar graph for 1–4.

1. Roxanne made this bar graph to show the number of birds that she saw at her bird feeder. How many more wrens than sparrows did Roxanne see?

_____

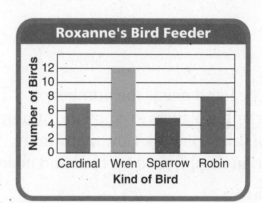

2. How many fewer sparrows than robins did Roxanne see?

_____

3. Roxanne saw 4 more of this kind of bird than robins. Which kind of bird is this?

_____

4. How many birds did Roxanne see at the feeder that were not cardinals?

_____

Use the Art Fair Projects bar graph for 5–6.

5. How many more students would have to make mobiles so that the number of mobiles equals the number of sculptures?

_____

6. List the art projects in order from the least number to the greatest number of students.

_____

Fill in the bubble completely to show your answer.
Use the Band Members bar graph for 7–9.

7. How many more flute players than
   triangle players are in the band?

   Ⓐ 22   Ⓒ 30

   Ⓑ 8   Ⓓ 14

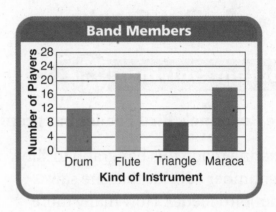

8. The band needs the number of
   triangle players to equal the number
   of drum players. How many more
   triangle players does the band need?

   Ⓐ 4   Ⓒ 8

   Ⓑ 12   Ⓓ 20

9. **Multi-Step** How many band
   members do NOT play the maracas?

   Ⓐ 18   Ⓒ 42

   Ⓑ 34   Ⓓ 60

Use the Kenji's Garden bar graph for 10–12.

10. Kenji wants to plant an equal
    number of corn and tomato plants.
    How many more corn plants does
    he need?

    Ⓐ 18   Ⓒ 48

    Ⓑ 30   Ⓓ 12

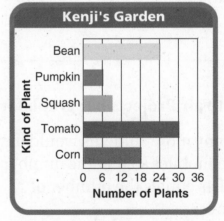

11. Kenji plants more pumpkin plants.
    There are double the number of
    pumpkin plants now. How many
    pumpkin plants are there?

    Ⓐ 6   Ⓒ 12

    Ⓑ 9   Ⓓ 15

12. **Multi-Step** How many fewer
    squash and pumpkin plants are
    there than corn and bean plants?

    Ⓐ 27   Ⓒ 15

    Ⓑ 42   Ⓓ 57

19.4 Solve Problems with Bar Graphs

TEKS Data Analysis—
3.8.A, 3.8.B

MATHEMATICAL PROCESSES
3.1.C, 3.1.D, 3.1.F, 3.1.G

Essential Question

How can you solve problems by using a bar graph?

Unlock the Problem

Jordan took a survey of his classmates to find out their favorite team sports. He recorded the results in the table at the right. How can he show the results in a bar graph?

Favorite Team Sport	
Sport	**Tally**
Soccer	卌 卌 II
Basketball	IIII
Baseball	卌 卌 IIII
Football	卌 IIII

Make a bar graph.

STEP 1

Write a title at the top to tell what the graph is about. Label the side of the graph to tell about the bars. Label the bottom of the graph to explain what the numbers tell.

STEP 2

Choose numbers for the bottom of the graph so that most of the bars will end on a line. Since the least number is 4 and the greatest number is 14, make the scale 0–16. Mark the scale by twos.

STEP 3

Draw and shade a bar to show the number for each sport.

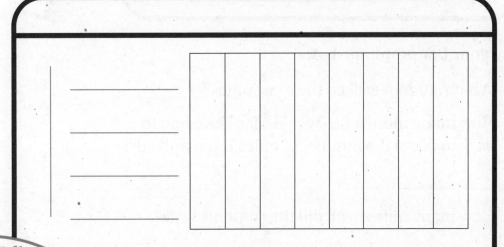

Math Talk

Mathematical Processes

How did you know how long to draw the bar for football?

Share and Show

Matt's school is having a walk-a-thon to raise money for the school library. Matt made a pictograph to show the number of miles some students walked. Make a bar graph of Matt's data. Use a scale of

0–_____, and mark the scale by _____.

School Walk-a-Thon					
Sam	👕	👕	👕	👕	👕
Matt	👕	👕	🔨		
Ben	👕				
Erica	👕	👕	👕	👕	

Key: Each 👕 = 2 miles.

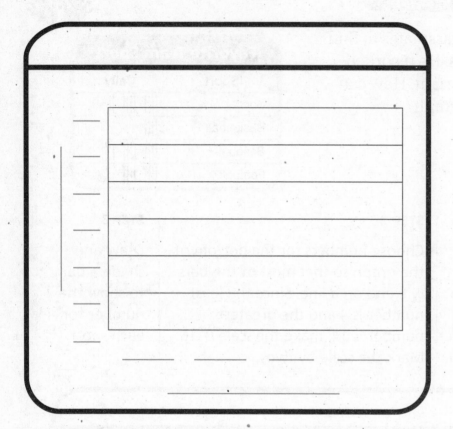

Math Talk
Mathematical Processes

Explain how the graph would change if another student, Daniel, walked double the number of miles Erica walked.

Use your bar graph for 1–4.

1. Which student walked the most miles? _____

2. How many more miles would Matt have had to walk to equal the number of miles Erica walked?

_____

3. How many miles in all did the students walk?

_____

4. Write the number of miles the students walked in order from greatest to least.

_____

Name _____

Points Scored	
Player	**Number of Points**
Billy	10
Dwight	30
James	15
Raul	25
Sean	10

5. **Use Tools** Susie recorded the number of points some basketball players scored. Use the data in the table to make a bar graph. Choose numbers so that most of the bars will end on a line.

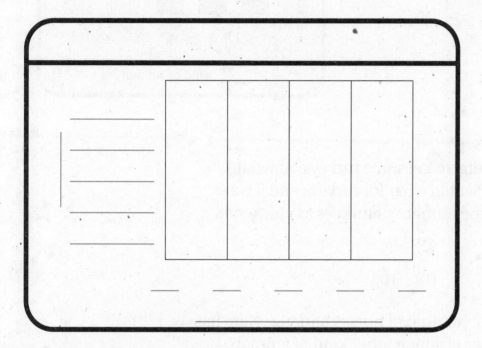

Use your bar graph for 6–9.

6. **Analyze** Which player scored the most points? _____

7. **H.O.T.** **Pose a Problem** Write and solve a new problem that matches the data in your bar graph.

_____

_____

8. **Analyze** Which player scored 10 fewer points than Raul?

_____

9. **H.O.T.** **Multi-Step** **What if** James scored 5 more points? How many points in all did the five players score?

_____

Daily Assessment Task

Fill in the bubble for the correct answer choice. Use the Farm Animals on Nate's Farm bar graph for 10–13.

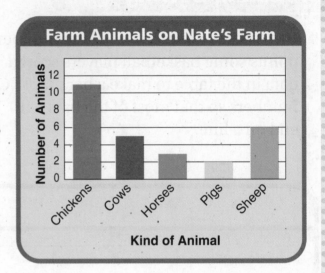

Farm Animals on Nate's Farm

10. Nate made this bar graph of the farm animals on his farm. How many horses does Nate have?

  Ⓐ 4

  Ⓑ 3

  Ⓒ 2

  Ⓓ 5

11. **Apply** Nate is planning to get some turkeys. At what number on the scale would a bar for turkeys end if Nate wants to have the same number of turkeys as chickens?

  Ⓐ 11   Ⓒ 9

  Ⓑ 12   Ⓓ 10

12. **Multi-Step** The total number of horses and pigs Nate has is equal to the number of which other kind of animal?

  Ⓐ chickens   Ⓒ cows

  Ⓑ sheep   Ⓓ horses

⭐ TEXAS Test Prep

13. **Multi-Step** How many farm animals in all are on Nate's farm?

  Ⓐ 21

  Ⓑ 12

  Ⓒ 17

  Ⓓ 27

644

Homework and Practice

Name _____

19.4 Solve Problems with Bar Graphs

Problem Solving

1. A scout troop collected cartons of food for a food drive. They recorded the number of cartons each team collected. Use the data in the tally table to make a bar graph. Choose numbers so that most bars will end on a line.

Food Drive	
Team	**Number of Cartons**
A	|||| |||| ||||	
B	||||	
C	|||| ||||
D	|||| ||||

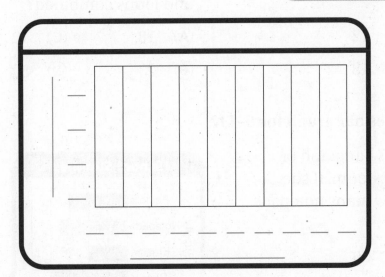

Use your bar graph for 2–5.

2. Which team collected the most cartons of food?

_____

3. How many cartons of food did all of the teams collect?

_____

4. How many more cartons of food must team C collect to equal the number of cartons that Team A collected?

_____

5. Which two other teams combined collected the same number of cartons that Team A collected?

_____

Fill in the bubble completely to show your answer.
Use the Runs Scored bar graph for 6–8.

6. Morris made this bar graph of the number of runs scored by teams in a softball league. How many more runs did the Wolves score than the Cubs?

   Ⓐ 18   Ⓒ 8

   Ⓑ 44   Ⓓ 26

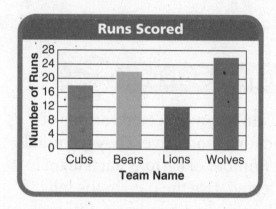

7. How many runs will the bar for Lions show if the Lions score 7 more runs?

   Ⓐ 19   Ⓒ 12

   Ⓑ 7   Ⓓ 18

8. **Multi-Step** How many fewer runs did the Bears score than the Cubs and Lions combined?

   Ⓐ 18   Ⓒ 12

   Ⓑ 23   Ⓓ 8

Use the School Supplies bar graph for 9–11.

9. Mrs. Susi makes this bar graph of supplies for her classroom. If she has 24 students, how many notepads will she have left?

   Ⓐ 35   Ⓒ 30

   Ⓑ 10   Ⓓ 11

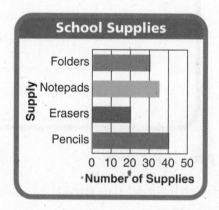

10. Mrs. Susi's class of 24 students is divided into 4 equal groups. How many pencils will each group get if the pencils are divided equally among the groups?

    Ⓐ 10   Ⓒ 8

    Ⓑ 12   Ⓓ 40

11. **Multi-Step** Mrs. Susi wants to have 40 more pencils than erasers. How many more pencils does she need to buy?

    Ⓐ 10   Ⓒ 20

    Ⓑ 30   Ⓓ 60

19.5 Dot Plots

Essential Question

How can you display and interpret data in a dot plot?

Unlock the Problem

A **dot plot** uses dots to record each piece of data above a number line. It helps you see groups in the data.

Some students took a survey of the number of letters in their first names. Then they recorded the data in a dot plot.

How many students have 6 letters in their first names?

Each dot stands for 1 student. →

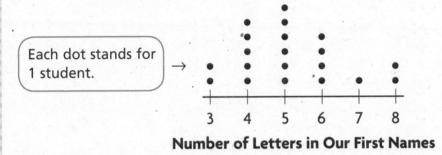

Number of Letters in Our First Names

← The numbers show the number of letters in a name.

Find 6 on the number line. The 6 stands for 6 _____.

There are _____ dots above the 6.

So, _____ students have 6 letters in their first names.

---

1. Which number of letters was found most often? _____

2. Write a sentence to describe the data. _____
   _____

3. How many letters are in your first name? _____

4. Put an a dot above the number of letters in your first name.

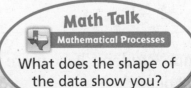

Math Talk
Mathematical Processes

What does the shape of the data show you?

Activity Make a dot plot.

Materials ■ number cube labeled 1 to 6

Each member of your group should toss a number cube 1 time. Combine your data with other groups' data. Then make a dot plot to show the data you collected.

STEP 1 Record the numbers tossed in the table.

STEP 2 Write a title below the number line to describe your dot plot.

STEP 3 Write the numbers tossed in order from left to right above the title.

STEP 4 Draw dots above the number line to show each number tossed.

Class Experiment	
Number Tossed	Tally

 Share and Show MATH BOARD

Use the Number of Pets dot plot for 1–3.

1. How many students have 1 pet?

   Think: How many dots are above 1?

   _____

2. What number of pets do 2 students have?

   _____

3. Do more students have more than 2 pets or fewer than 2 pets?

   _____

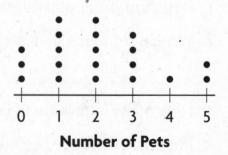

Number of Pets

648

Name _____

Problem Solving Real World

Use the table at the right for 4–7.

4. Use the data in the table to make a dot plot.

How Many Years Have You Owned Your Pet?	
Number of Years	Students
1	5
2	6
3	5
4	3
5	2

┼────┼────┼────┼────┼

How Many Years Have You Owned Your Pet?

5. How many students have owned a pet for 1 year? _____

6. **Analyze** Which number of years is found most often? _____

7. **H.O.T.** **Multi-Step** How many more students have owned a pet for 2 years or less than for 3 years or more?

_____

For 8–10, use the Baskets of Blueberries Picked dot plot.

8. **Representations** How many people picked 5 baskets of blueberries?

_____

9. **Multi-Step** How many more people picked 6 or fewer baskets of blueberries than picked 8 or more baskets of blueberries?

_____

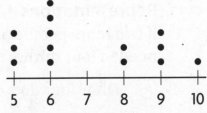

Baskets of Blueberries Picked

10. **H.O.T.** Is there any number of baskets for which there are no data? **Explain.**

_____

_____

Daily Assessment Task

Fill in the bubble for the correct answer choice.
Use the Number of Throws to Win dot plot for 11–14.

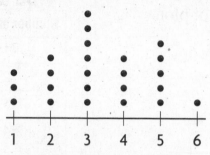

Number of Throws to Win

11. **Apply** For a penny toss game, players throw a penny into a tank of water and try to get it to land in a small glass. Jim recorded the number of throws it took a group of players to win the penny toss. How many players won on their first try?

Ⓐ 7   Ⓑ 3   Ⓒ 24   Ⓓ 1

12. **Multi-Step** How many players needed more than 3 throws to win?

Ⓐ 17   Ⓑ 6   Ⓒ 7   Ⓓ 10

13. **Representations** How would you change the dot plot if two more people played the game and each person needed four throws to win?

Ⓐ Draw four dots above 2.

Ⓑ Draw two dots above 4.

Ⓒ Draw two dots above 2.

Ⓓ Draw four dots above 4.

★ TEXAS Test Prep

14. **Analyze** How many more players needed 3 throws to win than 1 throw to win?

Ⓐ 3   Ⓑ 4   Ⓒ 7   Ⓓ 10

Name _____

19.5 Dot Plots

Use the Number of Books Read dot plot for 1–3.

1. The dot plot shows how many books students read during summer vacation. How many students read 6 books?

_____

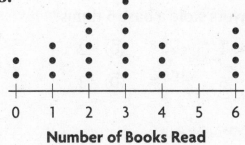

Number of Books Read

2. Did more students read more than 2 books or fewer than 2 books?

_____

3. How many students read either 0 books or 5 books?

_____

Problem Solving Real World

Use the table at the right for 4–6.

4. Use the data in the table to make a dot plot.

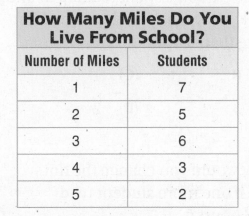

How Many Miles Do You Live From School?	
Number of Miles	Students
1	7
2	5
3	6
4	3
5	2

How Many Miles Do You Live From School?

5. How many students live less than 2 miles from school?

_____

6. How many students live exactly 4 miles from school?

_____

Fill in the bubble completely to show your answer.
Use the Number of Stolen Bases dot plot for 7–9.

7. The dot plot shows the number of bases stolen by each player during the softball season. How many players stole a base 5 times?

   Ⓐ 1   Ⓒ 2

   Ⓑ 5   Ⓓ 3

Number of Stolen Bases

8. Which number of stolen bases is found most often?

   Ⓐ 4   Ⓒ 6

   Ⓑ 5   Ⓓ 2

9. **Multi-Step** How many players stole bases during the entire softball season?

   Ⓐ 16   Ⓒ 12

   Ⓑ 21   Ⓓ 14

Use the Hours Spent Reading dot plot for 10–12.

10. The dot plot shows the number of hours students spent reading in one week. How many students read for more than 6 hours?

    Ⓐ 0   Ⓒ 1

    Ⓑ 3   Ⓓ 2

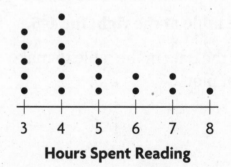

Hours Spent Reading

11. How would you change the dot plot if one more student read for 6 hours?

    Ⓐ Draw 1 dot above 6.

    Ⓑ Draw 6 dots above 1.

    Ⓒ Draw 1 dot above 1.

    Ⓓ Draw 6 dots above 6.

12. **Multi-Step** How many students spent 4 or more hours reading?

    Ⓐ 8

    Ⓑ 14

    Ⓒ 19

    Ⓓ 6

Name _____

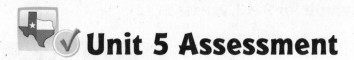 **Unit 5 Assessment**

Vocabulary

Choose the best term from the box.

Vocabulary
bar graph
dot plot
frequency table
pictograph

1. A _____ uses dots to record each piece of data above a number line. (p. 647)

2. A _____ is a table that uses numbers to record data. (p. 623)

3. A _____ uses bars to show data. (p. 635)

Concepts and Skills

Use the Dolphins Max Saw table for 4–6. ⬥ TEKS 3.8.A, 3.8.B

4. Max recorded in a table the number of dolphins he saw. How many dolphins did he see?

    _____

Dolphins Max Saw	
Day	**Number**
Friday	12
Saturday	15
Sunday	19

5. How many more dolphins did Max see on Sunday than on Friday? _____

6. If you made a bar graph of the data in the table, what labels would you use? _____

Use the Number of Goals Scored dot plot for 7–8. ⬥ TEKS 3.8.A, 3.8.B

7. Katie recorded the number of goals the players on her team scored during soccer practice. How many players scored 2 goals? _____

8. What was the least number of goals scored?

    _____

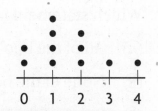

Number of Goals Scored

Fill in the bubble for the correct answer choice.
Use the Jim's Books pictograph for 9–13. TEKS 3.8.A, 3.8.B

9. Jim made a pictograph to show the types of books he has. How many puzzle books does Jim have?

   Ⓐ 16

   Ⓑ 4

   Ⓒ 14

   Ⓓ 3

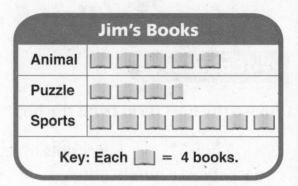

Jim's Books	
Animal	📖📖📖📖📖
Puzzle	📖📖📖📖
Sports	📖📖📖📖📖📖📖

Key: Each 📖 = 4 books.

10. How many animal books does Jim have?

    Ⓐ 5   Ⓒ 20

    Ⓑ 28   Ⓓ 16

11. How many books in all does Jim have?

    Ⓐ 15

    Ⓑ 62

    Ⓒ 20

    Ⓓ 31

12. How many more sports books than puzzle books does Jim have?

    Ⓐ 14   Ⓒ 4

    Ⓑ 24   Ⓓ 8

13. Which statement is true about the books Jim has?

    Ⓐ All of the books are puzzle books.

    Ⓑ None of the books is an animal book.

    Ⓒ Some of the books are computer books.

    Ⓓ Most of the books are sports or animal books.

◆ TEKS 3.8.A, 3.8.B

14. Robin collected shells during her vacation. She recorded the length of the shells to the nearest inch in a dot plot. How many shells were 9 inches long?

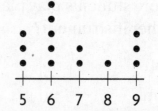

Length of Shells in Inches

   Ⓐ 3

   Ⓑ 2

   Ⓒ 4

   Ⓓ 5

15. How many shells were 6 inches long or longer?

   Ⓐ 5

   Ⓑ 6

   Ⓒ 11

   Ⓓ 8

16. How many more shells did Robin collect that were 5 inches long than 8 inches long?

   Ⓐ 2

   Ⓑ 3

   Ⓒ 1

   Ⓓ 4

17. How many shells were 7 inches long or shorter?

   Ⓐ 5

   Ⓑ 6

   Ⓒ 2

   Ⓓ 10

Fill in the bubble for the correct answer choice.
Use the Musical Instruments bar graph for 18–22.

⬥ TEKS 3.8.A, 3.8.B

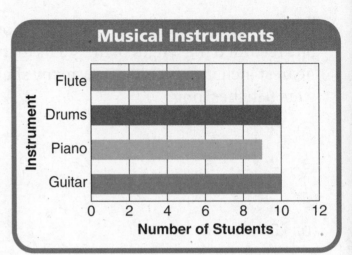

Musical Instruments

18. Three more students play piano than which other instrument?

    (A) flute

    (B) drums

    (C) violin

    (D) guitar

19. The same number of students play which two instruments?

    (A) guitar and drums

    (B) piano and drums

    (C) drums and flute

    (D) Not here

20. How many fewer students play flute and piano combined than play drums and guitar combined?

    (A) 11   (C) 5

    (B) 14   (D) 6

21. How many more students play piano and guitar combined than play drums?

    (A) 19   (B) 29   (C) 10   (D) 9

22. There are more students who play the trumpet than play the flute, but fewer students than play the guitar. **Explain** how you could change the bar graph to show the number of students who play the trumpet.

_____

_____

_____

Personal Financial Literacy

Show What You Know

Check your understanding of important skills.

Name _____

▶ **Practice Multiplication Facts** **Find the product.**

1. 7
   × 6

2. 4 × 8 =

3. 10 × 5 =

4. 9
   × 3

5. = 0 × 6

▶ **Record 2-Digit Addition and Subtraction** **Find the sum or difference.**

6. 63
   + 28

7. 72
   − 46

8. 39
   + 17

9. 94
   −59

10. 26
    15
   + 47

▶ **3-Digit Addition and Subtraction with Regrouping** **Find the sum or difference.**

11. 685
   + 259

12. 852
   − 356

13. 518
   − 349

14. 650
   + 362

15. 600
   − 159

16. 750
   − 230

17. 218
   + 390

18. 222
   + 759

GO
DIGITAL **Assessment Options:**
Soar to Success Math

Vocabulary Builder

▶ **Visualize It** ....

Use the checked words to complete the word map.

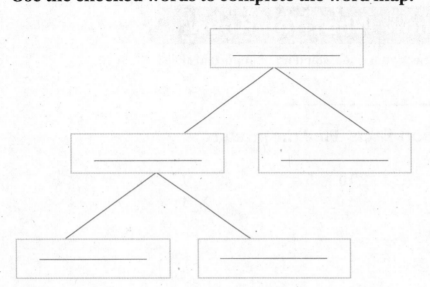

Preview Words

borrow

credit

human capital

✓ income

interest

labor

lend

✓ planned spending

purchase

resources

salary

✓ savings plan

✓ spend

✓ unplanned spending

▶ **Understand Vocabulary** ....

Complete the sentences by using the preview words.

1. You _____ something when you obtain it by paying money for an item or a service.

2. Money earned is called _____.

3. You _____ money when another person gives you money that you will need to pay back.

4. When you _____ money, you give it to someone else in exchange for something.

5. A _____ will help you save money regularly so you can reach your goals.

6. You _____ money to someone else by giving money that needs to be paid back.

• **Interactive Student Edition**
• **Multimedia eGlossary**

Name _____

Vocabulary

You can use coins to model problems about buying and spending.

On the way home from school, Janine spends 25 cents to buy a banana. She gives the grocer a $1 bill. The **change** is the amount of money she gets back. How much change should she get back?

Look at the coins in each box. Would Janine get the correct change if the grocer gave her these coins?

Write *exactly correct*, *not enough change*, or *too much change*.

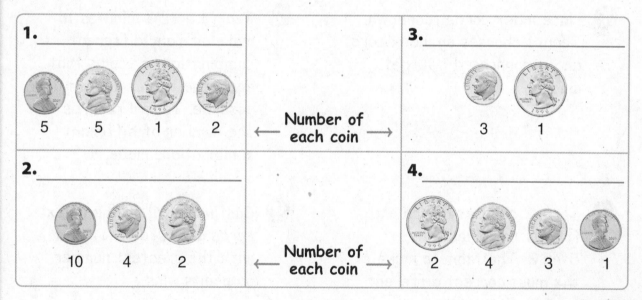

1. _____

5   5   1   2

← Number of each coin →

3. _____

3   1

2. _____

10   4   2

← Number of each coin →

4. _____

2   4   3   1

Writing Write about what you might spend money on.

Reading Look for this book in the library.
Jelly Beans for Sale, by Bruce McMillan

Count It Up!

Object of the Game Practice counting money amounts.

Materials

- set of 20 index cards with random money amounts up to one dollar
- play money (5 half-dollars, 5 quarters, 10 dimes, 15 nickels, and 50 or more pennies)
- clock or timer

Set Up

Divide students into pairs or small groups. Each pair or small group receives the same amount of play money.

Number of Players 2 teams of 2–4 players

How to Play

1 Place index cards facedown. Team 1 chooses an index card and announces the target amount.

95¢

2 Team 1 gets 3 minutes to make as many different combinations of coins that equal the target amount as possible. Team 1 records the number of different combinations made.

3 Team 2 chooses a card and follows the directions in Step 2. The team to make the most correct different combinations of coins scores 1 point.

4 Continue until all the index cards are used. The team with the greatest number of points wins.

Name _____

20.1 Making an Income

 TEKS Personal Financial Literacy—3.9.A
Also 3.2.D, 3.4.G, 3.4.K
MATHEMATICAL PROCESSES
3.1.A, 3.1.F

? **Essential Question**

What is the connection between your skills, abilities and knowledge, the amount of work you do, and the money you can earn?

Unlock the Problem (Real World)

Anita and Ruchi both want to buy a bicycle helmet that costs $40. They earn $3 for each week they complete their chores. **Labor** is the work that a person does. **Income** is money earned.

Labor and Income

A Look at the Work Completed table. Who will be able to buy her helmet at the end of 14 weeks?

Anita completed her chores for 10 weeks. Her income is

_____ × $3 = _____

_____ < $40, so _____ cannot buy her helmet.

Ruchi completed her chores for 14 weeks. Her income is

_____ × $3 = _____

_____ > $40, so _____ can buy her helmet.

If the rate of pay is the same, you can earn more

money if you do _____ work.

A person's knowledge and work skills can be called **human capital**.

Work Completed		
Week	Anita	Ruchi
1	✓	✓
2	✓	✓
3	✓	✓
4		✓
5	✓	✓
6		✓
7	✓	✓
8		✓
9	✓	✓
10	✓	✓
11		✓
12	✓	✓
13	✓	✓
14	✓	✓

Math Talk
Mathematical Processes
How can a person get more work skills? Explain.

Human Capital and Income

B Ruchi is 10 years old and Anita is 6 years old. Ruchi knows how to write, so she earns $1 extra to address letters for her mom. Anita earns 50¢ extra for putting stamps on the letters. How does what the girls know and do affect their income?

_____

Who can buy the item?

1. Mary and John earn $8 per hour. John works 42 hours. Mary works 29 hours. Who can buy a bicycle for $299?

_____

2. Jose and Karen earn $13 per hour. Jose works 8 hours. Karen works 7 hours. Who can buy a microscope for $89?

_____

3. Frank is a sports writer. Bob works in a fast food restaurant. Who do you think could possibly earn a higher salary? **Explain.**

_____

_____

> **Salary** is the amount of money a person can earn by being self-employed or by doing a job for another person or business.

Use the table for 4–7.

4. Matt is a plumber. What skills may he need for his job?

_____

5. Sofia is a medical secretary and needs professional knowledge for this position. What knowledge may be required?

_____

_____

Job	Starting Salary (per year)
Fashion designer	$38,233
Bank Teller	$21,465
Plumber	$34,447
College professor	$51,000
Store sales clerk	$15,500
Car mechanic	$27,756
Writer	$43,369
Computer scientist	$93,950
Medical secretary	$29,200

6. Dexter has worked 2 years as a computer scientist. He received a $1,500 raise after the first year. What was his salary for the second year? **Explain.**

_____

7. **Connect** What relationship do you notice between the jobs and the starting salary?

_____

_____

Name _____

 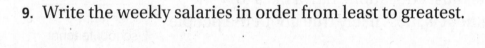
Use the table for 8–10.

Job	Starting Salary (per week)
Dentist	$2,634
Pharmacist	$2,109
Hair stylist	$383
Fire fighter	$604
Bookkeeper	$644
Webmaster	$1,086
Discount store clerk	$297
Fast food cook	$322
Computer engineer	$1,359
Surgeon	$5,208

8. **Write Math** ▶ Elaine is a salesperson in a discount store. She wants to be a bookkeeper. How much more can she possibly earn? **Explain** what she should do to become a bookkeeper.

_____

_____

_____

9. Write the weekly salaries in order from least to greatest.

_____

_____

10. Which starting salaries are about equal to earning $8 an hour for 40 hours a week? **Explain**.

_____

_____

_____

Write Math ▶
Show Your Work

11. **H.O.T.** **Multi-Step** Brianna has beautiful handwriting. She earns money by writing invitations to weddings. She gets $38 for each set of 5 invitations. If she does 2 groups of 45 invitations in one week, how much will she earn?

_____

_____

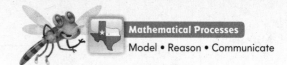
Daily Assessment Task

Fill in the bubble for the correct answer choice.

12. Marcia finished nursing school. Ben finished high school. Which statement about their job opportunities is most likely to be true?

Ⓐ Ben has more specialized skills than Marcia.

Ⓑ Marcia has fewer specialized skills than Ben.

Ⓒ Marcia may become a nurse.

Ⓓ Ben and Marcia may do the same job.

Use the table for 13.

13. **Reasoning** Andrew enjoys working in an office with other people. Chloe has the most education. Tanya likes to work outside. Which statement is most likely true about the people and jobs?

Ⓐ Chloe is the landscape worker.

Ⓑ Andrew is the legal secretary.

Ⓒ Andrew is the teacher.

Ⓓ Tanya is the legal secretary.

Job
Elementary school teacher
Landscape worker
Legal secretary

14. **Multi-Step** An elementary school teacher in one Texas city earns $47,730 a year. A fitness instructor earns $23,850. A legal secretary earns $14,360 less than the school teacher. What is the difference in salary between the fitness instructor and legal secretary?

Ⓐ $9,520   Ⓑ $10, 520   Ⓒ $33,370   Ⓓ $23,880

⭐ TEXAS Test Prep

15. Maeko went to school for 6 more years after graduating from a 4-year college to become an eye doctor. Which is most likely to be the amount of money she earns each week when she starts to work?

Ⓐ $200

Ⓑ $800

Ⓒ $2,000

Ⓓ $600

Homework and Practice

Name _____

20.1 Making an Income

Who can buy the item?

1. Jake and Charlene earn $9 per hour. Jake works 38 hours. Charlene works 42 hours. Who can buy a digital camera for $329?

   _____

2. Marta and Naji earn $12 per hour. On the same workday, Marta works 9 hours and Naji works 8 hours. Who can buy a computer desk for $100 with their income earned that day?

   _____

Problem Solving Real World

Use the table for 3–5.

Job	Starting Salary (per week)
Eye doctor	$2,450
Electrician	$655
Newspaper editor	$925
Waitress	$270
Office manager	$694
Librarian	$876
Typist	$472

3. Max is a typist. He wants to be an office manager. How much more can he possibly earn? **Explain** what he can do to become an office manager.

   _____

   _____

4. What is the difference in earnings between the highest starting salary and the lowest?

   _____

5. The starting salary for which job is about equal to earning $7 an hour for 40 hours each week? **Explain**.

   _____

   _____

Fill in the bubble completely to show your answer.

6. Ben earns $700 a week, Bradley earns $925 a week, and Russ earns $1,400 a week. Which statement about their knowledge and work skills is the most likely to be true?

Ⓐ Russ had no additional training past high school.

Ⓑ Bradley has the least training and work skills.

Ⓒ Ben has the least training and work skills.

Ⓓ Bradley went to medical school.

7. Kenneth went to college for 4 years, then went to graduate school for another two years. Which is most likely a job that Kenneth does based on his education?

Ⓐ auto mechanic

Ⓑ teacher

Ⓒ surgeon

Ⓓ clerk

8. Use the table at the right. Lu Chen enjoys playing the piano and singing. Alexis continues training in math and science. Hector enjoys working on trains. Which statement is most likely to be true about the people and their job opportunities?

Ⓐ Alexis is the aerospace engineer.

Ⓑ Hector is the college music teacher.

Ⓒ Hector is the home care aide.

Ⓓ Lu Chen is the railroad switch operator.

Job
Railroad switch operator
College music teacher
Home care aide
Aerospace engineer

9. **Multi-Step** Elio helps his grandfather rake leaves. He earns $3 an hour. Elio rakes leaves for 2 hours each day for two weeks. How much money does Elio earn?

Ⓐ $42   Ⓒ $84

Ⓑ $21   Ⓓ $32

10. **Multi-Step** Eileen wants to buy a CD headset for $64. She mows her family's lawn 3 times in one month. Eileen earns $8 for each mowing. How many more times does Eileen need to mow to buy the headset?

Ⓐ 40   Ⓒ 4

Ⓑ 5   Ⓓ 24

20.2 Cost of Resources

TEKS Personal Financial
Literacy—3.9.B
Also 3.2.D
MATHEMATICAL PROCESSES
3.1.A, 3.1.F

? **Essential Question**

How does the availability of resources affect their cost?

🔑 Unlock the Problem *Real World*

Ellen collects character toys. The toys come in sets named by colors. Some sets are hard to find because the toymaker does not make many of them. **Resources** are things that are produced and used. When many toy sets are made, the resources are plentiful. When few toy sets are made, the resources are scarce.

🔒 Resources and Cost

Toy Set Color	Blue	Orange	Red	Purple	Green
Number Made	50,000	50,200	500	50,350	50,850
Cost per Set	$32	$30	$99	$29	$28

Order the toy sets from the most to the least made.

_____

The toymaker made 50,000 or more of all the toy sets except

for the _____ set. Only _____ red sets were made.

Round each cost to the nearest ten dollars.

_____

Most toy sets cost about _____, but the _____ set costs about _____.

How does the number of toy sets made relate to the cost of the toy set?

When many toy sets are available, the cost for each set

is _____ (high, low).

When fewer toy sets are available, the cost for each set

is _____ (high, low).

Math Talk

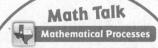
Mathematical Processes

If the toymaker makes only 100 toys sets in a new color, do you think the cost will be more than $99 or less than $99? **Explain.**

Anton collects baseball cards. He wants to buy a card that is very hard to find. Use the table for 1–2.

1. Order the baseball card prices from greatest to least.

_____

2. Which card do you think is the one Anton wants to buy? **Explain** using the term *resources*.

_____

_____

_____

Anton's Baseball Cards	
Baseball Cards	Price
Card A	$22
Card B	$39
Card C	$135
Card D	$3
Card E	$5

Mrs. Garcia is looking for a doll for her daughter Maria. The table shows how many of the dolls are available at some stores. Use the table for 3–4.

3. At which store do you think the price will be the lowest?

_____

4. **Explain** why a store might lower the price when it has too many of a particular resource?

_____

_____

Store	Number of Dolls
Tammi's Dolls	1
Place of Dolls	10
Toy Village	120
Midland Toys	20
Doll Town	10

The members of a service club want to raise money by selling muffins. The types of muffins are listed in the table below in order from the most muffins made to the least muffins made.

5. Use the prices $1, $2, $3, $4, and assign a price to each muffin. **Explain.**

Flavor	Chocolate	Banana	Bran	Plain
Price				

_____

_____

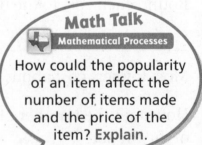

Math Talk
Mathematical Processes

How could the popularity of an item affect the number of items made and the price of the item? **Explain.**

Name _____

Problem Solving Real World

For 6–7, use the table.

Year Card was Made	Auction Price
1951	$4,810
1952	$1,550
1953	$999
1954	$1,210

6. **Write Math** ▶ Baseball cards of a famous player are sold at auctions. At an auction, people call out bids. A bid is the price they would pay for an item. In which year do you think the fewest cards for that baseball player were available? **Explain.**

_____

_____

_____

7. **H.O.T. Multi-Step** How much greater was the price for the 1951 card than prices for the 1952, 1953, and 1954 cards combined?

_____

Write Math ▶

Show Your Work

Leah will sell her headbands at a yard sale. She has 14 blue, 4 black, and 19 red headbands.

8. **H.O.T.** How should Leah price her headbands if she prices them based on availability of resources? Assign a price to each color. Then **justify** your answer.

_____

_____

_____

9. **Multi-Step** How much money will Leah earn if she sells all of her headbands at your prices?

_____

_____

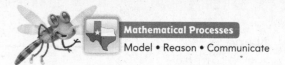
Daily Assessment Task

Fill in the bubble for the correct answer choice.
Use the Robot Toys table for 10–12.

10. A company makes toys that you can build into robots. The table shows how many of each robot design were made. Which shows the available resources, from most to least available?

Robot Toys	
Type of Robot	Number Made
Car	49,000
Plane	98,000
Train	800
Ship	9,000

Ⓐ   49,000; 800; 9,000; 98,000

Ⓑ   98,000; 9,000; 800; 49,000

Ⓒ   49,000; 98,000; 9,000; 800

Ⓓ   98,000; 49,000; 9,000; 800

11. **Apply** Which of the robots will sell for the greatest price?

Ⓐ plane   Ⓒ ship

Ⓑ train   Ⓓ car

12. **Multi-Step** If the toy company makes 1,000 more train robots, how many more ship robots will be available than train robots?

Ⓐ 7,200   Ⓒ 9,200

Ⓑ 8,200   Ⓓ 9,800

TEXAS Test Prep

13. **Analyze** Alana paid $15 for a rare stuffed animal. Then the toymaker announced that thousands more of that animal will be in stores next week. If Alana sells her stuffed animal online next week, which best describes what might happen?

Ⓐ   It will sell for more than $15 because there are more resources available.

Ⓑ   It will sell for $20 because it is a scarce resource.

Ⓒ   It will sell for $15 because it is a scarce resource.

Ⓓ   It will sell for less than $15 because there are more resources available.

TEKS **Personal Financial Literacy—3.9.B**
Also 3.2.D
MATHEMATICAL PROCESSES 3.1.A, 3.1.F

20.2 Cost of Resources

Edgar collects model cars. He wants to buy a car that is very hard to find. Use the table for 1–3.

Model Cars	
Car	Price
Rolls Royce	$23
Convertible	$12
Model T	$35
Pick-up Truck	$9
4-Door Sedan	$5

1. Write the names of the model cars in order from the greatest price to the least price.

   _____

   _____

2. Which car do you think Edgar wants to buy? **Explain**.

   _____

   _____

3. Which model car do you think will be the easiest for Edgar to find? **Explain**.

   _____

   _____

Problem Solving

Use the table at the right for 4–6.

4. Lucia collects models of famous ships. Write the names of the model ships in order from least number made to greatest number made.

   _____

   _____

Models of Famous Ships	
Ship	Number Made
Lusitania	21,000
Bismarck	5,000
Andria Doria	28,000
Titanic	48,000
HMS Victory	15,000

5. Which model ship do you think will be easiest for Lucia to find? **Explain**.

   _____

   _____

6. Which model ship will have the most expensive price? **Explain**.

   _____

   _____

Fill in the bubble completely to show your answer.

Use the Collectible Plates table for 7–9.

7. A company makes collectible nature plates. The table at the right shows how many plates of each type were made. Which of the plates will sell for the greatest price?

    Ⓐ Garden   Ⓒ Mountains

    Ⓑ Seaside   Ⓓ Forest

Collectible Plates	
Type of Plate	**Number Made**
Garden	17,500
Mountains	8,400
Seaside	12,800
Forest	2,200

8. Which shows the number of plates made in order from least to greatest?

    Ⓐ 2,200; 8,400; 12,800; 17,500

    Ⓑ 8,400; 12,800; 17,500; 2,200

    Ⓒ 17,500; 12,800; 8,400; 2,200

    Ⓓ 12,800; 8,400; 2,200; 17,500

9. **Multi-Step** The company makes another 2,000 Seaside plates. How many more Garden plates will there be than Seaside plates?

    Ⓐ 4,700   Ⓒ 14,800

    Ⓑ 19,700   Ⓓ 2,700

Use the Action Figures table for 10–12.

10. The table shows the price of some collectible action figures. Based on their prices, which action figure is the most available resource?

    Ⓐ Superhero   Ⓒ Gigantor

    Ⓑ Titan   Ⓓ Colossus

Action Figures	
Figure	**Price**
Superhero	$8
Titan	$12
Gigantor	$27
Colossus	$18

11. The action figure company announces that the Colossus action figure will no longer be made. In one year, which action figure will likely cost the most?

    Ⓐ Superhero   Ⓒ Gigantor

    Ⓑ Titan   Ⓓ Colossus

12. **Multi-Step** Zach buys 1 Titan and 2 Superhero action figures. He pays with two $20 bills. How much change does he receive?

    Ⓐ $28   Ⓒ $40

    Ⓑ $12   Ⓓ $8

TEKS Personal Financial Literacy—3.9.C
MATHEMATICAL PROCESSES
3.1.A, 3.1.G

20.3 Spending Decisions

? Essential Question

What are the benefits of planned spending decisions?

? Unlock the Problem Real World

To **purchase** is to obtain by paying money for an item or a service. When you **spend** money to purchase something, you give it to someone else in exchange for something.

Carlos wants to purchase a new baseball glove before summer vacation. He has saved $36. The glove costs $48. Carlos plans to save $4 each week. It is 3 weeks before summer vacation starts. Will he be able to save enough money to purchase the baseball glove?

Example Planned Spending

How much money will Carlos have saved before summer vacation?

_____ weeks × _____ = _____ $36 + _____ = _____

So, Carlos _____ (will, will not) be able to save enough money to buy the baseball glove.

Example Unplanned Spending

What if Carlos sees a team tee shirt on sale for $10 next week? Should he make the purchase?

If Carlos buys the tee shirt, he will have

$36 − _____ = _____.

In 3 weeks, he will have _____ + _____ = _____.

If he buys the tee shirt, Carlos _____ (will, will not) have enough money saved to buy the baseball glove before summer vacation starts.

Math Idea

Planned spending can help you reach a goal.

Unplanned spending is frequently not wise. Unplanned spending may prevent you from reaching a goal.

Math Talk
Mathematical Processes

What if Carlos sees the baseball glove on sale for $39 next week? Would it be a wise or unwise purchase? Explain.

1. Olga will be teaching a ceramics class, which starts in 6 weeks, and she needs to purchase clay. Fifty pounds of clay costs $54. Olga has saved $21. Her plan is to save $5 each week. Will she be able to save enough money to purchase the clay by the time the class starts?

   6 weeks × _____ = _____ $21 + _____ = _____

   _____

2. Will Olga have enough money to purchase the clay by the time the class starts if she saves $6 each week?

   _____ weeks × _____ = _____ $21 + _____ = _____

   _____

3. Suppose Olga does not have any money saved. How much money would she need to save each week to have enough money to purchase the clay by the time the class starts in 6 weeks? **Explain**.

   _____

4. Olga would like to purchase some sunglasses that cost $13. If she uses her savings to buy the sunglasses, and then she saves $8 each week, will she have enough money saved in 6 weeks to buy the clay?

   $21 − _____ = _____   6 weeks × _____ = _____

   In 6 weeks, she will have _____ + _____ = _____.

   _____

Math Talk

Mathematical Processes

Explain when you should not make an unplanned purchase.

5. Suppose Olga earns $100 a week. She spends $18 for transportation and $46 for food. She saves $30 each week to pay her rent at the end of the month. Can Olga also save $10 a week to buy clay? **Explain**.

   _____

   _____

   _____

Problem Solving Real World

$279

Use within 3 weeks to **save $50!**

6. **H.O.T.** **Multi-Step** Tony is saving for the tablet computer pictured. He has saved $169. How much money does he need to save each week if he plans to use the coupon to buy the tablet?

_____

7. **Write Math** ▶ Victoria has $36. She starts saving $10 a week to buy a stuffed bear for her cousin. The bear costs $59. Victoria will visit her cousin in 4 weeks. Would it be a wise unplanned spending decision for Victoria to purchase a pair of boots that cost $30? **Explain**.

Write Math ▶

Show Your Work

_____

_____

8. Tanya has $12 to spend. She will earn $10 a night for babysitting 2 nights next week. She wants to buy a backpack that costs $29. How much can Tanya spend today if she plans to buy the backpack in 2 weeks?

_____

9. **H.O.T.** Miguel wants to take his brother to a movie. The movie tickets cost $6. Miguel is saving $5 a week to buy a caboose for his train set, which costs $62. He has saved $54. Would his unplanned spending decision to go to the movies be wise? **Explain**.

Math on the Spot

_____

_____

_____

_____

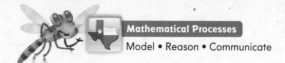
Daily Assessment Task

Fill in the bubble for the correct answer choice.

10. **Multi-Step** Sophie plans to spend $10 for a new dog toy. She saves $1 each week for 8 weeks. Then Sophie spends $3 on snacks. How many more weeks will Sophie have to save to have enough money to buy the toy?

Ⓐ 5 weeks   Ⓑ 6 weeks   Ⓒ 3 weeks   Ⓓ 4 weeks

11. **Reasoning** Olivia wants to buy a doghouse that costs $150. She saves $4 a week for 5 weeks and then receives a gift of $80. When the doghouse goes on sale for $99, she buys it. Which best describes her spending decision?

Ⓐ It is a wise unplanned spending decision, because her savings plus the gift allow her to buy the doghouse on sale.

Ⓑ It is an unwise unplanned spending decision because unplanned spending decisions never make sense.

Ⓒ It is a wise planned spending decision because she has already saved $150 in 5 weeks to buy the doghouse.

Ⓓ It is an unwise unplanned spending decision because the gift plus her savings are not enough to buy the doghouse.

 TEXAS Test Prep

12. Keesha plans to save $5 a week for a new skateboard. The skateboard costs $47, and she has $22 saved. Which will result in her NOT being able to buy the skateboard?

Ⓐ She continues to save and makes no unplanned purchases for 5 weeks.

Ⓑ She spends $3 and then saves $6 a week for 5 weeks.

Ⓒ She saves $5 a week for 2 more weeks and then uses some money to buy a book.

Ⓓ She saves $5 a week for 2 more weeks and then increases her savings to $8 a week for 2 weeks.

20.3 Spending Decisions

1. Theresa wants to buy a new skateboard that costs $48 before summer vacation starts in 4 weeks. She has saved $17. Her plan is to save $6 each week. Will she be able to save enough money to buy the skateboard?

   4 weeks × _____ = _____ $17 + _____ = _____

   _____

   _____

2. Suppose Theresa has only $8 saved. How much money will she need to save each week to have enough money to buy the skateboard in 4 weeks? **Explain**.

   _____

   _____

Problem Solving Real World

3. Deon wants to buy new car speakers that cost $66. He has saved $20 and he has a coupon to save $10. If he wants to buy the speakers in 4 weeks, how much money will he need to save each week?

   _____

4. Jared has $25. He starts saving $9 a week to buy a birthday present for his father that costs $45. Jared's father's birthday is in 3 weeks. Would it be a wise unplanned spending decision for Jared to spend $15 on a set of comic books? **Explain**.

   _____

   _____

Fill in the bubble completely to show your answer.

5. Which of the following is true about spending decisions?

Ⓐ Unplanned spending always helps you reach a goal.

Ⓑ Planned spending can help you reach a goal.

Ⓒ Planned spending means you can never purchase what you want.

Ⓓ Unplanned spending is always a wise decision.

6. Which of the following is a planned spending decision?

Ⓐ Spending all of your allowance each week

Ⓑ Buying a poster of your favorite singer with $10 that you found

Ⓒ Saving $12 a week for a trip, and spending half of it each week

Ⓓ Saving $15 a week for 5 weeks to buy a bicycle that costs $75

7. Rosa has $16 saved. She wants to buy a new cell phone in 6 weeks that costs $75. Which plan will help her reach her goal?

Ⓐ Save $10 each week for 6 weeks.

Ⓑ Save $14 each week for 4 weeks. Then buy a teeshirt that costs $12.

Ⓒ Save $7 each week for 6 weeks.

Ⓓ Save $5 each week for 11 weeks.

8. Carson has $13 to spend. He will earn $18 washing cars for his neighbors. He plans to buy a pair of jeans that cost $25. How much money will he have left after he buys the jeans?

Ⓐ $23

Ⓑ $9

Ⓒ $33

Ⓓ $6

9. **Multi-Step** Chelsea plans to buy a gift for her sister that costs $15. She saves $3 each week for 4 weeks. Then she spends $6 on school supplies. How many more weeks will Chelsea need to save to buy the gift?

Ⓐ 3 weeks   Ⓒ 12 weeks

Ⓑ 6 weeks   Ⓓ 9 weeks

10. **Multi-Step** Kalon has $80 saved. He earns $115 a week and spends $75 each week on gas and groceries. He plans to buy new tires for his car in 6 weeks that cost $140. How much should he plan to save each week?

Ⓐ $15   Ⓒ $10

Ⓑ $20   Ⓓ $12

20.4 Borrowing and Credit

TEKS Personal Financial Literacy—3.9.D
Also 3.4.F, 3.4.G, 3.4.K
MATHEMATICAL PROCESSES
3.1.A, 3.1.F

 Essential Question How does using credit to buy something that you want or need affect the cost?

 Unlock the Problem *Real World*

Borrowing

Emma wants to buy a new recorder for camp, but she does not have enough money. Her mother will lend Emma the money, but Emma must pay her mother back $5 each week from her allowance until the whole amount is paid back.

Emma will _____. Her mother will _____ Emma the money now, but she must pay back a given amount each week in the future.

Credit is paying for something with money that is borrowed and must be paid back, usually with interest.

Interest is the money paid by the borrower to the lender for the use of the lender's money.

> When you do not have enough money for something, you can borrow money. You **borrow** money when another person gives you money that you will need to pay back. A person **lends** money to someone else by giving money that needs to be paid back.

Credit

When Emma returns to school, she will take trumpet lessons. Her mother wants to buy her a trumpet that costs $150. She does not have enough money, so she will use credit. She arranges to pay back $50 a month, and she must pay $5 extra each month. If it takes her 3 months to pay back the money, how much will she pay for the trumpet?

Emma's mother needs to borrow _____. She pays back

_____ + $5, or _____ each month.

So, she will pay _____ × _____ = _____ for the trumpet.

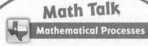 **Math Talk**
Mathematical Processes
Explain why Emma's mother has to pay more than $150 for the trumpet.

Since buying on credit often costs more, it is important to understand the difference between wants and needs.

Wants and Needs

Sometimes, you would like to have or buy something, but the item is not necessary at the time. Other things are real needs. Look at the sentences below. The words in red are either needs or wants. Write the words in red in the correct column in the table.

| Buy eyeglasses. Yours are broken. |
| Buy a backpack. Yours is muddy. |
| Buy a new baseball cap. Your team won! |
| Buy a snack right before supper. |
| Buy a book you saw at the bookstore. |
| Replace your friend's garden tool that you lost. |

Needs	Wants

- Choose an item from the table that you might have to use credit to purchase. Explain why your choice is reasonable.

I might use credit to buy _____ because _____

_____

Share and Show

1. Which of the following are examples of when you might use credit. Circle the boxes.

You have $20. You want some new jeans that cost $26, so you save $3 a week.	Your roof leaks. A roofer can make repairs for $1,200 but you do not have enough money.	You drive your car to take college classes, but your car broke down. It will cost $800 to repair.	A new flat screen TV costs $1,000. You have $2,000 in savings.

2. A chef uses credit to buy a new mixer for his restaurant. If he pays $63 a month for 9 months, plus interest of $7 a month, how much will he pay for the mixer?

_____

Problem Solving · Real World

For 3–4, circle the sentence that shows a need.

3. Your class is going on a field trip to an animal rescue farm.

   Ⓐ You are asked to bring a sandwich, fruit, and a juice box for lunch on the day of the trip.

   Ⓑ You decide to buy a new animal tee shirt for the trip.

4. Your grandmother is making a carrot cake for the fair.

   Ⓐ You are sent to the store with $2 to buy carrots.

   Ⓑ The carrots cost less than $2, so you buy yourself a snack.

5. **H.O.T.** **Multi-Step** Brianna's swimming lessons start tomorrow and she needs a new swimsuit. A swimsuit costs $35, but Brianna has saved only $7. Brianna borrows the money from her sister and pays her back $8 a week. Her sister does not make Brianna pay interest. Will Brianna be able to pay her sister back in 3 weeks? **Explain**.

_____

_____

6. **H.O.T.** **Apply** Write a problem about something you or your family needs that costs $100. Decide how much you have and how much you will need to borrow on credit, including how much you will pay back each month. Include an amount of interest to pay back each month. Then find how much you will pay back and the total cost.

Pose a problem.   **Solve your problem.**

Daily Assessment Task

Fill in the bubble for the correct answer choice.

7. **Multi-Step** John needs to have a textbook for a college class that starts tomorrow. The book costs $60. How much more will the book cost him to buy if he uses credit, pays $12 a month, and pays an extra $4 a month in interest?

Ⓐ $70   Ⓑ $20   Ⓒ $12   Ⓓ $60

8. Robin has $32. She needs to buy 3 soccer shirts that cost $15 each. Her father will lend Robin enough money to buy the shirts. How much will Robin need to borrow from her father on credit?

Ⓐ $13   Ⓑ $2   Ⓒ $45   Ⓓ $30

9. Jim has just enough money to pay his rent. He sees a coat at the mall that costs $50. His coat is old but usable. Which statement below is true?

Ⓐ He does not have enough to pay rent.

Ⓑ He needs the coat right away.

Ⓒ Using credit will not cost him any extra money.

Ⓓ He could buy the coat on credit.

⭐ TEXAS Test Prep

10. Mr. Diaz starts a basketball clinic for local youth, but he has no sports equipment. He needs to buy 3 basketballs that cost $30 each. Mr. Diaz has $45 saved and borrows the rest of the money. Which statement below is NOT true?

Ⓐ He is using $45 credit to buy the basketballs.

Ⓑ He can pay back $5 a week for 9 weeks.

Ⓒ He is using $90 credit to buy the basketballs.

Ⓓ He can pay back the loan faster if he pays $9 a week.

20.4 Borrowing and Credit

1. Look at the sentences below. The words in red are either needs or wants. Write the words in red in the correct column in the table.

Buy sneakers for gym class.
Buy a notebook for homework.
Buy cereal for breakfast.
Buy gasoline for the car.
Buy flowers for the table.
Buy a comic book.
Buy craft supplies for your hobby.
Buy a new sports T-shirt for your favorite team.

Needs	Wants

Problem Solving Real World

2. Pete needs to buy a new jacket that costs $33, but he has saved only $12. His parents will lend Pete the money, but he must pay them back $7 each week from his allowance. Who is the borrower? Who is the lender?

_____

3. Is Pete using credit? Is he paying interest? **Explain**.

_____

_____

_____

4. How long will it take Pete to pay back the money? **Explain**.

_____

Fill in the bubble completely to show your answer.

5. Chet needs to repair his broken bicycle so he can deliver newspapers. He uses credit to borrow $84. He will pay $12 each month. He must also pay $1 extra in interest each month. How much does he pay in all to have the bike repaired?

   (A) $91

   (B) $72

   (C) $84

   (D) $79

6. Ming wants to buy a new backpack that costs $28. She has $4 saved and will earn another $3 babysitting. How much money will Ming need to borrow if she wants to buy the backpack today?

   (A) $21

   (B) $35

   (C) $24

   (D) $25

7. Nyala is grocery shopping at the local market. Which of the following is most likely a need, rather than a want?

   (A) silk flowers

   (B) magazines

   (C) bread and milk

   (D) ice cream bars

8. Which of the following would you most likely use credit to buy?

   (A) food for a holiday meal

   (B) a light bulb for a lamp

   (C) a new basketball

   (D) material to fix a hole in the roof

9. **Multi-Step** Wendy needs to buy warm clothing for college. She borrows $200 and must pay the money back in equal amounts for 10 months. She must also pay $2 interest each month. What is her monthly payment, including interest?

   (A) $35   (C) $3

   (B) $12   (D) $22

10. **Multi-Step** Hakim has $15 saved. He wants to buy a barbeque grill for $75. He borrows the money he needs and pays an equal amount back for 6 months. The interest is $2 each month. How much money will he pay back in all?

    (A) $15   (C) $60

    (B) $75   (D) $72

Name _____

TEKS **Personal Financial Literacy—3.9.E**
Also 3.4.A
MATHEMATICAL PROCESSES 3.1.A

Essential Question

How and why should you save money?

Unlock the Problem

People save money for things they want or need in the future. When you save money, you keep it and do not spend it. There are many reasons that you and your family might make a plan to save money.

List some reasons to save money.

A **To reach a goal, such as going to college**

What other goals do you and your family save money for?

_____

B **To buy things that you want**

What things would you buy?

_____

C **To replace things that break or wear out**

What item might break or need to be replaced?

_____

D **To pay unexpected expenses**

What unplanned expenses might your family have?

_____

E **To help others**

What organizations can you help by donating money?

_____

Math Talk
Mathematical Processes

Explain why it is better to have a plan to save money than not to have one.

Savings Plan

A **savings plan** will help you save money regularly, so you can reach your goals.

 Make a savings plan.

Erika's family plans to save $75 every month to buy a new big screen television that cost $425. Complete the table to find how many months Erika's family needs to save money so they can buy the television.

Month	1	2	3	4	5	6
Money Saved	$75	$150				

So, Erika's family needs to save money for _____ months to buy the television.

- **Explain** why it is a good idea to make a savings plan.

_____

_____

 Share and Show MATH BOARD

1. Which things can a savings plan help you do? Circle all that apply.

Grow vegetables.	Buy a motor home.	Make friends.
Start your own business.	Travel overseas.	Attend college.
Buy gum.	Give to a charity.	Learn to knit.

2. Sonny plans to save $12 every month for a new video game that costs $59. Complete the table. How many months does Sonny need to save money so he can buy the video game?

Month	1	2	3	4	5	6
Money Saved	$12	$24				

Sonny needs to save money for _____ months to buy the video game.

686

Name _____

Problem Solving Real World

Avery's Reasons to Save Money	
Reason	**Money Needed**
Give money to Cindy's Cat Rescue	$40
Buy a bicycle	$90
Go to the dentist	$100
Replace a broken digital music player	$70

For 3–6, use the table at the right.

3. **Write Math** ▶ Which of Avery's reasons to save money could be an unexpected or unplanned expense? **Explain.**

_____

_____

4. **H.O.T.** **Multi-Step** Complete the table below to make a savings plan to help Avery save money to buy a bicycle in 6 months or less.

Month	1	2	3	4	5	6
Money Saved						

5. **H.O.T.** **Multi-Step** Suppose Avery saved $30 each month. How long would it be before she could pay for all four things listed in the table?

_____

6. **What if** Avery receives a new digital music player as a gift, and she adds the amount to her college savings that she would have needed to repair the broken music player. If she saves $25 each month for college, how much money will she have in all for college in 3 months?

_____

7. **Explain** how a savings plan could help you get a job when you are grown up.

_____

_____

_____

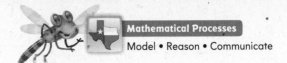

Daily Assessment Task

Fill in the bubble for the correct answer choice.

8. **Apply** Jeffrey is saving money so that he can give $25 to a children's museum improvement fund. Which of the following best describes Jeffrey's reason to save money?

   (A) to buy something he wants   (C) to replace something that broke

   (B) to help others   (D) to go on vacation

9. **Multi-Step** Destiny made a savings plan. She saved $21 each month for 9 months. Then she spent $135 on a computer language learning course. How much of her savings does she have left?

   (A) $45   (C) $54

   (B) $189   (D) $145

10. Which of the following is NOT a true statement about a savings plan?

    (A) It will always give you more money than you need to buy what you want.

    (B) It can help you save money for education.

    (C) It will help you decide when you can buy an item.

    (D) It can help you pay for unexpected expenses.

⭐ TEXAS Test Prep

11. **Apply** Mr. Gordon is saving money so that he can send his daughter to college. Which of the following best describes Mr. Gordon's reason to save money?

    (A) to repair a broken item   (C) to reach a goal

    (B) to go on vacation   (D) to buy an item he wants

20.5 Savings Plan

Problem Solving Real World

For 1–3, use the table at the right.

Ethan's Reasons to Save
Buy a new video game
Give money to a food drive
Buy new eyeglasses
Take music lessons

1. Which of Ethan's reasons for saving could help him reach a goal?

   _____

2. What other goals might Ethan have?

   _____

   _____

3. Which reason could be an unexpected expense? **Explain.**

   _____

   _____

4. Emily wants to buy a new tent before she goes on a camping trip in 6 months. The tent costs $240. Complete the table below to help Emily make a savings plan to buy the tent in 6 months.

Month	1	2	3	4	5	6
Money Saved	$40	_____	_____	_____	_____	_____

5. **What If** Emily already has $80 saved and the tent goes on sale for $200 in 3 months? Will Emily be able to buy the tent in less than 6 months? **Explain.**

   _____

   _____

Lesson Check

Fill in the bubble completely to show your answer.

6. Rachel is saving money so she can give money to the town to help build a new park. Which of the following best describes Rachel's reason to save money?

   Ⓐ to buy something she needs

   Ⓑ to help others

   Ⓒ to buy something she wants

   Ⓓ to go on vacation

7. Mrs. Keller is saving money so that she can add a deck to her house. Which of the following best describes Mrs. Keller's reason to save money?

   Ⓐ to go on vacation

   Ⓑ to help others

   Ⓒ to reach a goal

   Ⓓ to replace a broken item

8. Lindsay's savings plan will help her save money to repair a broken computer. The repairs will cost $125. By which month will Lindsay have enough money to repair the computer?

Month	1	2	3	4	5
Money Saved	$30	$60	$90	$120	$150

   Ⓐ Month 1   Ⓒ Month 3

   Ⓑ Month 4   Ⓓ Month 5

9. The chart shows Larry's plan to save money to buy a new desk for his office. The desk will cost $95. In how many weeks will Larry have enough money to buy the desk?

Week	1	2	3	4	5
Money Saved	$25	$50	$75	$100	$125

   Ⓐ 2 weeks   Ⓒ 5 weeks

   Ⓑ 4 weeks   Ⓓ 3 weeks

10. **Multi-Step** Savannah wants to save $120 in 8 weeks. She finds that her plan to save $8 each week is not enough to reach her goal. How much more money should she save each week in order to reach her goal?

    Ⓐ $6   Ⓒ $64

    Ⓑ $7   Ⓓ $56

11. **Multi-Step** Hiroki plans to save $9 each week for 10 weeks. He wants to buy a new sleeping bag for $92 and a canteen for $18. How much more money should he save each week to buy both items?

    Ⓐ $20   Ⓒ $2

    Ⓑ $90   Ⓓ $4

Name _____

20.6 Financial Decisions

TEKS Personal Financial Literacy—3.9.F
Also 3.4.A
MATHEMATICAL PROCESSES
3.1.A, 3.1.F

? Essential Question

What kinds of decisions can you make involving income, spending, saving, giving, and credit?

🔑 Unlock the Problem Real World

Make decisions about spending and saving. Follow the directions. See how much money you have at the end and how you can get what you need or want.

🔒 **Decision Mission**

Decision 1: Which item is your goal? _____

You earn $100 each week. You need $60 to pay living expenses.

How much do you have left? _____

_____

Decision 2: How much do you want to save each

week? _____

How much do you have left in your pocket? _____

Work for 10 weeks: How much do you save? _____

How much do you have in your pocket? _____

Your car breaks down. You need $90 to fix it.

_____

Decision 3: How will you pay–from your pocket or from

your savings? _____

How much is left? _____

You decide to give some of your pocket money to the

food bank. How much do you give? _____

How much do you have left? _____

Math Talk
Mathematical Processes

Explain how you might change your decisions in this mission to include regular donations to a charity that you like.

Decision 4: How much will you borrow and have to pay back? You don't want to wait to save for your goal. You want it now, so you use what you have saved and borrow the rest on credit.

$500 − _____ = _____.

You need to pay back $10 each week plus $1 interest each week. How much will you pay back in all? **Explain**.

_____

_____

Remember

Borrowing on credit means that you get money right away but must agree to pay back a given amount in regular payments until it is paid back, usually with interest.

Share and Show

Look at each decision. Circle the word or words that apply.

1. Buying some new socks

   income   spending   saving   credit   giving

2. Putting $25 aside each week for college expenses

   income   spending   saving   credit   giving

✓ 3. Donating to the Park Rebuilding Fund

   income   spending   saving   credit   giving

4. Borrowing $1,000 to pay for new garage door

   income   spending   saving   credit   giving

5. Starting a new job

   income   spending   saving   credit   giving

6. Buying gas to get to work

   income   spending   saving   credit   giving

✓ 7. **Write Math** ▶ **Explain** why you might need to use credit. Give an example.

_____

_____

_____

Problem Solving Real World

8. **Reasoning** Jenna has $38. She buys a toy on sale for her cousin for $4. She puts $5 in a savings account. She makes a bill payment of $15. She gets $3 for running an errand for her mother. How much does she have available for giving to charity?

_____

9. **H.O.T.** **Multi-Step** Alyssa earns money as a babysitter. She earns $15 per night. She plans to babysit 4 times during the next month. She will spend $10 on treats for the children. She also plans to spend $20 on new clothes for school. How much will Alyssa be able to save? **Justify**.

_____

_____

10. **H.O.T.** **Evaluate** Darren sees some boots that cost $100. He needs the boots in 6 weeks, and he has no money saved. He earns $50 a week. If he uses credit to buy the boots now, the total cost is $118. **Explain** what you would decide to do and why.

_____

_____

_____

11. **H.O.T.** **Multi-Step** Make a chart like the one at the right. Record your spending decisions. Make the amount you earn and the amount you spend equal. You can add as many rows as you need.

- You discover you need to pay $80 for a new tire. Adjust your chart.

My Savings Plan	
	Weekly Total
Income	$200
Expenses	
Donations	
Saving for College	
Unplanned Expenses	

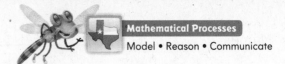

Daily Assessment Task

Fill in the bubble for the correct answer choice.

12. Jaxon earns $30 each month. He decides to give $5 to an animal charity. He also decides to buy 3 books at a sale for $5 each. Which of the following statements is NOT true?

Ⓐ His income is $30 a month.　　Ⓒ He spends $20.

Ⓑ He uses $15 of credit.　　Ⓓ He saves $10.

13. Kendra is looking for a summer job. She plans to spend $40 each month. She wants to save $40 each week for college. If she counts 4 weeks in a month, how much should she earn in one month to reach her goals?

Ⓐ $160　　Ⓒ $200

Ⓑ $120　　Ⓓ $80

14. **Multi-Step** Dexter earns $30 fixing and cleaning one bike. He plans to fix and clean 4 bikes during the next month. He will spend $20 on cleaning materials for the 4 bikes. He also plans to spend $30 on replacement parts for the 4 bikes. How much will Dexter be able to save?

Ⓐ $50　　Ⓒ $30

Ⓑ $15　　Ⓓ $70

 TEXAS Test Prep

15. Malia has a new job. Her income is $1,500 a month. She has $800 of expenses each month. Which of the following is NOT a reasonable decision about money?

Ⓐ spending $1,200 now for a flat screen TV

Ⓑ saving $250 a month for emergencies

Ⓒ donating $50 a month to charity

Ⓓ buying a new business suit on sale for $70

TEKS Personal Financial Literacy—3.9.F
Also 3.4.A
MATHEMATICAL PROCESSES 3.1.A, 3.1.F

20.6 Financial Decisions

Look at each decision. Circle the word or words that apply.

1. Setting $50 aside each month to buy a new washing machine

    income   spending   saving   credit   giving

2. Collecting and donating money to a local animal shelter

    income   spending   saving   credit   giving

3. Taking out a loan out to buy a new car

    income   spending   saving   credit   giving

Problem Solving

4. Martine has $43 in her savings account. She earns $12 doing chores and $9 walking her neighbor's dog each week. She wants to buy a new sweater for $18. She also wants to go to a bus trip that costs $52. Does Martine have enough money to buy the sweater and go on the bus trip this week? **Explain.**

    _____

    _____

    _____

5. Enrico earns $5 each day for taking care of his neighbor's cat while they are on vacation. The neighbors are away for 14 days. Enrico will spend $6 for paint brushes and $12 for a set of watercolor paints. How much money will Enrico be able to save? **Explain.**

    _____

    _____

    _____

Fill in the bubble completely to show your answer.

6. Lourdes earns $23 washing her neighbor's cars. Then she spends $12 to buy a new leash for her dog. Which words describes Lourdes decisions?

  Ⓐ income and spending

  Ⓑ credit and spending

  Ⓒ income and saving

  Ⓓ giving and credit

7. **Multi-Step** Xavier has a summer job. He will earn $50 each week for 8 weeks. At the end of summer, Xavier will use credit to buy a used car for $500. How much will he need borrow on credit?

  Ⓐ $400

  Ⓑ $900

  Ⓒ $100

  Ⓓ $550

8. Josette earns $60 a month. She decides to save $30 each month for an art course. If the art course costs $120, how many months will Josette need to save?

  Ⓐ 2 months

  Ⓑ 5 months

  Ⓒ 6 months

  Ⓓ 4 months

9. **Multi-Step** Carly earns $50 a month pet sitting and saves all of it. She decides to buy a jacket for $63 and a backpack for $28. If Carly decides to use her savings to buy the items, how much will she have saved after 3 months?

  Ⓐ $150

  Ⓑ $59

  Ⓒ $87

  Ⓓ $88

10. Jacie goes grocery shopping for his grandfather each week. He earns $20 for each shopping trip. He decides to save for 9 weeks to buy new skis for $175. Which describes Jacie's decision?

  Ⓐ buying on credit

  Ⓑ saving to meet a goal

  Ⓒ saving for an unexpected expense

  Ⓓ not saving enough to buy the skis

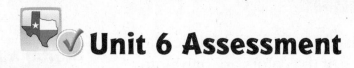

Unit 6 Assessment

Vocabulary

Choose the best term from the box.

1. _____ is the work that a person does. (p. 661)

2. You _____ money when another person gives you money that you will need to pay back. (p. 679)

3. Your _____ is the amount of money you earn by being self-employed or by doing a job for another person or business. (p. 662)

4. To _____ is to obtain by paying for an item or a service. (p. 673)

5. A _____ helps you save money regularly so you can reach your goals. (p. 686)

6. You _____ money when you give someone else money that needs to be paid back. (p. 679)

7. _____ is money earned. (p. 661)

8. When you _____ money, you give it to someone else in exchange for something. (p. 673)

9. _____ are things that are produced and used. (p. 667)

10. _____ is paying for something with money that you borrow and must pay back, usually with interest. (p. 679)

11. _____ is the money paid by a borrower to a lender for the use of the lender's money. (p. 679)

Vocabulary
borrow
credit
human capital
income
interest
labor
lend
purchase
resources
salary
savings plan
spend

A computer company released a new digital music player in five different colors. Some of the colors are harder to find and buy because the company did not make very many of them.

Digital Music Players	
Color	Number Made
black	80,000
silver	15,000
white	75,000
red	65,000
blue	70,000

Use the table for 12–13. TEKS 3.9.B

12. Order the digital music players from fewest made to most made.

_____

13. Which of the digital music player colors do you think will cost the most money to buy? **Explain**.

_____

_____

_____

Look at each decision. Circle the word or words that apply. TEKS 3.9.F

14. Buying a new pair of jeans.

   income   spending   saving   credit   giving

15. Borrowing $500 to buy a new bicycle.

   income   spending   saving   credit   giving

16. Donating $25 to a pet shelter.

   income   spending   saving   credit   giving

17. Starting work at a computer store.

   income   spending   saving   credit   giving

Fill in the bubble for the correct answer choice.

18. A store sells magnets of the animals in a popular cartoon. The table at the right shows the price for each magnet. If the store bases it prices on available resources, which magnet did the magnet company make the fewest of? ⬅ TEKS 3.9.B

Cartoon Magnets	
Type of Stickers	**Price**
Dog	$3
Bird	$1
Cat	$8
Horse	$3

   Ⓐ bird   Ⓒ horse

   Ⓑ cat   Ⓓ dog

19. Which of the following is most likely to be an unplanned spending decision? ⬅ TEKS 3.9.C

   Ⓐ paying for college course   Ⓒ paying to go to the movies

   Ⓑ buying a new car   Ⓓ buying plane tickets for a vacation

20. Jose finished high school. Lauren went to work right after graduating from high school. Alyssa went to college and then on to graduate school for more training. Who is most likely to have the specialized skills for more job opportunities? ⬅ TEKS 3.9.A

   Ⓐ Alyssa   Ⓒ Ethan

   Ⓑ Lauren   Ⓓ Jose

21. Which of the following is NOT a true statement about credit? ⬅ TEKS 3.9.D

   Ⓐ You have to pay back the money you borrow.

   Ⓑ You spend less money when you use credit.

   Ⓒ Most of the time you will need to pay interest to the lender.

   Ⓓ You use credit when something you want or need costs more than you can pay.

22. Kristin is saving money so that she can buy a new cell phone. Which of the following best describes Kristin's reason to save money? ⬅ TEKS 3.9.E

   Ⓐ to help others   Ⓒ to go on vacation

   Ⓑ to repair a broken item   Ⓓ to buy an item she wants

23. Amelie needs to buy 2 leotards for a dance recital. Each leotard costs $25. She has $32 saved and will borrow the rest of the money from her father. Amelie will pay her father back $6 a week. Which of the following describes what Amelie and her father are doing? ⬇ TEKS 3.9.D

Ⓐ Amelie is using credit.   Ⓒ Not here

Ⓑ Amelie will pay back $50.   Ⓓ Amelie's father is borrowing money.

24. Which of Luis's decisions best shows charitable giving? ⬇ TEKS 3.9.F

Ⓐ Luis works at the library on weekends.

Ⓑ Luis buys a book for $20 and donates it to the library.

Ⓒ Luis borrows $20 to pay for an overdue library book that he lost.

Ⓓ Luis puts $20 in the bank every month for college.

25. Cameron sees a pair of inline skates for $50 which she cannot afford. Which statement best shows planned spending? ⬇ TEKS 3.9.C

Ⓐ She suddenly decides to use credit to buy the skates.

Ⓑ She waits and hopes for a $50 birthday gift.

Ⓒ She saves $8 a week until she has enough money.

Ⓓ She saves $10 for 2 weeks and then spends the money on a video game.

26. Nevaeh saved $300 of the $585 she needs for a summer course. She borrows the money she needs and pays back $57 a month. She pays interest of $6 each month for this arrangement. **Explain** the financial decision she has made. Complete the chart to show how long it will take to pay the money back. How much will she pay back in all? ⬇ TEKS 3.9.D, 3.9.F

_____

_____

Month	1				
Amount Saved	$57				

Glossary

Pronunciation Key

a	add, map	f	fit, half	n	nice, tin	p	pit, stop	yōō	fuse, few
ā	ace, rate	g	go, log	ng	ring, song	r	run, poor	v	vain, eve
â(r)	care, air	h	hope, hate	o	odd, hot	s	see, pass	w	win, away
ä	palm, father	i	it, give	ō	open, so	sh	sure, rush	y	yet, yearn
b	bat, rub	ī	ice, write	ô	order, jaw	t	talk, sit	z	zest, muse
ch	check, catch	j	joy, ledge	oi	oil, boy	th	thin, both	zh	vision, pleasure
d	dog, rod	k	cool, take	ou	pout, now	ŧħ	this, bathe		
e	end, pet	l	look, rule	ōō	took, full	u	up, done		
ē	equal, tree	m	move, seem	ōō	pool, food	û(r)	burn, term		

ə the schwa, an unstressed vowel representing the sound spelled a in above, e in sicken, i in possible, o in melon, u in circus

Other symbols:
- • separates words into syllables
- ′ indicates stress on a syllable

A

addend [a′dend] **sumando** Any of the numbers that are added in addition
Examples: 2 + 3 = 5

     ↑   ↑

   addend   addend

addition [ə•dish′ən] **suma** The process of finding the total number of items when two or more groups of items are joined; the opposite operation of subtraction

A.M. [ā•em] **a. m.** The time after midnight and before noon

analog clock [an′ə•log kläk] **reloj analógico** A tool for measuring time, in which hands move around a circle to show hours and minutes
Example:

angle [ang′gəl] **ángulo** A figure formed by two rays that share an endpoint (p. 481)
Example:

Word History

When the letter *g* is replaced with the letter *k* in the word **angle**, the word becomes *ankle*. Both words come from the same Latin root, *angulus*, which means "a sharp bend."

area [âr′ē•ə] **área** The measure of the number of unit squares needed to cover a surface (p. 513)
Example:

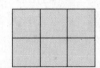

Area = 6 square units

array [ə•rā′] **matriz** A set of objects arranged in rows and columns (p. 191)
Example:

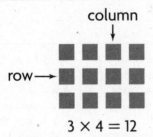

$$3 \times 4 = 12$$

Associative Property of Addition [ə•sō′shē•āt•iv präp′ər•tē əv ə•dish′ən] **propiedad asociativa de la suma** The property that states that you can group addends in different ways and still get the same sum (p. 113)
Example:
$$4 + (2 + 5) = 11$$
$$(4 + 2) + 5 = 11$$

Associative Property of Multiplication
[ə•sō′shē•āt•iv präp′ər•tē əv mul•tə•pli•kā′shən] **propiedad asociativa de la multiplicación** The property that states that when the grouping of factors is changed, the product remains the same (p. 243)
Example:
$$(3 \times 2) \times 4 = 24$$
$$3 \times (2 \times 4) = 24$$

bar graph [bär graf] **gráfica de barras** A graph that uses bars to show data (p. 635)
Example:

borrow [bôr′ō] **pedir o tomar prestado** You **borrow** money when another person gives you money that you will need to pay back. (p. 679)

capacity [kə•pas′i•tē] **capacidad** The amount a container can hold (p. 589)
Example:
1 liter = 1,000 milliliters

cent sign (¢) [sent sīn] **símbolo de centavo (¢)** A symbol that stands for *cent* or *cents*
Example: 53¢

centimeter (cm) [sen′tə•mēt•ər] **centímetro (cm)** A metric unit used to measure length or distance; 1 meter = 100 centimeters
Example:

1 cm

circle [sûr′kəl] **círculo** A round closed plane figure
Example:

closed figure [klōzd fig′yər] **figura cerrada** A figure that begins and ends at the same point
Examples:

Commutative Property of Addition
[kə•myōōt′ə•tiv präp′ər•tē əv ə•dish′ən] **propiedad conmutativa de la suma** The property that states that you can add two or more numbers in any order and get the same sum (p. 113)
Example:
$$6 + 7 = 13$$
$$7 + 6 = 13$$

Commutative Property of Multiplication
[kə•myōōt′ə•tiv präp′ər•tē əv mul•tə•pli•kā′shən] **propiedad conmutativa de la multiplicación** The property that states that you can multiply two factors in any order and get the same product (p. 198)
Example:
$$2 \times 4 = 8$$
$$4 \times 2 = 8$$

compare [kəm·pâr′] **comparar** To describe whether numbers are equal to, less than, or greater than each other

compatible numbers [kəm·pat′ə·bəl num′bərz] **números compatibles** Numbers that are easy to compute with mentally (p. 107)

cone [kōn] **cono** A three-dimensional, pointed figure that has a flat, round base (p. 505)
Example:

base

congruent [kən·groo′ənt] **congruente** Figures that have the same size and shape (p. 499)
Example:

counting number [kount′ing num′bər] **número positivo** A whole number that can be used to count a set of objects (1, 2, 3, 4 . . .)

cube [kyoōb] **cubo** A three-dimensional figure with six square faces of the same size (p. 505)
Example:

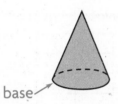

cup (c) [kup] **taza (tz)** A customary unit used to measure capacity (p. 589)

credit [krĕd′ĭt] **crédito** Paying for something with money that is borrowed and must be paid back, usually with interest (p. 679)

cylinder [sil′ən·dər] **cilindro** A three-dimensional figure that is shaped like a can (p. 505)
Example:

data [dāt′ə] **datos** Information collected about people or things

decagon [dek′ə·gän] **decágono** A polygon with ten sides and ten angles
Example:

decimal point [des′ə·məl point] **punto decimal** A symbol used to separate dollars from cents in money
Example: $4.52

⌐ decimal point

denominator [dē·näm′ə·nāt·ər] **denominador** The part of a fraction below the line, which tells how many equal parts there are in the whole or in the group (p. 49)
Example: $\frac{3}{4}$ ← denominator

difference [dif′ər·əns] **diferencia** The answer to a subtraction problem
Example: 6 − 4 = 2

⌐difference

digital clock [dij′i·təl kläk] **reloj digital** A clock that shows time to the minute, using digits
Example:

digits [dij′its] **dígitos** The symbols 0, 1, 2, 3, 4, 5, 6, 7, 8, and 9

dime [dīm] **moneda de 10¢** A coin worth 10 cents and with a value equal to that of 10 pennies; 10¢
Example:

Distributive Property [di•strib′yoo•tiv präp′ər•tē] **propiedad distributiva** The property that states that multiplying a sum by a number is the same as multiplying each addend by the number and then adding the products (p. 229)
Example: 5 × 8 = 5 × (4 + 4)
    5 × 8 = (5 × 4) + (5 × 4)
    5 × 8 = 20 + 20
    5 × 8 = 40

divide [də•vīd′] **dividir** To separate into equal groups; the opposite operation of multiplication (p. 313)

dividend [div′ə•dend] **dividendo** The number that is to be divided in a division problem (p. 320)
Example: 35 ÷ 5 = 7
      ↑__dividend

divisible [də•viz′ə•bəl] **divisible** A number that is a counting number and can be evenly divided (p. 352)
Example: 18 is divisible by 3.

division [də•vizh′ən] **división** The process of sharing a number of items to find how many groups can be made or how many items will be in a group; the opposite operation of multiplication

divisor [de•vī′zər] **divisor** The number that divides the dividend (p. 320)
Example: 35 ÷ 5 = 7
      ↑__divisor

dollar [däl′ər] **dólar** Paper money worth 100 cents and equal to 100 pennies; $1.00
Example:

dot plot [dŏt plŏt] **diagrama de puntos** A graph that records each piece of data on a number line (p. 647)
Example:

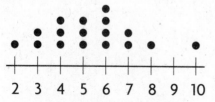

2 3 4 5 6 7 8 9 10
**Height of Bean Seedlings
to the Nearest Centimeter**

edge [ej] **arista** A line segment formed where two faces meet (p. 506)

edge

eighths [ātths] **octavos**

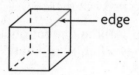

These are eighths.

elapsed time [ē•lapst′ tīm] **tiempo transcurrido** The time that passes from the start of an activity to the end of that activity (p. 565)

endpoint [end′point] **extremo** The point at either end of a line segment

equal groups [ē′kwəl groopz] **grupos iguales** Groups that have the same number of objects (p. 173)

equal parts [ē′kwəl pärts] **partes iguales** Parts that are exactly the same size (p. 37)

equal sign (=) [ē′kwəl sīn] **signo de igualdad (=)** A symbol used to show that two numbers have the same value
Example: 384 = 384

equal to (=) [ē′kwəl too] **igual a (=)** Having the same value (p. 29)
Example: 4 + 4 is equal to 3 + 5.

equation [ē•kwā′zhən] **ecuación** A number sentence that uses the equal sign to show that two amounts are equal (p. 320)
Examples:
   3 + 7 = 10
   4 − 1 = 3
   6 × 7 = 42
   8 ÷ 2 = 4

equivalent [ē•kwiv′ə•lənt] **equivalente** Two or more sets that name the same amount

equivalent fractions [ē•kwiv'ə•lənt frak'shənz] **fracciones equivalentes** Two or more fractions that name the same amount (p. 87)
Example:

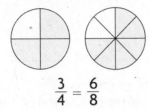

$$\frac{3}{4} = \frac{6}{8}$$

estimate [es'tə•māt] *verb* **estimar** To find about how many or how much

estimate [es'tə•mit] *noun* **estimación** A number close to an exact amount (p. 107)

even [ē'vən] **par** A whole number that has a 0, 2, 4, 6, or 8 in the ones place

expanded form [ek•span'did fôrm] **forma desarrollada** A way to write numbers by showing the value of each digit (p. 11)
Example: 721 = 700 + 20 + 1

experiment [ek•sper'ə•mənt] **experimento** A test that is done in order to find out something

expression [ek•spresh'ən] **expresión** A part of a number sentence that has numbers and operation signs but does not have an equal sign (p. 455)

face [fās] **cara** A polygon that is a flat surface of a solid figure (p. 506)

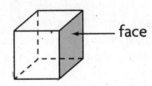
face

factor [fak'tər] **factor** A number that is multiplied by another number to find a product (p. 174)
Examples: 3 × 8 = 24
    ↑ ↑
   factor factor

foot (ft) [foot] **pie (ft)** A customary unit used to measure length or distance; 1 foot = 12 inches

fourths [fôrths] **cuartos**

These are fourths.

fraction [frak'shən] **fracción** A number that names part of a whole or part of a group (p. 43)
Examples:

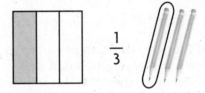

$$\frac{1}{3}$$

Word History

Often, a *fraction* is a part of a whole that is broken into pieces. *Fraction* comes from the Latin word *frangere*, which means "to break."

fraction greater than 1 [frak'shən grāt'ər than wun] **fracción mayor que 1** A number which has a numerator that is greater than its denominator
Examples:

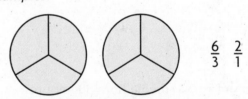

$$\frac{6}{3} \quad \frac{2}{1}$$

frequency table [frē'kwən•sē tā'bəl] **tabla de frecuencia** A table that uses numbers to record data (p. 623)
Example:

Favorite Color	
Color	**Number**
Blue	10
Green	8
Red	7
Yellow	4

gallon (gal) [gaʹlən] **galón (gal)** A customary unit used to measure capacity; 1 gallon = 4 quarts (p. 589)

gram (g) [gram] **gramo (g)** A metric unit used to measure mass; 1 kilogram = 1,000 grams (p. 607)

greater than (>) [grātʹər <u>than</u>] **mayor que (>)** A symbol used to compare two numbers when the greater number is given first (p. 29)
Example:
Read 6 > 4 as "six is greater than four."

Grouping Property of Addition [groōpʹing prӓpʹər•tē əv ə•dishʹən] **propiedad de agrupación de la suma** *See* Associative Property of Addition.

Grouping Property of Multiplication [groōpʹing prӓpʹər•tē əv mul•tə•pli•kāʹshən] **propiedad de agrupación de la multiplicación** *See* Associative Property of Multiplication.

half dollar [haf dolʹər] **moneda de 50¢** A coin worth 50 cents and with a value equal to that of 50 pennies; 50¢
Example:

half hour [haf our] **media hora** 30 minutes
Example: Between 4:00 and 4:30 is one half hour.

halves [havz] **mitades**

These are halves.

hexagon [hekʹsə•gän] **hexágono** A polygon with six sides and six angles
Examples:

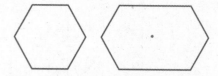

horizontal bar graph [hôr•i•zäntʹl bär graf] **gráfica de barras horizontales** A bar graph in which the bars go from left to right (p. 636)
Example:

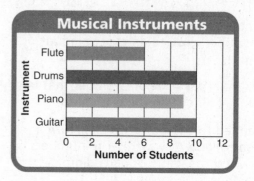

hour (hr) [our] **hora (h)** A unit used to measure time; in one hour, the hour hand on an analog clock moves from one number to the next; 1 hour = 60 minutes

hour hand [our hand] **horario** The short hand on an analog clock

human capital [hyoōmən kăpʹĭ•tl] **capital humano** Knowledge and work skills (p. 661)

Identity Property of Addition [ĭ•denʹtə•tē prӓpʹər•tē əv ə•dishʹən] **propiedad de identidad de la suma** The property that states that when you add zero to a number, the result is that number
Example: 24 + 0 = 24

Identity Property of Multiplication [ĭ•denʹtə•tē prӓpʹər•tē əv mul•tə•pli•kāʹshən] **propiedad de identidad de la multiplicación** The property that states that the product of any number and 1 is that number (p. 204)
Examples: 5 × 1 = 5
1 × 8 = 8

inch (in.) [inch] **pulgada (pulg.)** A customary unit used to measure length or distance; 1 foot = 12 inches
Example:

income [ĭn'kŭm] **ingreso** Money earned (p. 661)

interest [ĭn'trĭst] **interés** The money paid by a borrower to a lender for the use of the lender's money (p. 679)

intersecting lines [ĭn•tər•sekt'ing līnz] **líneas intersecantes** Lines that meet or cross
Example:

inverse operations [ĭn'vûrs ăp•ə•rā'shənz] **operaciones inversas** Opposite operations, or operations that undo one another, such as addition and subtraction or multiplication and division (p. 145)

key [kē] **clave** The part of a map or graph that explains the symbols (p. 629)

kilogram (kg) [kil'ō•gram] **kilogramo (kg)** A metric unit used to measure mass; 1 kilogram = 1,000 grams (p. 607)

labor [lā'bər] **trabajo o labor** Work that a person does (p. 661)

lend [lĕnd] **prestar** A person **lends** money to someone else by giving money that needs to be paid back. (p. 679)

length [lengkth] **longitud** The measurement of the distance between two points

less than (<) [les <u>than</u>] **menor que (<)** A symbol used to compare two numbers when the lesser number is given first (p. 29)
Example:
Read 3 < 7 as "three is less than seven."

line [līn] **línea** A straight path extending in both directions with no endpoints
Example:

Word History

The word *line* comes from *linen*, a thread spun from the fibers of the flax plant. In early times, thread was held tight to mark a straight line between two points.

line segment [līn seg'mənt] **segmento** A part of a line that includes two points, called endpoints, and all of the points between them
Example:

liquid volume [lik'wid väl'yōōm] **volumen de un líquido** The amount of liquid in a container (p. 595)

liter (L) [lēt'ər] **litro (L)** A metric unit used to measure capacity and liquid volume; 1 liter = 1,000 milliliters (p. 595)

mass [mas] **masa** The amount of matter in an object (p. 607)

meter (m) [mēt'ər] **metro (m)** A metric unit used to measure length or distance; 1 meter = 100 centimeters

midnight [mid'nīt] **medianoche** 12:00 at night

milliliter (mL) [mil'i•lēt•ər] **mililitro (ml)** A metric unit used to measure capacity and liquid volume; 1 liter = 1,000 milliliters (p. 595)

minute (min) [min'it] **minuto (min)** A unit used to measure short amounts of time; in one minute, the minute hand on an analog clock moves from one mark to the next; 1 hour = 60 minutes

minute hand [min'it hand] **minutero** The long hand on an analog clock

multiple [mul'tə•pəl] **múltiplo** A number that is the product of two counting numbers (p. 217)
Examples:

$$
\begin{array}{cccc}
6 & 6 & 6 & 6 \\
\underline{\times\ 1} & \underline{\times\ 2} & \underline{\times\ 3} & \underline{\times\ 4} \\
6 & 12 & 18 & 24
\end{array}
$$
counting numbers ←
multiples of 6 ←

multiplication [mul•tə•pli•kā'shən] **multiplicación** The process of finding the total number of items in two or more equal groups; the opposite operation of division

multiply [mul'tə•pli] **multiplicar** To combine equal groups to find how many in all; the opposite operation of division (p. 174)

nickel [nik'əl] **moneda de 5¢** A coin worth 5 cents and with a value equal to that of 5 pennies; 5¢
Example:

noon [nōōn] **mediodía** 12:00 in the day

number line [num'bər līn] **recta numérica** A line on which numbers can be located
Example:

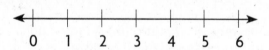

0   1   2   3   4   5   6

number sentence [num'bər sen'təns] **oración numérica** A sentence that includes numbers, operation symbols, and a greater than symbol, a less than symbol, or an equal sign
Example: $5 + 3 = 8$

numerator [nōō'mər•āt•ər] **numerador** The part of a fraction above the line, which tells how many parts are being counted (p. 49)

Example: $\frac{3}{4}$ ← numerator

octagon [äk'tə•gän] **octágono** A polygon with eight sides and eight angles
Examples:

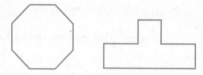

odd [od] **impar** A whole number that has a 1, 3, 5, 7, or 9 in the ones place

open figure [ō'pən fĭg'yər] **figura abierta** A figure that does not begin and end at the same point
Examples:

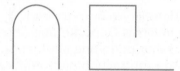

order [ôr'dər] **orden** A particular arrangement or placement of numbers or things, one after another

order of operations [ôr'dər əv äp•ə•rā'shənz] **orden de las operaciones** A special set of rules that gives the order in which calculations are done

Order Property of Addition [ôr'dər präp'ər•tē əv ə•dish'ən] **propiedad de orden de la suma** *See* Commutative Property of Addition.

Order Property of Multiplication [ôr'dər präp'ər•tē əv mul•tə•pli•kā'shən] **propiedad de orden de la multiplicación** *See* Commutative Property of Multiplication.

ounce (oz) [ouns] **onza (oz)** A customary unit used to measure weight; 1 pound = 16 ounces (p. 601)

parallel lines [pâr'ə•lel līnz] **líneas paralelas** Lines in the same plane that never cross and are always the same distance apart (p. 481)
Example:

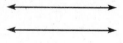

parallelogram [pâr•ə•le′lə•gram] **paralelogramo** A quadrilateral with two pairs of parallel sides and two pairs of sides of equal length (p. 482)
Example:

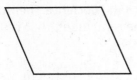

partial products [pär′shəl prŏd′əkts] **productos parciales** A method of multiplying in which the ones, tens, hundreds, and so on are multiplied separately and then the products are added together (p. 293)

pattern [pat′ərn] **patrón** An ordered set of numbers or objects in which the order helps you predict what will come next (p. 443)
Examples:
2, 4, 6, 8, 10

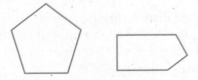

pentagon [pen′tə•gän] **pentágono** A polygon with five sides and five angles
Examples:

perimeter [pə•rim′ə•tər] **perímetro** The distance around a figure (p. 545)
Example:

perpendicular lines [pər•pən•dik′yōō•lər līnz] **líneas perpendiculares** Lines that intersect to form right angles
Example:

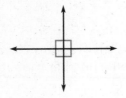

pictograph [pĭk′tə•grăf] **pictografía** A graph that uses pictures to show and compare information
Example:

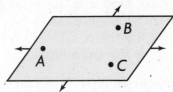

How We Get to School	
Walk	✳ ✳ ✳
Ride a Bike	✳ ✳ ✳ ✳
Ride a Bus	✳ ✳ ✳ ✳ ✳ ✳
Ride in a Car	✳ ✳
Key: Each ✳ = 10 students.	

pint (pt) [pīnt] **pinta (pt)** A customary unit used to measure capacity; 1 pint = 2 cups (p. 589)

place value [plās val′yōō] **valor posicional** The value of each digit in a number, based on the location of the digit

plane [plān] **plano** A flat surface that extends without end in all directions
Example:

plane figure [plān fĭg′yər] **figura plana** A figure in a plane that is formed by curves, line segments, or both
Example:

P.M. [pē•em] **p. m.** The time after noon and before midnight

point [point] **punto** An exact position or location

polygon [päl'i•gän] **polígono** A closed plane figure with straight sides that are line segments
Examples:

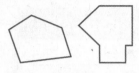

polygons   not polygons

Word History

Did you ever think that a **polygon** looks like a bunch of knees that are bent? This is how the term got its name. *Poly-* is from the Greek word *polys*, which means "many." The ending *-gon* is from the Greek word *gony*, which means "knee."

---

pound (lb) [pound] **libra (lb)** A customary unit used to measure weight; 1 pound = 16 ounces (p. 601)

product [präd'əkt] **producto** The answer in a multiplication problem (p. 174)
Example: 3 × 8 = 24
            ⤴product

purchase [pûr'chĭs] **comprar** To obtain by paying money for an item or a service (p. 673)

quadrilateral [kwäd•ri•lat'ər•əl] **cuadrilátero** A polygon with four sides and four angles (p. 482)
Example:

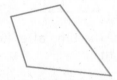

quart (qt) [kwôrt] **cuarto (ct)** A customary unit used to measure capacity; 1 quart = 2 pints (p. 589)

quarter [kwôrt'ər] **moneda de 25¢** A coin worth 25 cents and with a value equal to that of 25 pennies; 25¢
Example:

quarter hour [kwôrt'ər our] **cuarto de hora** 15 minutes
Example: Between 4:00 and 4:15 is one quarter hour.

quotient [kwō'shənt] **cociente** The number, not including the remainder, that results from division (p. 320)
Example: 8 ÷ 4 = 2
                  ⤴quotient

ray [rā] **semirrecta** A part of a line, with one endpoint, that is straight and continues in one direction
Example:

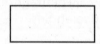

rectangle [rek'tang•gəl] **rectángulo** A quadrilateral with two pairs of parallel sides, two pairs of sides of equal length, and four right angles (p. 482)
Example:

rectangular prism [rek•tang'gyə•lər priz'əm] **prisma rectangular** A three-dimensional figure with six faces that are all rectangles (p. 505)
Example:

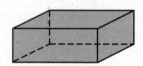

regroup [rē•grōōp'] **reagrupar** To exchange amounts of equal value to rename a number
Example: 5 + 8 = 13 ones or 1 ten 3 ones

related facts [ri•lāt'id fakts] **operaciones relacionadas** A set of related addition and subtraction, or multiplication and division, number sentences (p. 339)
Examples: 4 × 7 = 28   28 ÷ 4 = 7
            7 × 4 = 28   28 ÷ 7 = 4

remainder [ri•mān'dər] **residuo** The amount left over when a number cannot be divided evenly

resource [rē'sôrs] **recurso** Something that is produced and used (p. 667)

results [ri•zults'] **resultados** The answers from a survey

rhombus [räm'bəs] **rombo** A quadrilateral with two pairs of parallel sides and four sides of equal length (p. 482)
Example:

right angle [rīt ang'gəl] **ángulo recto** An angle that forms a square corner (p. 481)
Example:

round [round] **redondear** To replace a number with another number that tells about how many or how much (p. 23)

rule [rōōl] **regla** An instruction that tells you the correct way to do something (p. 444)

salary [săl'ə•rē] **salario** The amount of money a person can earn by being self-employed or by doing a job for another person or business (p. 662)

savings plan [sā'vĭngs plăn] **ahorros** A **savings plan** will help you save money regularly so you can reach your goals (p. 686)

scale [skāl] **escala** The numbers placed at fixed distances on a graph to help label the graph (p. 635)

side [sīd] **lado** A straight line segment in a polygon

sixths [siksths] **sextos**

These are sixths.

skip count [skip kount] **contar salteado** A pattern of counting forward or backward
Example: 5, 10, 15, 20, 25, 30, . . .

solid figure [sä'lid fĭg'yər] **cuerpo geométrico**
See three-dimensional figure.

spend [spĕnd] **gastar** When you **spend** money, you give it to someone else in exchange for something. (p. 673)

sphere [sfir] **esfera** A three-dimensional figure that has the shape of a round ball (p. 505)
Example:

square [skwâr] **cuadrado** A quadrilateral with two pairs of parallel sides, four sides of equal length, and four right angles (p. 482)
Example:

square unit [skwâr yōō'nit] **unidad cuadrada** A unit used to measure area such as square foot, square meter, and so on (p. 513)

standard form [stan'dərd fôrm] **forma normal** A way to write numbers by using the digits 0–9, with each digit having a place value (p. 11)
Example: 345 ← standard form

subtraction [səb•trak'shən] **resta** The process of finding how many are left when a number of items are taken away from a group of items; the process of finding the difference when two groups are compared; the opposite operation of addition

sum [sum] **suma o total** The answer to an addition problem
Example: $6 + 4 = 10$

$\qquad$ sum

survey [sûr'vā] **encuesta** A method of gathering information

tally table [tal'ē tā'bəl] **tabla de conteo** A table that uses tally marks to record data
Example:

Favorite Sport	
Sport	**Tally**
Soccer	ЖⱧ |||
Baseball	|||
Football	ЖⱧ
Basketball	ЖⱧ	

thirds [thûrdz] **tercios**

These are thirds.

three-dimensional figure [thrē də•men'shə•nəl fig'yər] **figura de tres dimensiones** A figure that has length, width, and height (p. 505)
Example:

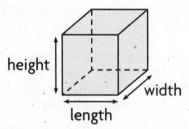

time line [tīm līn] **línea cronológica** A drawing that shows when and in what order events took place

trapezoid [trap'i•zoid] **trapecio** A quadrilateral with exactly one pair of parallel sides (p. 482)
Example:

triangle [trī'ang•gəl] **triángulo** A polygon with three sides and three angles
Examples:

triangular prism [trī•ang'gyə•lər priz'əm] **prisma triangular** A solid figure that has 3 faces that are rectangles and 2 faces that are triangles (p. 505)
Example:

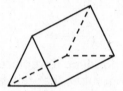

two-dimensional figure [tōō də•men'shə•nəl fig'yər] **figura de dos dimensiones** A figure that has only length and width
Example:

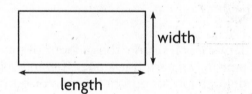

unit fraction [yōō'nit frak'shən] **fracción unitaria** A fraction that has 1 as its top number, or numerator (p. 43)
Examples: $\frac{1}{2}$ $\frac{1}{3}$ $\frac{1}{4}$

unit square [yōō'nit skwâr] **cuadrado de una unidad** A square with a side length of 1 unit, used to measure area (p. 513)

Venn diagram [ven dī′ə•gram] **diagrama de Venn**
A diagram that shows relationships among
sets of things (p. 493)
Example:

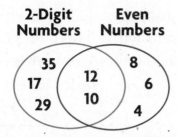

2-Digit Numbers   **Even Numbers**

35   12   8
17   6
29   10   4

vertex [vûr′teks] **vértice** The point at which
two rays of an angle or two (or more) line
segments meet in a plane figure or where
three or more edges meet in a solid figure
(pp. 481; 506)
Examples:

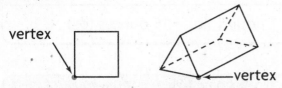

vertex

vertex

vertical bar graph [vûr′ti•kəl bär graf] **gráfica
de barras verticales** A bar graph in which the
bars go up from bottom to top (p. 636)
Example:

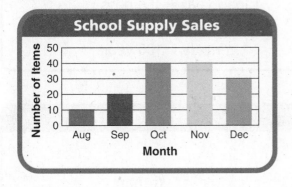

School Supply Sales

Number of Items

50
40
30
20
10
0

Aug Sep Oct Nov Dec
Month

weight [wāt] **peso** The heaviness of an object
(p. 601)

whole [hōl] **entero** All of the parts of a shape or
group (p. 37)
Example:

$\frac{2}{2} = 1$

This is one whole.

whole number [hōl num′bər] **número entero**
One of the numbers 0, 1, 2, 3, 4, . . .
The set of whole numbers goes on
without end

word form [wûrd fôrm] **en palabras** A way
to write numbers by using words (p. 11)
Example: The word form of 212 is
two hundred twelve.

Zero Property of Multiplication [zē′rō
präp′ər•tē əv mul•tə•pli•kā′shən] **propiedad
del cero de la multiplicación** The property
that states that the product of zero and
any number is zero (p. 204)
Example: $0 \times 6 = 0$

Table of Measures

METRIC | ## CUSTOMARY

Length

1 centimeter (cm) = 10 millimeters (mm)
1 decimeter (dm) = 10 centimeters (cm)
1 meter (m) = 100 centimeters
1 meter (m) = 10 decimeters
1 kilometer (km) = 1,000 meters

1 foot (ft) = 12 inches (in.)
1 yard (yd) = 3 feet, or 36 inches
1 mile (mi) = 1,760 yards,
       or 5,280 feet

Liquid Volume and Capacity

1 liter (L) = 1,000 milliliters (mL)

1 pint (pt) = 2 cups (c)
1 quart (qt) = 2 pints
1 gallon (gal) = 4 quarts

Mass/Weight

1 kilogram (kg) = 1,000 grams (g)

1 pound (lb) = 16 ounces (oz)

TIME

1 minute (min) = 60 seconds (sec)
1 hour (hr) = 60 minutes
1 day = 24 hours
1 week = 7 days

1 year = 12 months (mo),
     or about 52 weeks
1 year = 365 days
1 leap year = 366 days
1 decade = 10 years
1 century = 100 years

MONEY

1 penny = 1 cent (¢)
1 nickel = 5 cents
1 dime = 10 cents
1 quarter = 25 cents
1 half-dollar = 50 cents
1 dollar ($) = 100 cents

SYMBOLS

< is less than
> is greater than
= is equal to